Learning to Improve

Learning to Improve

How America's Schools
Can Get Better
at Getting Better

ANTHONY S. BRYK
LOUIS M. GOMEZ
ALICIA GRUNOW
PAUL G. LEMAHIEU

HARVARD EDUCATION PRESS
CAMBRIDGE, MASSACHUSETTS

Fifth Printing, 2017
Copyright © 2015 by the President and Fellows of Harvard College

Library of Congress Control Number 2014959079

Paperback ISBN 978-1-61250-791-0
Library Edition ISBN 978-1-61250-792-7

Published by Harvard Education Press,
an imprint of the Harvard Education Publishing Group

Harvard Education Press
8 Story Street
Cambridge, MA 02138

Cover Design: Saizon Design
Cover Image: daz2d/Digital Vision Vectors/Getty Images
The typefaces used in this book are Minion Pro and ITC Stone Sans

*To all of the educators whose work and learnings
are described in this volume. They trusted
in an idea and in a group of colleagues.
They made improvement come alive.*

Contents

Preface

IN THE FALL OF 2007, the American Enterprise Institute organized a conference titled the "Supply Side of School Reform" in Washington, DC. The conference created an occasion for two of the authors of this volume, Tony Bryk and Louis Gomez, to draw together a set of ruminations, based on over a decade of collaboration on work to improve student outcomes in the Chicago Public Schools. The "Ruminations" paper offered a sober appraisal.[1] Something was seriously wrong with the ways the field of education sought to connect research to practice improvement. One could see small successes here and there, but the overall processes of improvement were very fragile and much too slow. The forces at work in large urban school systems were competing tsunamis of change. Each hot new idea seemed well intentioned, but often impervious to evidence. The cumulative effect of various reforms, layered one on top of another, was often less than helpful. It seemed clear that if educational reformers continued to do what they had always done, education would continue to get more of the same—great variability in outcomes that often further disadvantages the most disadvantaged in our society.[2]

We questioned how our nation could possibly improve our schools without a transformation in the ways it develops and supports school professionals and the materials, ideas, and evidence with which they work. We noted that when other sectors of society confront mounting challenges, such as those facing education today, leaders naturally turn to their research and development communities for guidance. Unfortunately, the research and development infrastructure for school improvement is weak and fragmented. The core institutional arrangements among public education, universities, and the commercial sector are failing our schools. Moreover, even when constructive efforts operate, they occur within a political environment that continues to seek quick fixes rather than investing in the sustained work necessary to advance quality outcomes reliably at scale.

Our universities reward faculty members for their scholarly research contributions; the individually authored paper in a refereed journal is the prized accomplishment. This institutional culture and its academic incentives are not conducive to teams working together on the kinds of design, development, and refinement activities that are necessary to solve educational problems.[3] To be sure, valuable knowledge is emerging from schools of education and across the social sciences. This knowledge has salience and *could* improve schooling significantly. It is just not happening at the speed and scope of what is needed and is possible.

Likewise, while individual educators may develop considerable knowledge through their daily work, no mechanisms exist to test, refine, and transform this practitioner expertise into a professional knowledge base.[4] School districts are not especially proactive in developing and improving instructional materials, practices, and programs based on careful design and testing. Systematic evidence-based improvement is just not in the fabric of their work. Instead, educational leaders move quickly to implement untested solutions in responding to ever-changing government and foundation initiatives. Educators are constantly running from behind, seeking to keep up before the next new reform—often disconnected from the last reform—sweeps over them.

Not surprisingly, the commercial sector is also lacking in this context. It responds quickly to changes in policy and funding priorities by bringing forth many new products and services, but individual firms rarely initiate and commit to the kind of sustained R&D necessary to improve schools. There is just too much market uncertainty to warrant such longer-term risk taking.

The Ruminations paper sketched a design for an R&D enterprise that would specifically focus on improving our nation's schools and colleges. In brief, the paper argued that we needed to

- Focus on improving the actual day-to-day work in classrooms, schools, and districts
- Orchestrate diverse expertise among researchers, practitioners, designers, and developers to solve practical problems
- Embrace an approach that focused on multiple quick tests of change and iterative refinement of promising ideas
- Recognize that variation in organizational contexts is a core design and development challenge rather than just some externality to be ignored
- Reframe the overall mission as accelerating how a field learns to improve its core work

All of this seemed very sensible to us, yet very little research was actually organized this way. We wondered whether these ideas could actually work.[5]

And then something unexpected happened.

Inspiration—seeing a complex problem through fresh eyes—arises on occasion in most unexpected ways. In the summer of 2008, we were approached by Jim Kohlmoos, then the executive director for the Knowledge Alliance, a Washington-based association of major applied research organizations in the United States. Some of its members had read Ruminations and were intrigued. The Knowledge Alliance invited us to present at a conference it was organizing for that December at Snowbird, Utah. It was there that we first met Donald Berwick, then-president and cofounder of the Institute for Healthcare Improvement (IHI). As Don talked, we realized that this organization, which had been around for nearly twenty years, was actually living the ideas and doing the kind of work in the health-care sector that we had been speculating about for education. Don, who was trained as a pediatrician, subsequently invited us to visit IHI to see all of this firsthand. Little did we know at the time that he had just opened a door for us to an extraordinary high-performing organization.

At the conclusion of our first visit to IHI, Don shared a copy of *The Best Practice* by Charles Kenney.[6] The book offers a narrative account of the emergence of improvement research in health care. Over two decades ago, a few extraordinary leaders in health care recognized the challenges confronting their field. These leaders borrowed the discipline and culture of quality improvement, pioneered by Japanese industry, and then applied it to the complex enterprise that is modern health care.[7] Under their influence, medical institutions have reduced harm, saved lives, and enhanced patients' experiences while also controlling costs.[8] Their efforts to promote a system in which "continuously improving is what we do here" became our inspiration.[9] At several points in Kenney's text, one could easily substitute the words *teachers* and *students* for *doctors* and *patients* and believe that this was actually a discourse about education. We were convinced that if those in health care could learn useful lessons from studying industrial quality improvement, there was a good chance that educators could learn something in turn from them.

So we became serious students of IHI—how it organized its work and why and how it had come to do so as it did.[10] IHI generously opened its doors to us. We have participated in several of its professional training programs. Its staff and associates have been our mentors as we sought to adapt to education many of the principles, tools, and routines of improvement science that have been so successfully deployed in health care.

Along the way, I (Tony) had the privilege of being invited to serve on an Institute of Medicine committee. Through these discussions, I came to understand better why leaders in this field were seeking to promote a more dynamic and vigorous learning-to-improve health-care system. The medical field attracts bright, well-trained professionals and compensates them well. It draws from a vast reservoir of basic and applied research and cutting-edge technology applications. But even with the best of people, tools, and technical knowledge, tremendous variability exists in health-care outcomes. Many hospitals aren't as good as they could be because they focus too little attention on how to bring their talent and technology together effectively day-in and day-out on behalf of patients. Their systems do not support their many professionals effectively, and they do not sufficiently address the complex and often very trying conditions under which they work.[11]

As an organizational sociologist who has spent many years seeking to improve urban schools and districts, the implications seemed obvious. Education too has a serious learning-to-improve problem. Even as we await better knowledge, tools, and other resources, we must accomplish more with what we already know and the resources we already have. We believe this is achievable in education, as is now occurring in select health-care institutions, when leaders seriously commit to systematic quality improvement.

ANALOGICAL SCAVENGERS

Our deep dive into health-care quality improvement shaped a practical orientation that continues to guide our efforts. We authors of this volume have come to think of ourselves as a new breed of birds, the "analogical scavenger." We are constantly looking to other fields that share a concern about improving practices and that have made some significant progress. We study these deeply, reflecting on commonalities with the education field, while also scrutinizing critical differences. How do these ideas fit? Where are adaptations needed, and how do we discern which are most appropriate?

Learning to Improve draws on some of the best ideas emerging in education itself in the form of communities of practice, teacher action research, lesson study, and the scholarship of teaching and learning.[12] We also acknowledge close colleagueship with a set of practices labeled developmental evaluation.[13] Likewise, we are indebted to a growing scholarship around user-centered and design-based implementation.[14] We have also drawn liberally on the practical strategies developed in commercial design firms, such as IDEO, and in related academic centers such as the Hasso Plattner Institute of Design at Stanford. In each instance, we have scavenged for good ideas and practices that have worked in other contexts but may not yet have received their due attention in education.

Consequently, we owe debts to many others for the basic principles and practical tools detailed in this book. Our main contribution in this regard is as an integrative agent, drawing together the best of what we have found and melding it into a coherent system of principles and methods for accelerating learning to improve. Ultimately, this led us to the concept of *networked improvement communities* (NICs). This new form for educational R&D joins together the discipline of improvement science with the dynamism and creative power of networks organized to solve common problems. NICs are about helping America's schools get better at getting better.

LEARNING-BY-DOING

In tandem with our scavenging activity, we also set out to test and refine these ideas, methods, and tools by seeking to use them to address important improvement problems in colleges and schools. One of our goals in the book is to share our early experiences at the Carnegie Foundation for the Advancement of Teaching in attempting to make two NICs come alive.

In 2010 we initiated a Community Colleges Pathways NIC focused on the extraordinarily high failure rates in developmental mathematics courses in community colleges. Unable to acquire necessary college credits, these students cannot transfer to a four-year institution nor qualify for entry into specialized technical and occupational training programs. These courses literally function as a gatekeeper to opportunity for hundreds of thousands of students every year. By July 2011 some twenty-seven colleges had joined the Pathways NIC to attack this problem. Where historically only 5 percent of the students assigned to developmental math classes received college math credit in one year, 50 percent of students participating in the Statway® and Quantway® programs developed by the network now achieve college mathematics credit in a year. Measured improvements have emerged in virtually every participating college and for every subgroup of students. These success rates have been sustained over three years even as the NIC has expanded to more than fifty colleges and to many more faculty. The network actively continues to learn from its data in efforts to further improve its students' outcomes.

In the fall of 2011, the Carnegie Foundation launched a second and smaller NIC focused on the weak systems that bring new teachers into public schools, fail to support them in learning to teach well, and consequently under-educate the children in their classrooms. These systems function as a revolving door where many new teachers leave the profession and the process just recycles with a new group over and over. District teams in Baltimore, Maryland; Austin, Texas; and the New Visions for Public Schools Network in New York City joined together to attack this problem. While each district initially pursued some different change ideas, the network eventually focused on two processes that strongly affect new teachers' lives: the quality of feedback that new teachers receive for improving their teaching and the degree of support that new teachers sense in their relationship with their primary supervisor, the school principal. New feedback and support processes were developed, tested, refined, and adapted to work reliably across different kinds of schools. A measurement infrastructure is now in place that allows local improvement teams to track process measures about the frequency and quality of these interactions and how this in turn connects to teacher reports about job satisfaction and burnout and to key longer-term outcomes—measures of teaching effectiveness and decisions about possibly leaving teaching. This network has directly engaged teachers, principals, and other school-based educators in improvement research. In our view, the improvement paradigm that we introduce in this book has passed a key practitioner test. Increasing numbers of school leaders in these districts now want to learn how to use improvement methods to address a broader array of local problems.

These two NICs began somewhat differently and as a result provide complementary and contrasting experiences. The Community College Pathways NIC formed quickly as a network around the design, development, and scaling of new courses of instruction in developmental mathematics. It offers key insights about the early stages of network formation. The second NIC, which we call Building a Teaching Effectiveness Network (BTEN), began by immersing district leaders and school principals in rapid, small tests of change seeking to improve the quality of feedback and support that new teachers receive. It offers key insights about the mechanics of introducing such disciplined inquiries into day-to-day school affairs. Interwoven throughout this book are brief illustrations of select tools and processes now being used by these two NICs. We also detail some issues that have surfaced as educators begin to take up active roles as improvement researchers and as academic researchers attempt to interact in very different ways with their clinical colleagues.

Learning to Improve seeks to make these ideas and this emergent know-how accessible to a larger audience. This book is merely a starting point. It is an introduction to a new way of tackling problems in education and an invitation to join in the journey of building the capacity for quality improvement in our nation's schools and colleges.

Introduction

A Better Way

*The history of American education includes a graveyard
of good ideas condemned by pressure for fast results.*

—JAMES HIEBERT, RON GALLIMORE, AND JIM STIGLER[1]

BY THE LATE 1990s, many policy advocates and educational reformers
had concluded that U.S. high schools were too big and too impersonal.
In attempting to be everything to everyone, comprehensive high schools
failed many students, especially those from disadvantaged backgrounds.
Anonymity bred apathy and alienation among students and teachers alike.
Far too many students dropped out, and many of those who did persist to
graduation were ill prepared for work or higher education.

A reform movement emerged. One of its most articulate advocates was
Tom Vander Ark, the senior program officer for education at the Bill &
Melinda Gates Foundation. Testifying before a congressional committee
in 2001, he pressed for smaller, more personalized school settings, places
where faculty and students would really know each other, leading to a
strong sense of shared commitment to each other and to academic success.[2] Vander Ark described how visionary leaders at Central Park East
and Urban Academy in New York City and other small schools had created impressive examples of truly engaging learning environments.[3] These

1

compelling stories were buttressed by a growing body of research showing that high schools with fewer than 400 students produced significant
benefits, including higher student attendance and graduation rates; improved school climate and safety; greater parent and community involve-
ment; and higher staff satisfaction. Moreover, research found that smaller
schools benefitted economically and socially disadvantaged students the
most.[4] Vander Ark urged federal leaders to promote the redesign of the
American high school.

The Gates Foundation pursued that goal aggressively over the next several years. It spent some $2 billion promoting the dissolution of large high
schools and the creation of some 2,600 smaller ones in forty-five states and
the District of Columbia.[5] New York City alone created more than two
hundred such schools. The scope and pace of change was breathtaking.
Embedded here is a remarkable story of how a single philanthropic institution leveraged its resources to transform the institutional landscape of
American public education in a few short years.

Yet all was not well. While the number of small schools grew at an
astounding rate, so did the problems. Only a small number of urban educators had ever worked in small high schools, let alone started them. Even
fewer had taken on the more difficult task of transforming large dysfunctional high schools into multiple smaller units that could coexist under
a single roof. Few educational leaders knew how to maneuver effectively
through the swamp of day-to-day problem solving required to bring this
new institutional form to life.

Equally problematic were the on-the-ground politics of change. Many
school staff were resistant to the small school idea. They saw it as just one
more instance of change being imposed from outside by reformers who
knew little about the conditions that teachers and principals actually confronted. The human and social resources necessary to engage meaningful
change of any sort were also lacking in many of the Gates-funded schools.
Teachers reported extremely low levels of satisfaction in their jobs, little inclination to try new things, and little trust in each other.[6] Breaking
large comprehensive high schools into smaller units also challenged the
long-standing authority of department heads and other leaders in tradi-

tional high schools. Not surprisingly, there was much wrangling over details that proved time-consuming and divisive.[7]

Most significant, many of the new, smaller high schools that emerged from the Gates initiative developed in ways very different from places like Central Park East and Urban Academy that had been held out as models. Those successful small schools had started with a select group of faculty; built up gradually by adding a grade each year; and learned from trial and error, changing and improving over time.[8] In essence, their leaders brought what design professionals refer to as a design and development orientation to the task of new school creation.[9]

In contrast, under the Gates initiative, districts often compelled staff in large existing high schools to redesign themselves into clusters of small schools to be housed in the same facility. School faculties who were already working under exceedingly difficult conditions and who had no prior experience in school redesign were charged with essentially reinventing themselves, often in less than a year. There was little opportunity to start small, fail, learn, and iterate toward success. Rapid large-scale change was being called for under conditions least likely to produce success.[10]

So a good idea found itself embedded in a bad development strategy with weak collective will, limited capacity to execute, and an unrealistic timetable. Educators across the country were confronting common challenges and trying to solve complex problems. Many learned valuable lessons that could have propelled the small schools initiative toward success. Unfortunately, most were working on this effort largely on their own. There was no organized system to capture their learning, refine it, and transform it into a collective force accelerating wider-scale improvements. That many small schools struggled and some failed, especially early on, is not surprising.[11] This reform was ambitious and quite novel, and much of the practical knowledge required to make it work was unknown at the outset. That failures were likely to occur under these circumstances is not a fatal flaw; but that the field failed to learn quickly from these failures was, and is.

Although some notable exceptions did subsequently emerge, such as the New Century High Schools in New York City, by late fall of 2008 the

Gates Foundation came to acknowledge that its efforts to rapidly develop small high schools were not the panacea that it had hoped.[12] Another promising reform idea had failed to deliver.

With this effort in the rearview mirror, the foundation moved on to another big transformative idea to fix education.

> [The Gates Foundation] has shifted its considerable weight behind an emerging consensus—shared by U.S. Education Secretary and Gates ally Arne Duncan—that quality of teaching affects student performance and that increasing achievement is as simple as removing bad teachers, identifying good ones, and rewarding them with more money.[13]

A pressing new concern had come into view. Media accounts, such as the "Rubber Room" article in the *New Yorker*, focused attention on teachers whom districts appeared unable to fire.[14] In a full-length motion picture, *Waiting for Superman,* Americans were told that test scores were low because there are so many bad teachers.

Policy leaders quickly jumped on a new reform bandwagon: rigorous teacher evaluations tied to financial incentives and employment decisions. A complex statistical procedure called value-added analysis, which previously had been employed by only a very select group of microeconomists and statisticians, quickly became the centerpiece for these new evaluation systems.

As with small high schools, this reform idea, too, was anchored in a growing body of academic research. In this instance, numerous studies had documented wide variability in student learning among different classrooms. Less clear was how to interpret these findings and to discern their practical implications.[15] Regardless, policy makers quickly came to believe that the new teacher evaluation protocols coupled with new data systems would now be able to tell district leaders who to fire and who to reward.

But here, too, reformers got ahead of themselves. States and districts, supported by resources from both the Gates Foundation and the U.S. Department of Education, moved quickly to implement teacher evaluation procedures even though very significant technical and logistical issues remained unsolved.[16] As with high school redesign, reformers had rapidly launched a major change strategy in public education with a lack of requisite knowledge, skill and organizational capacity, and not surprisingly with considerable resistance from teachers.

THE CHRONIC FAILURE OF PROMISING REFORM IDEAS

While teacher evaluation and high school redesign are high-profile cases, they are not anomalies. Over and over, change efforts spread rapidly across the education landscape, despite an absence of knowledge as to how (or even whether it is possible) to effect improvements envisioned by reform advocates.

When reformers focused attention on the generally poor quality of professional development efforts to help teachers improve their classroom teaching, a new organizational role—the instructional coach—was introduced into schools.[17] However, what coaches actually needed to know and be able to do, and the requisite work conditions necessary in schools for them to do their jobs successfully, was left largely unspecified. When reformers recognized the importance of principal leadership, principals were asked to take on an expanded role as instructional leaders even though demands on their time were already excessive.[18] When policy makers were unsatisfied with the rate of school improvement, high-stakes accountability schemes were introduced, but unintended consequences abounded, some of them hurting the very students the reforms were designed to help.[19] Reaching back a bit further, when corporate downsizing was the rage some years ago, school districts moved quickly to embrace the concept of site-based management. But, the roles and responsibilities of newly empowered school-based decision makers were often left unclear and the resources needed for carrying out school-based decisions often lacking.[20]

In each instance there was a real problem to solve, and in most cases there was at least a germ of a good reform idea. Educators, however, typically did not know how to execute on the ideas. Districts and states lacked the individual expertise and organizational capacity to support these changes at scale, and policy makers regularly ignored arguably the most important instrument for any of this to work: engaging the minds and hearts of our nation's teachers and principals on behalf of the reforms.

Educational leaders continue down this path today, believing that they must disrupt the educational system substantially and quickly. They expend great energy rolling out large-scale changes across whole districts and, sometimes, whole states.[21] These initiatives make extraordinary demands on leaders' time, as they seek to advance broad changes while also working hard to sustain political support in the face of inevitable implementation problems. Teachers, principals, students, and parents are taxed too. Directives change, guidance is absent, and key provisions sometimes don't work at all. When the data are crunched, the same disappointing conclusions emerge. The press to quickly push good ideas into large-scale use rarely delivers promised outcomes. Results are typically modest and vary from school to school. In some locales a reform might work; in many places it does not; and in some instances it might even do harm.

At base is a common story of *going fast and learning slow*. We consistently fail to appreciate what it actually takes to make some promising idea work reliably in practice. We become disappointed when dramatic positive results do not readily emerge, and then we just move on to the next new reform idea. This should trouble all of us. If we continue to seek improvement in the ways we have always done, we are likely to continue to get what we have always gotten.

IMPROVEMENT SCIENCE AND NETWORKED COMMUNITIES

Each reform case, mentioned previously, sought to implement fast and wide and then fix problems later. This strategy has failed again and again. Comforting in a somewhat perverse way, such results are not peculiar to education. They are also seen in other sectors that have sought to improve their productivity in similar ways.[22] Experiences across many different fields now caution humility about how much must be learned in order to transform successfully a change idea into new human capabilities, into day-to-day practices that work reliably, and into the redesign of organizational arrangements necessary to support all of this. Achieving successful change in complex work systems means recognizing that one cannot predict ahead of time all of the details that need to be worked through nor the unintended negative consequences that might also ensue. This is just an operational fact of life about the nature of complex organizations. And as we detail in chapter 4, contemporary educational institutions are indeed complex.

Understanding this dynamic presses a fundamental shift in how we think and act, a shift toward *learning fast to implement well*.[23] It also calls out for very different organizational arrangements to accomplish this end. As we elaborate across the pages of this volume, the concept of *networked improvement communities* (NICs) offers an attractive alternative. A NIC unites the conceptual and analytic discipline of improvement science with the power of networked communities to innovate and learn together. In embracing improvement science, educators are able to draw upon a well-established set of tools and deep practical experiences. Many different kinds of institutions have learned faster and better by using these methods. In carrying out this activity through networked communities organized to solve a shared problem, it is possible to accelerate improvements even further and to engage actively many different individuals and institutions in the process. Moreover, this strategy is broadly useful whether the target for improvement is the classroom, school, faculty network, or school-community partnership; or a whole college, school district, or state education system.

Improvement Science Disciplines Inquiries

Over the past half-century, notable successes for improvement science have occurred first in industry and then more recently in social sectors such as health care.[24] The lesson those experiences teach is that problems ranging from defective products to hospital-induced infections do not stem primarily from an absence of basic research or inferior workforces. Rather, they result from the ways that work systems are designed and thereby shape how individuals carry out their responsibilities.

Improvement science addresses this reality by focusing on the specific tasks people do; the processes and tools they use; and how prevailing policies, organizational structures, and norms affect this. Applying improvement science to education would direct greater attention to how better to design and fit together the many elements that shape the way schools work. The latter is key to making our educational institutions more effective, efficient, and personally engaging.

Analytically, improvement research entails getting down into the micro details as to how any proposed set of changes is actually supposed to improve outcomes. Unfortunately, such careful on-the-ground systems thinking rarely characterizes most educational reforms. Typically, a reform's logic of action is vague and almost always underspecified. When such reforms are scrutinized closely, zones of wishful thinking—gaps in understanding, questionable assumptions about causes and effects, and tacit beliefs of the form "and then something good will happen"—regularly abound.[25]

In response, improvement science deploys rapid tests of change to guide the development, revision, and continued fine-tuning of new tools, processes, work roles, and relationships. The approach is explicitly designed to accelerate learning-by-doing. As iterative cycles of change proceed, previously invisible problems often emerge, and improvement activities may need to tack off in some new directions. The objective here is quite different from the traditional pilot program that seeks to offer a proof of concept. Improvement research, in contrast, is a focused learning journey. The overall goal is to develop the necessary *know-how* for a reform idea ultimately to spread faster and more effectively.

This strategy draws on a natural human instinct.[26] Much practical learning occurs every day in schools. Individual teachers learn when they introduce a new practice in their classroom and then carefully evaluate the resulting student work. Likewise, individual schools learn as staff examine data together on the effectiveness of current practices and test improvement ideas against evidence of changes in students' work. Organizations across numerous fields have become much more productive by acknowledging this natural inclination and by building on it in deliberate and systematic ways.

A commitment to empirical evidence anchors this learning orientation. Participants are constantly asking three *core improvement questions*: "What is the specific problem I am now trying to solve? What change might I introduce and why? And, how will I know whether the change is actually an improvement?" Change ideas are tested and refined based on evidence from what actually happened, both intended and otherwise. When a change fails to produce expected results or creates unintended consequences, it forces deeper thinking about what meaningful improvements will actually entail. As subsequent cycles of redesign and testing unfold, a better understanding evolves of the actual problem or problems that need to be solved and more workable interventions begin to emerge.

Improvement science also promotes a different angle of view on efforts to spread effective change. The latter is no longer assumed to be simply a matter of implementing mechanically some processes designed by others. To be sure, well-designed tools and processes matter. But even when such resources are at hand, achieving quality outcomes at scale demands sustained attention to solving a diverse array of local issues. So these too become grist for improvement research.

At its most basic and human level, improvement science is not some set of specialized studies carried out exclusively by external researchers. Learning to improve demands the active, full engagement of educators. This provision challenges prevailing arrangements in which researchers study schooling, design interventions, and analyze policies; and then teachers, principals, and education leaders are cast as *users* of this research in their work.[27] Improvement science, in contrast, brings educators into regular interaction with a broad array of academic and technical experts. Participants in an improvement network form as a colleagueship of expertise—academic, technical, and clinical—deliberately assembled to address specific problems. All involved are now *improvers* seeking to generate strong evidence about how to achieve better outcomes more reliably.

We use in this book a number of related terms that are commonly found in writings about improvement in other fields. Formally, we define them here, even though on occasion we may be a bit more casual in their use. *Improvement science* is a methodology that disciplines inquiries to improve practice. Undergirding it is a distinctive epistemology about what we seek to learn and how we may come to understand it well.[28] Particular acts of inquiry are *improvement research* projects. These projects aim for *quality improvement*.[29] In the context of education, this refers to the capacity of an organization to produce valued outcomes reliably for different subgroups of students, being educated by different teachers and in varied organizational contexts. Since improvement research is an iterative process often extending over considerable periods of time, it is also referred to as *continuous improvement*. Each term offers a somewhat different angle of view on the overall enterprise, and hopefully all will become clear as we illustrate their application in the chapters ahead.

We also note that in embracing the phrase *improvement science* we aim to distinguish sharply from the language commonly used in educational circles today about "research for policy and practice."[30] Generating better guidance for educational policy and improving work practices to make schooling more effective are very different activities. Each makes different information demands and entails different processes through which such information is developed and its utility assessed. Yoking these two needs together may afford some rhetorical convenience in arguing for public funding, but it also does disservice to building the kind of knowledge that is truly useful for improving schools. We firmly believe that a robust methodology—a highly practical form of rigorous inquiry—exists and can be matched to this most important societal need. In this monograph, we detail its guiding principles, some of its key tools and inquiry processes, and its social organization as a scientific community.

Networks Accelerate Learning

As noted previously, teachers, principals, and educational leaders regularly experiment with new approaches seeking to improve outcomes for their students. Given the size and scope of American education, this experimentation occurs on a grand scale. From this angle of view, the lack of wide-scale improvement in educational practice appears anomalous.

Individual educators and institutions are learning much every day, yet as a field we fail to organize, refine, and build on these lessons.

In other contexts, networks are now forming to attack and quickly solve problems that had once been thought difficult and even intractable.[31] For instance, when a mysterious and deadly new virus emerged, subsequently called SARS, a network of labs working separately, but in regular communication with the World Health Organization (WHO), quickly identified the virus and opened the door for new diagnostic testing and future vaccine development. Multiple investigators, each taking a somewhat different tack on the problem, shared day by day what they were learning. The WHO hub facilitated these exchanges and catalyzed conversations about emerging implications and new hypotheses to examine. What under other circumstances might have taken months or years to discover occurred in just a matter of weeks.[32] Ambitious efforts of this sort are emerging all across the biological and physical sciences. Large networks, engaging diverse participants often including nonscientists, are now mapping DNA, carrying out inquiries into the structure of the universe, and resolving complex mathematical theorems.[33]

These science networks represent a new organizational form, deliberately designed to enable effective collective action on solving complex problems and for developing complex products.[34] By breaking up thorny problems and possible solutions into smaller discrete parts, it becomes possible for many more individuals and organizations to offer meaningful contributions.[35] This strategy capitalizes on the fact that key insights often emerge in unusual places. By working through organized networks, the likelihood increases that these ideas may surface, be systematically examined, and if promising, moved rapidly into testing and refinement. In addition, promising practices emerging in the network are likely to diffuse more rapidly and are further tested and refined as others take them up. Accumulating the practical knowledge generated from these multiple tests of change is essential to making a reform work reliably as diverse individuals engage with it across varied contexts. It provides the strongest assurance that as a change scales, what is implemented is actually an improvement.

A *network hub* plays a key role in structuring and supporting this distributed activity.[36] The hub is responsible for detailing the problem to be solved and for developing and maintaining the coherence of the evolving framework that guides efforts among many different participants. It establishes the processes and norms governing how individuals and groups work together and the evidentiary standards for warranting claims. The hub also provides technical resources and supports the open communication mechanisms necessary to accelerate learning networkwide.

Imagine if these vibrant networks were used to solve practical problems in education. They could harness the field's many efforts at improvement and transform them into collective knowledge building. Fortunately, educators have already taken some steps in this direction. Since the early 2000s interest has grown in activity labeled variously as professional learning communities, communities of practice, and faculty inquiry groups.[37] Typically, these communities coalesce around a common problem. As individuals share their experiences, they stimulate insights among others. Networked science appreciates the value of this social learning and seeks to take it a step further by bringing scientific discipline to bear on how plausible change ideas are detailed, tested, and further refined against evidence. Networked science aims to exploit how the social intelligence of a group can accelerate not just individual learning, but a whole profession's capacity to learn and improve.

THE IMPROVEMENT PRINCIPLES

We elaborate over the course of the next six chapters on the basic ideas sketched out quickly in the preceding sections. Each chapter focuses on a distinct principle. Taken together as a set, these principles represent the foundational elements for improvement science carried out in networked communities. We introduce the principles briefly here.

Make the Work Problem-Specific and User-Centered

Anchoring all activity in a NIC is a specific problem to be solved. Detailing this problem statement often proves harder than it sounds. Initial versions are typically quite general. For example, early conversations with college leaders, which eventually led to the initiation of the Community College Pathways NIC mentioned in the preface, focused on improving student success in program completion. Framing problem statements in this fashion directs attention toward valued social goals—in this instance the important role that community colleges can and should play in creating opportunities for a better job and better life. Such problem framing affords powerful rhetoric for mobilizing political action but provides little guidance as to what actually needs to happen to improve how these organizations function. It indicts many different problems operating across many different departments and jurisdictions both within and outside the colleges. Improvement research, in contrast, demands focus—"What specific problem or small set of problems are we trying to solve?"

Equally important is examining the problem from the point of view of the user—the person who is experiencing it firsthand. In the community college case, a network initiation team scrutinized the success problem from the point of view of the students. What is it that they experience from the time they arrive at the community college doorstep through to successfully completing a program of study? The team considered a myriad of factors that shaped these trajectories and then zeroed in on arguably the single biggest impediment to student success: the high failure rates in developmental mathematics courses. This became the specific problem to be addressed by the NIC.

Focus on Variation in Performance

Variability in performance is the natural state of affairs in complex organizations. Reducing harmful variation and improving overall quality form the prime targets for improvement efforts. In the context of schooling, this means more consistently producing positive outcomes for diverse students being educated by different teachers and in varied contexts.

Adopting this orientation responds to a common educational finding that change ideas work in some places but not others. It directs attention away from simplistic thinking about solutions in terms of "What works?" toward a more realistic appraisal of "What works, for whom, and under what set of conditions?" As detailed in chapter 2, a NIC seeks to identify and target for change those key processes where major differences in outcomes take root. Improving how this work is carried out can change the overall distribution of outcomes that ensue.

See the System That Produces the Current Outcomes

Our third principle directs attention to the question, "Why do we continue to get the undesirable outcomes observed?" In developing its improvement agenda, a NIC examines how work is actually carried out in classrooms, schools, and colleges and how larger institutional forces shape this. Results from prior research assist in these efforts (i.e., "What is it that we already know about these factors?"). Likewise, educational practitioners are actively engaged throughout the processes of conceptualizing the problem, examining possible change ideas, and learning about improvement as these changes are tried out.

Adopting a systems perspective makes visible many of the hidden complexities actually operating in an organization that might be important targets for change. It generates an interrelated set of hypotheses that form a working theory of improvement for a NIC. This in turn guides the change efforts to be tested, organizes results from this activity as an accumulating body of evidence, and creates an evolving framework for collective action across an improvement community. Chapter 3 introduces a set of processes and tools to assist in this regard.

We Cannot Improve at Scale What We Cannot Measure

Chapter 4 focuses on the centrality of measurement for improvement. Operationalizing this principle directs us to identify the specific measurable aims that the NIC seeks to accomplish. Regular reporting on these outcomes disciplines the work of the community and holds it internally accountable. Absent continuous feedback of such data, one can easily maintain a belief in the efficacy of one's actions even when the warrant for this remains uncertain or nonexistent. Psychologically, leading improvement requires living on the boundary of belief (about the importance of what one is trying to accomplish) and doubt (as to whether real progress is occurring). Evidence is essential to operating productively on this boundary.

Informing improvement, however, requires more than just measuring targeted outcomes. This is a direct consequence of adopting a systems view about change. First, it is rare to find an educational intervention that consists of a single action that has direct and immediate effect on some targeted aim. Rather, interventions are typically of the form of a "causal cascade": we need to improve "a" in order to achieve "b," which in turn is essential to accomplishing "c." For example, instructional coaching reforms seek to strengthen the relevance and quality of professional development afforded teachers in order to transform their classroom practices in order to improve students' learning. In many instances, educational interventions actually involve multiple interacting causal cascades of this sort. For example, referencing instructional coaching again, these reforms also have to attend to (a) the selection, (b) the initial training, and (c) the continuing professional development of coaches in order to enhance their expertise in working with teachers in order to increase teachers' expertise in carrying out instruction that results in better student learning. Improvement requires attending to each of the component processes that combine together to determine how well the overall system functions.

Adding a second layer of complication, the ultimate aim for a NIC will often be somewhat removed temporally from the activities that are the immediate targets for improvement. For example, in the Building a Teaching Effectiveness Network (BTEN) mentioned in the preface, the ultimate goal was to improve the retention of effective new teachers. These outcomes can take several years to emerge. The NIC's working theory about how to achieve these outcomes, in contrast, targeted a set of processes that begin within the first weeks and months of employment.

Consequentially, improvement research requires gathering data about the specific processes targeted for change, intermediate outcomes directly linked to these processes, and other key markers on the pathway toward achieving the network's ultimate aims. Unfortunately, such data are not routinely collected. This opens up a whole new demand for measurement in education, but with a very different purpose—helping educators improve what they do. It also raises significant new logistical issues—how can measurement of this sort be easily woven into the day-to-day work of students and educators rather than added as still one more demand on top of what is an already overburdened work system? Chapter 4 includes an example of such practical measurement and introduces a set of guiding principles and tools to assist in building them.

Use Disciplined Inquiry to Drive Improvement

The methods used in improvement research have been tuned to focus on learning quickly and cheaply. In education, this means minimizing intrusions into ongoing schooling activities (since we expect failures to occur, but we just don't know exactly where), while also generating empirical guidance as to what to try next. Improvement typically entails a sequence of inquiries, where the results from each test of change offer guidance for the next test. Formally, each test is akin to a small experiment; the overall arch of activity is an improvement investigation.

The methodology also offers an explicit process for learning how to scale improvements. Inevitably, as new programs, tools, processes, and roles move out into new contexts, they will need to be changed some in order to be integrated into these contexts. Tackling this problem of *adaptive integration* is a standard aspect of improvement research. As practices that have worked in one or few places move out to more diverse contexts, new improvement cycles are launched. The focus now is on "What will it take to make the intervention work under these new conditions?" This is how improvement research iterates toward quality outcomes reliably at scale.

Interestingly, significant by-products result from this approach to spreading improvement. As this activity proceeds, it is also building organizational resources for broader-based change. The educators involved in the early stages of improvement research become a key human resource in subsequent efforts to spread these changes. They have developed know-how—that is, how to make some set of changes actually work—and can now teach and mentor others along this same path. In addition, because these same individuals have personally experienced success, they are now poised to become evangelizing leaders, building will with colleagues for wider-spread implementation.

In sum, improvement research consists of a highly integrated set of methods for developing the necessary technical knowledge to transform good ideas into practices that work, building human capabilities necessary for this learning to spread, and directly addressing a major challenge in every improvement effort—building will for change. Addressing each of these is essential to scaling change faster and more effectively.

Accelerate Learning Through Networked Communities

In chapter 6, we explore how a NIC, organized as a scientific community, accelerates broad-based improvements. We detail the organizational resources, formal agreements, and normative understandings shared among participants that are necessary for such collective actions to occur.[38] Drawing on experiences from the two Carnegie-initiated networks and those of others, we describe the relationships that operate among network participants and how practical knowledge develops through their efforts and is taken up productively by others.

Membership in a NIC means placing priority on solving a problem together, rather than pursuing a theoretical predilection, methodological orientation, or personal belief. The latter are all resources, but advancing them is not the primary goal. At the most fundamental level, NIC participation challenges the long-standing norm of autonomy in practice that educators have traditionally prized. It means recognizing that today's problems cannot be solved through isolated individual actions. Each participant holds expertise that is valuable in solving a given problem, but each also recognizes that he or she must join together with others to solve it. Consequently, the life of a NIC entails a profound normative shift. It vitalizes a core belief that we can accomplish more together than even the best of us can accomplish alone.

WHY ALL OF THIS MATTERS NOW

Our nation's schools are, and have been for decades, in a constant state of reform.[39] By many accounts they are actually getting better.[40] Unfortunately, our aspirations for schools are accelerating at a faster rate. Consequently, a growing chasm exists between these noble aspirations and what schools can actually achieve.

Today we ask more of our public schools than ever before. The No Child Left Behind Act of 2001 compelled attention to the learning of all of our nation's students, not just some. The new Common Core State Standards substantially raise the bar as to what this learning entails. So as a first priority, we want our schools to become more effective in advancing deeper learning for all students. Second, we live in a time in which tremendous pressures exist on the public purse. For several decades, education commanded increasing public resources. Now the expectation is that our schools should not only get better results but also do so more efficiently. Third, far too many students remain disengaged, walking out the doors of our high schools and colleges and never completing their education. Turnover among teachers, principals, and superintendents is also unacceptably high, and morale is at an all-time low.[41]

A significant advance on any one of these three aims—greater academic effectiveness, cost efficiency, and human engagement—would be a major accomplishment. Simultaneously improving on all three counts would be extraordinary. Yet this is precisely what our educational institutions must now do.

We return to the example with which we began—the movement toward small high schools. The alienating quality of large urban high schools motivated this reform. Small schools promised, and often delivered, much more engaging environments for both students and teachers. But many advocates for this reform largely ignored questions about how instruction would actually improve in small schools. And then suddenly, when they were confronted with an economic downturn and increasing fiscal pressures, policy shifted toward consolidating smaller schools. It was now argued that larger schools provided access to a wider array of courses and services and were more cost efficient. But what about the implications for student and faculty engagement? And how would this change actually enable more effective instruction?

Attaining the *Triple Aims of Educational Improvement*—improved effectiveness, greater efficiency, and enhanced engagement—seems inconceivable to us so long as we continue to pursue reforms as we typically do.[42] Success will elude educational leaders and each new cadre of educational reformers unless they and their institutions are equipped with better ways of understanding the practical problems needing address and with more systematic approaches toward their improvement.

This book is about setting out a new path—a more dependable way for educators to improve their schools. Our goal is to unleash the dynamism of networked improvement communities. They are our best hope for crossing the growing quality chasm in education.

1

Make the Work Problem-Specific and User-Centered

The problem is that managing quality is not just an intellectual endeavor; it is a pragmatic one. The point is not just to know what makes things better or worse; it is to make things actually better.

—DONALD BERWICK[1]

CONSISTENT AND SUSTAINED improvement has been hard to achieve in education. Despite the best efforts of researchers and policy makers, the policies and programs that educators are asked to implement and the tools they are asked to use often don't help schools improve. Sometimes they even produce perverse effects. A story from an unlikely source offers a fresh perspective on how we might better approach these tasks in the future.

UNCOVERING THE PROBLEM: DESIGNING A BETTER SOAP?

In the mid-1990s, executives at Procter & Gamble (P&G) were worried.[2] Although the company maintained a lion's share of the market for floor-cleaning products, its competitive position was eroding. Other companies' products did pretty much the same thing, and floor cleaning remained a difficult and unpleasant task. P&G's leaders concluded that they needed a new product—one that made floor-cleaning better—to reestablish their market dominance. So they turned to their industrial chemists, some of the finest in the world, to create something new. The chemists immediately set out to design a better soap.

Making a better detergent to clean floors, it turns out, is a tough chemical engineering task. Make the detergent too mild, and the floor won't get cleaned. Make the detergent too strong, and you risk irritating the customer's skin or ruining the floor's finish. A new detergent would need to do a good job of grabbing the dirt and adhering to the mop. But better adherence would also make the mop more difficult to rinse. Finding the right balance was challenging. Even after several years of experimenting, P&G's scientists and engineers weren't very close to their goal.

P&G's then-CEO, John Pepper, chose a new direction. He named Craig Wynett to direct a new innovation unit within P&G. Wynett decided to take a fresh approach and sought the advice of Harry West, CEO of Continuum, a well-respected design and innovation team. West reckoned that his team could never outdo P&G's scientists when it came to chemical engineering. If they were to make progress on this problem, insight would need to be found elsewhere.

What did Continuum do? Its designers got out of the lab and went into the field. They spent a lot of time on the job floor—literally observing customers as they mopped floors in their homes. They learned that mops were unwieldy. They were OK at absorbing dirt, but rinsing the mop in the bucket and then squeezing out the water was hard work. If the bucket became really dirty, the water had to be dumped, a new solution had to be made, and the mop thoroughly rinsed. The Continuum designers noticed that users actually spent more time cleaning the mop than washing the floors. Gradually, the designers came to understand that the real problem was how to make cleaning floors easier. A solution might entail something different than simply making a better soap.

Continuum noticed along the way that some people actually cleaned their floors before the designers visited their homes. These housekeepers wanted their guests to see a clean home, even if the guests were there to talk about dirty floors. Since a precleaned floor was a problem in terms of Continuum's learning goals, its designers would sometimes intentionally spill coffee on the floor to see what would happen. Often housekeepers would immediately reach for a paper towel, moisten it with a bit of water from the faucet, wipe the floor, and then throw away the paper towel.

Suddenly, an idea for a very different solution emerged: it wasn't about the soap. It was about the mop. From these observations, designers invented the Swiffer—a disposable wipe attached to a mop handle.[3] In short, a work-around created by housekeepers had inspired a brand new product.

Continuum's key to success was getting very clear about the specific problem to solve. The P&G chemists, drawing on their own academic and technical expertise, had jumped immediately to a solution: design a better soap. Seeing the problem as a chemical engineering task is what chemists naturally do. Continuum, in contrast, began by observing the actual experiences of those who used the floor-cleaning products. They drew insights from these observations to both understand the problem better and visualize a new way to do the job better.

Interestingly, even after Continuum's work had coalesced around the idea for the Swiffer, it was not immediately accepted inside P&G. Before taking Swiffer to market, P&G resorted to its traditional method for testing a potential new product by providing a consumer test group with a written description of the Swiffer. Housekeepers seemed reticent to abandon their tried-and-true mops for some kind of "wipe on a stick." Continuum convinced P&G to forgo the written descriptions of the mop in favor of an actual prototype that housekeepers could really try out. When P&G did this—essentially revisiting the job floor—the test consumers liked the product a lot more. And, as they say, the rest is history: Swiffer has become one the most popular and profitable floor-cleaning products ever invented.

DIAGNOSING SOLUTIONITIS:
AN EDUCATION REFORM DISEASE

Why is the Swiffer example instructive for educational improvement? When a problem presents itself, it is natural for people to formulate a solution based on their past experiences, professional knowledge, and beliefs about what seems appropriate. P&G has deep expertise in chemical engineering and employs an extraordinary group of industrial chemists who have had great success in creating solvents. So when they were faced with finding a more effective way to clean floors, the obvious path seemed to lie in redesigning the soap. If you have a hammer, it's human nature to believe that a problem can be fixed by just pounding away. This strategy is not peculiar to P&G; it simply reflects how individuals, groups, and organizations tend to think and act. And it can easily lead to a phenomenon that we call *solutionitis*.

Solutionitis is the propensity to jump quickly on a solution before fully understanding the exact problem to be solved. It is a form of groupthink in which a set of shared beliefs results in an incomplete analysis of the problem to be addressed and fuller consideration of potential problem-solving alternatives. When decision makers see complex matters through a narrow lens, solutionitis lures them into unproductive strategies.

This sort of siloed thinking is especially problematic in education. With its professionals and institutions under constant scrutiny, education has become an easy target for new suddenly popular ideas to move quickly across the field.[4] As noted in the introduction, this was the case with the calls for small high schools and the push for more intensive teacher evaluations. Other examples abound. There was a time, for example, when educational policy leaders were enthralled with downsizing. They argued that if empowered, teachers, parents, and community members would make better local decisions than some distal, often unresponsive central bureaucracy. Then the field discovered James Coleman's research on the significance of social capital, and developing it seemingly became the solution to most every problem. More recently, we have heard a lot about data-driven decision making. As big ideas like these gain currency, they begin to take on the character of solutions in search of problems to solve. In short, the hot idea becomes the new hammer.

The Teacher Incentive Solution

Some of the strongest voices in the chorus of educational reformers today are public policy analysts trained in microeconomics. In this community, financial incentives are a coin of the realm, and not surprisingly, they are now a common point of conversation in many educational circles. As we have noted, the recent introduction of more rigorous teacher evaluation systems is directly tied to the use of financial incentives. With more empirically based teacher evaluations, schools would now have the necessary data to institute a system in which teachers were paid according to performance.

Supporters of pay-for-performance see improvements resulting through three interrelated mechanisms. First, as the theory goes, attracted by the prospect of better pay, more capable people will enter the profession and teaching will thereby improve. Second, effective teachers will more readily persist in a teaching career because of increased salaries. Third, and most sweeping, productivity will increase systemwide as financial incentives encourage all teachers to improve their students' learning. Once the policy community focuses on an idea like this, solutionitis spreads rapidly.

In 2006, the U.S. Department of Education launched the Teacher Incentive Fund (TIF). Under this initiative, funded at $1.6 billion through FY 2012, districts were motivated to offer performance bonuses to teachers who improved student outcomes. The federal Race to the Top (RTT) competition, begun in FY 2010, expanded this discretionary district-level program to one of statewide mandates, funding it with another $5 billion. Then in 2011, the education department allowed states to apply for waivers to certain requirements of the federal No Child Left Behind Act. To qualify for a waiver, states had to pledge improvements to their teacher evaluation systems, and they were strongly encouraged to include performance pay incentives. The prospect of receiving RTT funds during a major economic recession, along with likely relief from inevitable NCLB sanctions, proved powerful motivators for districts and states.[5]

The rapid spread of performance pay from a handful of districts in 2007 to a nationwide movement in 2011 was not slowed by research findings, which suggested that even well-executed reforms to teacher compensation might not be especially effective in improving student outcomes.[6] Ironically, at a time when so many are calling for federal education policy to ground itself more solidly in evidence, no research whatsoever was cited in the original design of these policies. And today, we still lack evidence to warrant such a major experiment in public education.[7]

So here is yet one more example of how a reform idea—financial incentives—took on great salience. States and districts move quickly to implement changes with little understanding of how to accomplish them, modest capacity at best to execute on them, and no real evidence to predict what might actually happen. Not surprisingly, huge problems with implementation have ensued. At a most basic level, it remains unclear how districts and states will even be able to finance these initiatives once outside funding ends.

School reform, like the creation of Swiffer, is an act of design. Firms like Continuum have a record of making good progress on hard problems by following a golden rule: observe and consult the people on the ground who know the most about the problem. Translating this practice into education means that if we want to improve the quality of teaching, we should pay close attention to the work teachers actually do and to what really matters to those who do it.

Fortunately, we know a lot about teachers' work, why they are attracted to the profession, why they stay or not, and in most basic terms, what sustains their efforts.[8] This knowledge provides a good starting point for a more user-centered and problem-specific approach to improving teaching and learning.

We know, for example, that the principal rewards that teachers' experience and value are intrinsic in character. It is in the lives that teachers touch, "seeing the lights turn on" as their students learn, and contributing significantly toward social well-being. To be sure, teachers would appreciate and deserve better remuneration, but, historically at least, money is not what makes them go. So, introducing significant financial incentives into this mix creates a brand new world for teachers. It has the potential to induce profound and largely unknown change in the meaning and values that educators associate with this work of human betterment. Could this be productive? Possibly. Could it also do great harm? Yes, quite possibly too. We simply don't know.

As for the hypothesized effects on student learning associated with improving the quality of new recruits, we can project likely results based on evaluations of the Teach For America (TFA) program. TFA has been highly effective in bringing extraordinary young people into teaching in some of our nation's most troubled schools; it is hard to imagine any large school system recruiting as well.[9] This point is significant, because evaluations of TFA document modest positive effects in select areas, particularly in middle and high school mathematics instruction, but not in other areas such as teaching children to read. Most important, the distribution of learning gains among TFA classrooms is just as wide as that found in non-TFA classrooms.[10] So while recruiting more of our nation's best talent into schools would surely be a good thing, on its own it is not likely to make quality teaching occur more regularly in our nation's schools.

Likewise, we know a fair amount about the factors affecting teacher retention. Some schools are far more challenging places to work in than others, and they are likely to experience greater teacher turnover. Even in the most challenging situations, however, the key to teacher persistence is the quality of collegial ties and the supportiveness of the school principal.[11] Recognizing the significance of these factors would direct consideration toward how state and district actions might strengthen these school-based professional connections. Performance pay is not an obvious response if this is the problem one seeks to solve.

We also know that the vast majority of teachers work hard at their jobs.[12] This fact is important because extrinsic incentives (e.g., paying people for performance) are most likely to be effective for cases in which increasing individual effort is a major concern.[13] However, improving teaching is not primarily a matter of getting teachers to work harder; it's about getting them to work smarter. Put differently, if teachers knew how to teach better, they would surely do it. This perspective demands closer attention to the systems that prepare people to teach and then support their continued development in our nation's schools. Here, too, financial incentives do not seem especially relevant for the improvements that need to occur.

Our point here is not to argue against financial incentives. Rather, we cite this case to reinforce our first principle, that of being user- and problem-centered. Applying this principle to efforts aimed at improving the quality of teaching means engaging teachers and focusing on the factors that shape how their work is carried out. Educational leaders gain unexpected insights when they do attend to these details. An initiative of Baltimore Public Schools, as part of their engagement with the Building a Teaching Effectiveness Network (BTEN), opens a window to the kind of on-the-ground improvement work actually required to help teachers get better at what they do.

Taking a Step Back: A Learning-to-Improve Example

New teachers have a lot on their plates. Among other things, they have to master classroom routines, develop empathetic relationships with students and parents, and build good working relationships with colleagues. While they are grappling with all these things, they have to master both the curriculum and ways to teach it engagingly to students. And they must orchestrate all of these elements day after day. To develop such a complex sets of skills, new teachers need regular feedback.

State-mandated teacher evaluations in Maryland are generating information about teaching that might be useful for such feedback. Typically, a district would form a team, develop a protocol for providing feedback, and move as quickly as possible to roll out this new process systemwide. But Jarrod Bolte, formerly the director of teacher development for Baltimore Public Schools, had a different idea. Building on what he was learning through his participation in BTEN, Bolte and his team went out first to talk with new teachers about what was actually happening to them and the kinds of feedback they were receiving. What they learned was surprising.

"Many times, we think the answer is to do more," says Bolte, "when actually, if you do less, in a focused way, you get better results."[14] Bolte and colleagues created a simple protocol asking new teachers to keep track of who visited with them to provide advice and feedback. As it turned out, some new teachers were already receiving lots of feedback—in some cases from ten or more different sources. In figure 1.1, Bolte and colleagues illustrate the maze of advice-giving that these new teachers confront.

At the same time, the improvement team also learned that other new teachers received almost no feedback. So Baltimore had two quite different problems to solve. For some teachers, the problem was too much feedback from too many different people—feedback that was uncoordinated, often incoherent, and sometimes in outright conflict with one another. Elsewhere, the problem was not enough feedback; the challenge was how to assure that all new teachers received regular advice that might actually help them improve their teaching.

Figure 1.1   Many new teachers experience a blizzard of guidance.

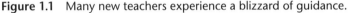

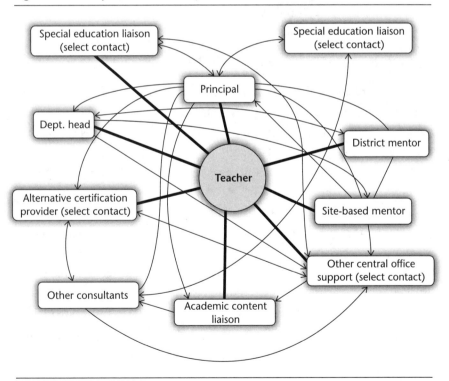

As with the Swiffer case, seeing the issue from the users' perspectives (looking closely at the feedback teachers were actually experiencing) created a deeper understanding of the problems to be solved. The "aha moment" was recognizing the great variability in how this process was currently being carried out. One thing seemed clear: Baltimore had a complex and highly varied system of processes that needed improvement. Layering another centrally developed and mandated protocol on top of all of this was not likely to help.

The Swiffer case and the Baltimore schools case share some commonalities. In Baltimore, as at P&G, Bolte and his colleagues interrupted the standard protocol for change. They embraced instead an improvement science orientation. They sought to learn more about actual teacher needs and the contexts in which these needs occur. Baltimore could easily have succumbed to another instance of solutionitis, in which leaders, lacking a deep understanding of teachers and their problems, are led down a garden path to initiatives that don't work.

BECOMING USER- AND PROBLEM-FOCUSED IN EDUCATION

Before the 1980s, the state of the art was to write manuals to guide people through what were often poorly designed products and services. How easy or difficult it might be for individuals to use these items was largely an afterthought. Ideas about engaging users in the initial design process and the continued refinement of these products and services was a totally foreign concept.

Today, a very different set of practices guides the design enterprise. This field has come to learn that good designs emerge through a multistage process. Designers now regularly seek to (1) observe people as they carry out their work; (2) understand how contextual factors shape this work activity; (3) visualize how individuals might engage with new tools and routines; (4) develop, evaluate, and refine changes in prototypes based on users' experiences with them; and (5) exploit the insights generated through these processes to engineer better goods and service for use effectively at scale. In these ways, leaders such as Tom Kelley at IDEO along with Harry West at Continuum and others have transformed how design activity is now carried out across many different industries.

In writings that presaged the advent of firms like IDEO and Continuum, psychologist Don Norman revolutionized design thinking with his groundbreaking book *The Psychology of Everyday Things*.[15] Norman recounts the travails of people trying to navigate poorly designed objects— from telephone systems to TV remote controls. He envisioned a better way. According to Norman, good design focuses first on people (the users). It identifies the problems that characterize the products and services that people use; then it sets out to build new ones that better fit their needs. Even though Norman's work centered on the design of physical objects, his insights are broadly relevant from designing large-scale educational policies to the microprocesses of work in classrooms and schools.

By and large, today's educational interventions proceed as though uninformed by the revolution in user-centered design.[16] In the teacher quality case, we highlighted how solutions have emerged out of a conceptual silo dominated by microeconomic thinking imported from outside educational practice. We could just as easily have detailed other thought communities that suffer their own strain of solutionitis.

For example, teacher educators in our nation's colleges and universities have labored for decades to establish legitimacy for a professional knowledge base about teaching. This thought community supported the development of national board certification and now advocates for a national "bar exam" for new teachers. In a way, the bar exam idea shares common ground with Teach For America in that both focus on changing how individuals enter the classroom. As with Teach For America, the introduction of a bar exam would surely improve the basic quality of talent coming into the field. Yet even a rigorous bar exam is unlikely to reduce much the wide variation in student outcomes found across classrooms and schools. Considerable variability, for example, persists today even among classrooms with national board-certified teachers.[17] A bar exam also is not likely to change the school conditions that affect how teachers work together, support each other to create more engaging environments for students, and continuously improve teaching. And it would not directly address on-the-ground organizational problems such as those the BTEN team identified in Baltimore.

Teacher education researchers have carried out many studies that offer rich analyses of teaching, teacher learning, professional development, and other topics. Numerous conceptual perspectives guide these inquiries and sometimes yield significant theoretical insights.[18] However, the premium in these studies is on conceptual originality, on detailing fine differences among alternative frameworks for examining teaching and learning. The development of original theories, rather than the solving of specific problems, is typically placed in the first position. Consequently, these studies rarely provide the detailed practical guidance that educators need to improve educational quality at any kind of scale.

Likewise, an enormous educational research and evaluation industry has become expert at identifying shortcomings in existing educational policies and new program interventions. These studies, in contrast to the more theory-based educational research described previously, are highly applied. But documenting that there is a problem with a new policy or intervention is not the same as knowing how to solve it. How actually to improve teaching and how better to organize classrooms, schools, and districts to support learning depend on a distinctive form of empirically grounded know-how—how to make things work. It is this target—making things work better—that improvement research places in the first position.

Management and organization experts Jeffrey Pfeffer and Robert Sutton have called this disconnection the "knowing–doing gap."[19] In essence, they argue that it is one thing to know that some bit of knowledge is germane to a problem and quite another to turn that knowledge into action. Effective problem solving demands that a premium be placed not just on *what* needs to be fixed but also on knowing *why* systems currently work as they do and learning *how* they might be reformed toward the goal of greater efficacy at scale.

Becoming more user-centered is key to accomplishing these goals. At its most basic level, being user-centered means respecting the people who actually do the work by seeking to understand the problems they confront. It means engaging these people in designing changes that align with the problems they really experience.[20] And this in turn requires different relationships among educational practitioners, researchers, and those holding various types of technical expertise. Now the nature of these connections may take on varied forms, depending on the problem and its contexts. For example, even in a very technical domain such as developing a better house-cleaning product, the key design insight for Swiffer came through observing a work-around invented by housekeepers (i.e., the wet paper towel they used to clean a coffee spill). The technical expertise of P&G scientists was then drawn in to engineer the chemistry of a good wipe cloth and the design of a cheap and effective mop handle.

In chapter 3, we describe a very different form of a design partnership. An experimental intervention, originating in basic social psychology, had demonstrated that it is possible to change students' mindsets about their ability to learn math. The key question was whether this experimental intervention could be translated into a practice that actually helped community college students. Inventing this practice entailed iterative cycles of design, tryout, and refinement among the original academic researchers, community college faculty, and their students. Each had distinct insights that needed to be blended together.

In still other situations, practicing educators may take on the lead role as improvers, and academic researchers become primarily advisors and coaches. We detail an instance of this in chapter 5 where the Austin, Texas, public school district also took on the problem of improving teacher feedback. School principals became improvement leaders, working in tandem with their own teachers, a district team, and an improvement coach. Their goal was ambitious: to create more effective and reliable processes for feedback that would work across many different school contexts in the Austin district.

Whatever the example, our general point is simple: engaging insights from the job floor can break the susceptibility to solutionitis and the prevailing one-size-fits-all approach to educational reform.

The experience of the teaching profession during the twentieth century, and into the twenty-first, has not been one in which teachers' expertise has shaped major efforts to improve practice and designed policies more conducive to these outcomes.[21] Teachers have far less input than do other professionals into the factors that affect their work. Far too many efforts at improvement are designs delivered *to* educators rather developed *with* them. Not surprisingly, then, when teachers are presented with new ideas for change, they may just mutter, "This, too, shall pass."

The pursuit of quality, across many different sectors and industries, has taught us an important lesson: it is essential that all involved in the work be active agents in its improvement. This means that all those engaged in educating students must own the outcomes of their efforts and be actively learning how to improve these outcomes. This notion stands in sharp contrast to the current situation, in which many seem to believe that those who stand apart from the work—whether they are researchers, policy pundits, or lawmakers—are somehow "better knowers." Likewise, it stands in sharp contrast to a reform nostrum that educators should just "implement programs as others have designed them." The latter attitude tends to encourage thinking along the lines of, "I did what you told me to do, and beyond this I am not responsible for any outcomes that may ensue." The endemic quality problems that result from this way of working were lessons hard-learned by American industry from its Japanese counterparts.[22]

Finally, and most profoundly, a user-centered philosophy assigns great dignity to, and shows great respect for, all who work in our nation's schools. As a lot, educators are creative, rational, and well-intentioned human beings. Design arrangements can and should do a better job of according their work the status it deserves. At the same time, it is important to recognize that professional status does not accrue simply by virtue of a position held or a claim about some academic knowledge.[23] Rather, a profession knows how to *do* something; it knows how to make some socially valued outcomes occur reliably, over and over. Building this kind of knowledge is the goal of networked improvement communities.

2

Focus on Variation
in Performance

*[V]ariation itself is nature's only irreducible essence. Variation is the hard
reality, not a set of imperfect measures for a central tendency.*

—STEPHEN JAY GOULD[1]

GOULD'S INSIGHT POINTS toward a second principle guiding improvement efforts. Achieving improvements at scale is not about what works on average. It is about getting quality results under a variety of conditions. Understanding the sources of variation in outcomes, and responding effectively to them, lies at the heart of quality improvement. This principle is true whether one is making cars in different factories, flying commercial airliners manned by different crews, or teaching reading in different classrooms. We should expect well-built cars regardless of the assembly line; safe, efficient flights regardless of the crew; and successful readers regardless of who is teaching them. To introduce this principle, we look to an example from health-care quality improvement.

IMPROVING THE TREATMENT OF ADOLESCENT ASTHMA

Dr. Mona Mansour is the director of primary care at Cincinnati Children's Hospital. Her close colleague Jeffrey Simmons is associate director of clinical operations for hospital medicine. Their work together places them at the front line of efforts to improve how the hospital provides care to the children of Cincinnati. The discrepant health outcomes among children and adolescents with asthma troubled them.

Asthma is a chronic health condition for many young people. Symptoms of the ailment include coughing, wheezing, and shortness of breath. Contact with dust mites, tobacco smoke, mold, rodents, and cockroaches can trigger these symptoms. The disease is the number one source of hospital admissions for children nationally and the cause of over one thousand five hundred annual admissions to Cincinnati Children's alone.[2]

Although there is no cure for asthma, its symptoms can be effectively managed through well-established protocols that include using medication and alleviating conditions in the home environment that can trigger asthma attacks.[3] These prevention and treatment strategies, however, didn't seem to work for nearly a quarter of Cincinnati Children's asthma patients. These children returned to the hospital over and over again. Mansour and Simmons wanted to know why.

To attack the problem, Mansour and Simmons assembled a diverse group from throughout the hospital, including doctors and nurses from emergency medicine, pulmonary care, and pediatrics. The team also involved social workers from local health clinics and other community agencies. The team's first task was to understand better whom the system was failing and why. Team members knew from national studies that children from low-income families and those who lived in poorer neighborhoods experienced more emergency room visits, hospitalizations, and deaths due to asthma than the general population.[4] So the team reviewed clinical records that provided information about the demographics and home environments of the patients who were making repeated trips to the hospital. They also began to look more closely at exactly how health and social services were being provided to these children and their families.

One important clue in the patients' health records was that nearly a quarter of the children and adolescents treated for asthma under the Medicaid insurance program returned to Cincinnati Children's within ninety days. In contrast, the return rate for children with private insurance was half that. As Mansour, Simmons, and their Asthma Control Team dug deeper, a set of precipitating factors began to emerge. The medical records for readmitted patients were often incomplete. Especially significant, intake interviews often lacked detail about home conditions that might trigger asthma attacks. In addition, because of employment instability, housing problems, and concerns about neighborhood safety, poor and immigrant families in Cincinnati are more mobile than the population at large. So their children tend to receive treatment at multiple medical facilities, and their health-care records often don't move smoothly with them. In contrast, privately insured children were much more likely to consistently go to the same health-care providers in the same facility. Thus, their records tended to be much more thorough. The team knew that well-documented patient records were essential to effective plans for comprehensive care. So one part of the problem came into view.

The practices of health-care professionals themselves represented a second important consideration. In the press of emergency room practice, the team found, providers sometimes failed to record key pieces of information in patients' files. In other instances, some staff hesitated to ask questions about home circumstances for fear of embarrassing parents. Consequently, environmental triggers in the homes of these children may have gone unnoticed, and referrals to appropriate social agencies may not have been made.

The Asthma Control Team took several steps in response to what they had learned. First, to ensure more complete patient profiles, they developed an asthma-specific intake template to ensure that Cincinnati Children's staff ask the right questions every time. The form required specific information about possible asthma-related triggers in patients' lives and whether patients had received asthma-related care from other providers. The team's goal, according to Simmons, "was to construct a template that engineered bad intake practices out of the system."[5] Although it took some time to refine the initial prototype into workable practice, once the template was used regularly, environmental histories were documented for virtually all patients. Referrals to agencies that could address asthma triggers in patients' homes were now occurring in much greater numbers.

Based on what the Asthma Control Team had learned, Cincinnati Children's also took the lead in forging partnerships with other health-care providers outside its system. These new partnerships eased the exchange of patient information in ways not previously the case; health-care providers could now access complete patient records regardless of where the patients were being served. This better access to full patient records had broad significance for improving the quality of health care across the neighborhoods of Cincinnati.

As efforts were proceeding on improving record keeping, the Asthma Control Team's attention shifted toward what happened to their patients after they left the hospital. Intake interviews indicated that many of the readmitted patients were not using prescribed medicines and that regular access to these medications was an issue. Some families lived in neighborhoods with no pharmacy nearby, and some pharmacies would not fill Medicaid-reimbursed prescriptions. Working with the hospital's pharmacy and outside insurance carriers, the Asthma Control Team developed a procedure that made sure patients would leave the hospital with their medication already in hand. They also made certain, through a new exit protocol, that patients were informed about the importance of taking these medications regularly.

Collectively, these new strategies changed the way Cincinnati Children's and its patients managed chronic asthma. The results were impressive. In less than eighteen months, the return rate for low-income patients declined substantially, and the difference in rates between publicly and privately insured patients virtually disappeared. The health-care system was now working well for both affluent and less-affluent patients alike.

The success of the Cincinnati Children's Asthma Control Team was remarkable, but not magical. While the hospital already followed a research-based treatment regime for asthma, the team had to learn how to make this protocol actually work for all of its patients. By interviewing patients and analyzing clinical records, the Asthma Control Team was able to discern who was responding to treatments and who was not. They also began to better understand the reasons for negative outcomes among the latter group. Variations in how key processes were being carried out—the intake interview, referrals to agencies to remediate environmental problems, co-ordination of patients' records, and access to and regular use of prescribed medication—were producing many of the undesirable outcomes. These observations led the Asthma Control Team to come up with a few new processes they hoped would improve results. As they introduced each of these processes, they tracked results and refined the processes based on the data. Using the methods of improvement research, Mansour, Simmons, and colleagues were able to close what initially seemed to be an intractable gap in health-care outcomes associated with a patient's race, ethnicity, and family income.

APPRECIATING PERFORMANCE VARIATION IN EDUCATIONAL SYSTEMS

Improvement science offers a very systematic but also highly practical set of principles and methods for advancing this same kind of learning in educational settings. To highlight the contrast between the improvement research case just described and existing research practices in education, we consider another past school reform effort: the introduction of instructional coaches.

Does Instructional Coaching Work?

A new role for education professionals—that of the instructional coach—began to emerge in U.S. schools early in the 1990s. Most notable in this regard were the efforts in District 2 in New York City. An account of these efforts, *High Performing Learning Communities,* reported remarkable improvements in student test scores.[6] Equally if not more significant, most everyone who had a chance to observe teaching and learning in the district's classrooms came away deeply impressed with the intellectual quality of the student work and with the expertise demonstrated by coaches in supporting teachers to improve this work.

Instructional coaching became the hot new reform idea. And as with other promising ideas, it was quickly taken up by districts nationwide. While District 2 had developed quality coaching in a very deliberate fashion over the course of almost a decade, other school districts went from zero to sixty in a matter of weeks. Not surprisingly, many of their efforts suffered from the problems we noted earlier: a lack of know-how for turning a good idea into workable practice, inadequate capacity to execute this new role with quality at scale, and resistance from some teachers, in this case, about the perceived intrusion of another educator into the privacy of their classroom. Our point is not to rehash further the propensity of educational leaders to implement fast and learn slow. Rather, we focus now on how the educational research enterprise intersects with reforms of this sort. Gould's insight about the fundamental character of variation proves prescient.

Because federal funding largely supported many of these new coaching initiatives, the federal government's educational research arm, the Institute of Education Sciences (IES), saw a need for a rigorous evaluation of coaching effectiveness. It commissioned a randomized control trial.[7] Even before the study began, however, the researchers encountered a clear problem. The coaching initiatives that were springing up so rapidly across the country were not all the same. Schools districts varied considerably in how they specified the goals for coaching and how they defined the coaches' roles. Consequently, coaches varied greatly in how they carried out their work. The field trial sponsored by the IES would look narrowly at only new coaches working at one grade level (grade 2) for one year. The coaches in the field trial were trained and supported through a professional development initiative specifically designed for the trial. (No district had ever used this particular instantiation of coaching and coach preparation before.) The final report concluded that instructional coaching produced no measurable effects on student learning. This finding appears in the What Works Clearinghouse (WWC), a federally supported initiative whose goal is to provide educational leaders with the information they need to improve school effectiveness.

Now, might instructional coaches actually have been effective in some of the field sites, with some teachers, and under certain conditions? We don't know. As is typically the case in a randomized control trial, the study focused primarily on comparing mean differences between two groups: those who received coaching and those who did not. In this research paradigm, the core quality improvement concern—understanding variation in performance—just disappears into the background. Because the study sought a precise answer about the average effectiveness of just one kind of coaching, carried out for just one year and in just one context, it told us virtually nothing about the efficacy of coaching as it was actually being enacted in many districts across the country. It also told us little about how coaching practices might be improved. To be clear, this is not a critique of the quality of this particular field trial. Rather, our comments are about the significance of the questions chosen to investigate and the methods used to pursue them.

Interestingly, IES also supported a field-initiated study of instructional coaching that took a different tack. The investigators examined the performance of one of the largest and oldest examples of literacy coaching in the United States: the Literacy Collaborative. The program has detailed coaching standards connected to a well-specified program for teaching and literacy learning.[8] It requires a full year of preparation for all new coaches.[9] Even under these conditions, arguably among the best-in-class, the investigators assumed that they would find variability both in the coaching and in the outcomes that resulted from it.

Coaching is by its very nature a complex intervention. Its effects depend on a host of considerations, including the quality of the coach, the nature of the school context where the coach works, and the content and amount of coaching that each teacher receives. Achieving quality outcomes requires detailed knowledge about how coaches might best carry out their work, about how best to respond to differences among teachers so that coaches might interact more effectively with them, and about critical aspects of school leadership necessary to develop and sustain this activity.

So the investigators set out to examine the effects of coaching, but now they did so based on a working theory about factors that might contribute to variation in student outcomes. The team developed a research design, measurement, and analysis strategy to explore this theory. During a baseline year of no treatment, they estimated an annual learning gain in each participating classroom and school. They then estimated the changes in student learning gains over each of the next three years, as classroom teachers were coached to improve their literacy teaching.

What did they learn? When one is open to seeing it, variation abounds. First, the effects of the Literacy Collaborative program varied over time. Researchers detected a small on-average positive effect on student learning in the first year as novice coaches began to take up their new roles. This effect more than doubled over the next two years. Three years in, students in Literacy Collaborative classrooms were learning 38 percent more on average than did their peers during the baseline year.[10] Improving teaching and improving coaching in support of this are complex change processes that require time to develop. Consequently, it is reasonable to expect that the effects of an intervention in this domain might change as the initiative matures. Thus, studying a coaching intervention in only its first year, as was the case in the IES field trial, can be misleading in assessing its ultimate value.

Second, the study team learned that the effects of coaching varied across the primary grades, with the largest improvements accruing in kindergarten. This finding prompted the Literacy Collaborative team to consider how they might make their coaching more powerful in grades 1 and 2.

Third, as expected, effects varied considerably across schools (see figure 2.1). The successful introduction of a coach into a school requires the formation of a new set of work relationships among the principal, coach, and school faculty. Developing supportive social connections was an initial challenge for all schools. Unfortunately, productive relationships never fully developed in a few schools, and effects appeared weaker there.[11]

This finding has implications for how a district thinks about allocating its resources. Rather than the quick introduction of coaches systemwide to every school, it encourages district leaders to consider how best to target coaching initiatives. Where is coaching most likely to add value quickly, and where must other considerations be addressed first in order to assure readiness for instructional coaching to take deep root? This finding also had implications for the Literacy Collaborative's own efforts to continue to improve. How might it, for example, strengthen its

Figure 2.1 Variation in value-added effects over three years of Literacy Collaborative program implementation for seventeen different schools (These effects are over and above performance in the baseline year.)

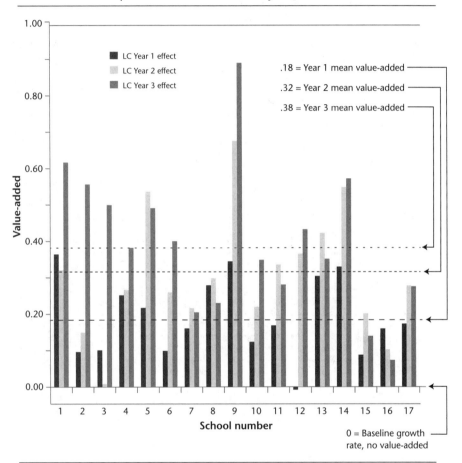

Source: Graph by Gina Biancarosa, Anthony S. Bryk, and Emily R. Dexter. © 2010 by The University of Chicago. http://www.press.uchicago.edu/ucp/journals/journal/esj.html

program to better support coaches who are placed in schools not especially conducive to this work?

Fourth, coaching had variable effects on teachers. A few teachers showed little or no change in student learning. Others more than doubled their student learning gains (figure 2.2). Particularly informative, the study

Figure 2.2   Variation in teacher value-added effects over the first three years of Literacy Collaborative program implementation. (Separate box plots are shown for each school and year.)

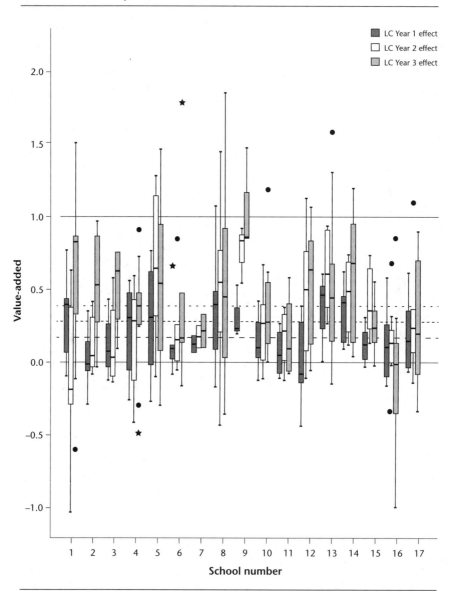

Source: Graph by Gina Biancarosa, Anthony S. Bryk, and Emily R. Dexter. © 2010 by The University of Chicago. http://www.press.uchicago.edu/ucp/journals/journal/esj.html

documented considerable variability in the amount of coaching that different teachers received. Teachers who received more coaching were more likely to improve.[12] This finding points to a basic quality improvement challenge: how to make sure that coaching happens consistently for more teachers.

Lastly, the study's findings moved the Literacy Collaborative to scrutinize more deeply the actual quality (not just frequency) of coaching occurring in their schools. Among other actions, leaders of the Literacy Collaborative developed a formative assessment rubric to gauge the progress of coaches as they were being prepared and as they were growing in the job. Through the process of creating this measurement tool, Literacy Collaborative leaders developed more explicit and shared understandings about the fundamentals of good coaching. It sharpened their attention to a core set of questions: What do our coaches actually see in the classrooms? How do they interpret what they see? And what should they subsequently say and do? Historically, these deep details about coaching are largely relegated to the domain of a private practice carried out by individual coaches. There were now reasons to believe that systematic improvement research focused on key aspects on these key questions might well yield better quality overall.

All of these insights were derived from one study of variation in performance in seventeen schools. Now, imagine if a national network of teachers and schools (a topic we will take up in chapter 6) were engaged with researchers and program developers to generate data of this same sort, year in and year out, and from many more places. The compendium of evidence would inform educators as to what is more likely to work, where, and under what conditions. Moreover, as educators used this evolving knowledge, the evidence itself would be further tested and refined through practical applications. Equally important, such evidence would provide critical guidance to program designers about how to sustain efficacy in response to inevitable local adaptations that will occur as the intervention is taken up in many different schools and districts.

In short, getting smarter about how to successfully replicate results under diverse conditions is the key analytic challenge for quality improvement. As with the IES randomized control trial, the Literacy Collaborative study produced an estimate of the "on-average effect" of its coaching.[13] But it also told us that the intervention appeared to work better in some places than others; it generated evidence about the contours of this variation and plausible factors that might be contributing to it. Educators need precisely this kind of information to identify opportunities for quality improvement. Unfortunately, no governmental or professional infrastructure currently exists for engaging educators in developing and testing such practice-based knowledge and synthesizing what is being learned along the way.

PURSUING QUALITY IN STANDARD WORK PROCESSES

As you walk into a classroom, what do you look at? Should you attend to what the teacher is saying or to the conversations that may be occurring among students? Should you focus on the subject matter students are working on? Or perhaps how the room is physically arranged? Does the environment appear orderly and safe? Do all students seem motivated and actively engaged? The list of features that might grab your attention grows long quickly. This phenomenon is characteristic of work in complex environments.

The key to improvement is seeing the actual organization of work amidst this complexity.[14] At Cincinnati Children's, for example, Mansour and Simmons zeroed in on a few key processes that had important consequences for both asthma patients and their caregivers. Improving the intake interview, for example, helped the hospital staff determine which caregivers to assign to patients and how the staff should engage with them. And by redesigning the exit process, the hospital staff improved patients' access to and use of the medicines they needed to stay healthy.

A general finding applies here. All work, regardless of profession or sector, involves sets of processes. In the complex organizations that characterize modern life, multiple related processes typically occur simultaneously. Each of these processes, in turn, may link to other processes that sequence out over time. Quality improvement—getting more of the outcomes one wants—requires attention to how these various processes are currently conducted, to identifying opportunities for carrying them out better, and to testing these changes over time against data. This is exactly what Mansour and Simmons did in seeking to improve outcomes for their asthma patients.

Within any organized system of activity, the individual work process is the basic unit for improvement-focused inquiry. Since an organization's capacity to engage in improvement efforts is limited at any given point in time, choices inevitably must be made. Educators will often want to concentrate on *high-leverage processes*. Such processes have the following properties: (1) they consume substantial resources, especially teacher or student time; (2) their execution and outcomes vary considerably; and (3) there are reasons to believe that changes in these processes might yield significant improvements. Such processes abound in schooling and often suffer from poor execution. Improvement research here can make a big difference.

High-leverage processes become attractive targets for detailing out as *standard work*. The concept of standard work is central to quality improvement, but it is also a multifaceted and carefully nuanced idea. It can be easily confused, for example, with efforts to de-skill professional practice. Its goal is exactly the opposite. The development of standard work aims to better support the activities that professionals engage in so that they are more likely to achieve positive outcomes reliably over and over. In this chapter, we aim simply to introduce the concept and offer a rationale for it. We will return to and elaborate further on it over the next several chapters.

Atul Gawande, in his book *Better*, cites an early exemplar of detailing standard work in health care.[15] Up through the 1920s, infant and maternal mortality rates were very high in childbirth; one in every one hundred fifty pregnancies ended in the death of the mother. Forceps were commonly used in difficult deliveries, and different doctors, responding to different conditions, invented a variety of forceps moves. Some became quite skilled, others much less so. The practice demanded considerable dexterity to be executed well, and learning to "feel" proved very difficult to teach to new physicians. So great variability in outcomes was inevitable. Too often, a misuse of forceps proved fatal to both mother and child. In sharp

contrast, the medical profession was able to detail an alternative procedure, the Cesarean section, so that many different doctors could execute
the procedure successfully, even under relatively primitive conditions.
Use of the C-section has greatly improved childbirth and substantially reduced maternal deaths.[16]

Gawande's account drives home the point that standard work processes help practitioners better address complex problems. Psychological
research has documented that humans have limited attention capacity
and that this capacity is especially challenged in situations that are emo-
tionally charged.[17] When individuals confront complex tasks, such as delivering a child safely or teaching a classroom of students well, human
errors will occur. Even the smartest, best educated, and most committed
professional can (and will) get it wrong when tasks become too demanding. Critical observations are missed; key steps are forgotten; miscommu-
nication happens. Improvement research is about achieving better quality
results under these difficult conditions.

In a seminal study, cognitive scientist Edwin Hutchins examined how
highly skilled airline pilots reliably execute demanding tasks that require
concentrated attention.[18] Hutchins shows that planes land successfully hundreds of times every day because airlines have created standard work. Over
time, they have developed numerous routines and supportive tools that coordinate the interaction of highly skilled people and intricate machines.
Because these procedures are now routine, they reduce the cognitive load
on pilots at critical junctures in their work and create spare attention capacity to focus on the unexpected, the particular, and the unusual.

So a general point emerges. Developing standard work processes is key
to reducing the stress and cognitive overload associated with carrying out
complex tasks. To the extent that at least select aspects of work can be
formulated as routines, human attention is freed to focus more sharply on
details particular to the immediate situation.[19] This creates conditions that
are more conducive to quality outcomes occurring more reliably. Put simply, as tasks become more complex, we need more good routines to rely on.

Forming standard work processes also responds to a second class of
problems that arise out of organizational complexity. In health care, for

example, patients may be harmed during shift changes, as various specialists and nurses interact with one another, and as patients move from one medical service to another.[20] Likewise, when educational activities are poorly aligned, students often lose out. They may fall through the cracks as they move from one school to the next, or from the general classroom to supplemental instruction. Breakdowns also occur as students and teachers interact with counselors, social workers, family members, and others both inside and outside school. The improvement research objective in confronting such organizational complexity is to synchronize better the efforts of various individuals and organizational units. It directs explicit attention to how individuals occupying different work roles engage one another and the norms that undergird how their interactions play out.

Despite seemingly obvious benefits, the idea of standard work processes can trigger negative reactions. In health care, for example, opponents argued that every patient was different, so efforts to formalize practices seemed nonsensical. It is not uncommon to hear similar statements in educational settings about every child, every classroom, every school, every district, and so on. Indeed, whether in medicine or education, the concept of standard work does challenge professional cultures that traditionally have prized individual autonomy and where one's professional identity is reflected in expressions about "*my* course," "*my* classroom," "*my* surgical theater," and so on.

It is important to recognize that the uniqueness of human interactions, whether between doctor and patient or teacher and student, is not the target of standard work. Students, like patients, are not interchangeable widgets and should not be treated as such. It also true, however, that a vast array of work processes operate in these interpersonal exchanges, and it is in the details of these processes where much of the variability in outcomes is introduced. Identifying the processes and creating good protocols for executing them make it possible to achieve greater quality more reliably at scale.[21] The members of the Asthma Control Team at Cincinnati Children's did not turn health-care providers into automatons; rather they created routines that enabled these practitioners to better achieve what they really cared about—serving all their patients well.

Returning to the educational context, pursuing quality through developing standard work processes is not a criticism of how educators do their job. As a whole, teachers work hard and want only the best for their students. Rather, the need for standard work processes simply reflects the complexity of the tasks that educators undertake and the systems through which they carry them out. Absent the supports provided by standard routines, highly variable consequences are the inevitable end result.

The educational context for this discussion is a long-standing, divisive, and largely dysfunctional debate. In one corner are the voices that say: "Every child, classroom, and school is unique, and therefore, each educator is a craftsman who must invent her own practice." This philosophy creates great variability in execution and outcome. As with the doctors and their forceps, instruction in some classrooms is superb, but in others sadly lacking.[22] In the opposite corner—responding to manifest weaknesses in the craftsman view—are those who are trying to teacher-proof instruction by scripting lessons to be followed "no matter what"—no matter who the students are, what may have just happened in the classroom, or what insights a teacher might have.[23] The aim of these reformers is literally to take the teacher out of the instructional equation—a goal that is naïve as well as demeaning to those whose good efforts are essential to the outcomes we desire.

Thus, placing the development of standard work processes at the heart of improvement research holds to a middle ground. It acknowledges that variability in performance is a major problem to solve, while also affirming that individual professional judgment will continue to play a central role in practice. Standard work processes are designed to assist, not replace, the deeply intellectual work of educating children. As in the case of the airline pilots, good standard work processes can free practitioners to better focus where they must and enhance their capabilities to exercise professional judgment well.

Correspondingly, the learning goal of a networked improvement community is to build an accumulating base of such processes through its improvement research efforts. To be clear, standard work processes are not some seemingly arbitrary standards imposed from outside or delivered from above. Rather, the community through its disciplined inquiries actively creates them, tests them, and refines them over time. To earn its warrant, a standard work process is anchored in evidence—*practice-based evidence*—that demonstrates that the process can work under a variety of conditions and that quality outcomes will typically ensue.[24] At any point in time, a set of standard work processes represents the NIC's best-practice knowledge. As in other scientific communities, this knowledge will evolve as participants continue to use these processes and learn how to further improve them.

An Example from Primary Literacy Instruction

Comprehensive literacy instruction is common in many U.S. primary schools. It is organized around a set of six regular practices: interactive read aloud, shared reading, interactive writing, writers' workshop, word study, and guided reading.[25] Among these, guided reading, in which a teacher typically teaches different students in three or four small groups each day, is arguably the highest-leverage activity. Guided reading consumes a lot of time—typically sixty to ninety minutes per day—and, if well executed, it is likely to support major gains in student learning.

At this point, some clarifying language is in order. Educators often refer to the activities such as those used in comprehensive literacy instruction as *practices*. But this term often has multiple meanings. In keeping with definitions common in improvement research, we refer to such activities as work *processes*. Each of the six practices mentioned here is actually a *macro-process* in that its execution typically entails a sequence of more detailed actions, each of which might be termed a *micro-process*.[26]

For example, six distinct micro-processes form the standard work of guided reading. (These are illustrated in figure 4.2 in chapter 4.) The first step is selecting an appropriate text for a given group of students. This is followed by two activities in which the teacher first introduces the text to students and then engages them in a prereading conversation to activate relevant knowledge they may already have about the topic. Next, as students attempt to read the text, the teacher provides support calibrated to where students are in their development as readers. The reading group concludes with two more micro-processes: assessing students' comprehension of the text and summarizing the learning objectives for that group on that particular day.

Each of these six micro-processes is scaffolded by a set of tools and routines. For example, texts are categorized by levels of difficulty. Data on students' current reading skills from a running record and other formative assessments, such as STEP assessments, help teachers select appropriate texts.[27] The texts are also organized by topic. This, too, guides selection, since engaging topics can motivate students to persist in the hard work of decoding. Even so, teachers must exercise considerable judgment as this standard work plays out in each reading group. This can be seen in teachers' planning for individual sessions as well as their in-the-moment decision making as instruction proceeds.

Although these micro processes are standard, they are not static; they continue to evolve as new evidence accrues. One might learn, for example, that some texts are categorized at the wrong level or that some are much better than others for advancing a particular learning objective. This continuous learning in practice informs periodic updates to libraries of leveled texts.

Finally, quality in execution is operationally defined for each micro process. For example, within the Literacy Collaborative, the conversation that the teacher has with students after they have read the text is designed to afford student practice in learning to comprehend the ideas in the text. The teacher's objective is to drive home the point that reading is much more than saying words aloud; it is a meaning-making activity. The quality of the lesson depends on whether the teacher is able to catalyze a rich conversation about the text just read. Tools now exist to guide coaches' observations of such teaching, and Literacy Collaborative coaches can reliably document differences between weaker and stronger lessons. These data in turn are useful in supporting more personalizing professional development for individual teachers and inform larger efforts to continue to improve how the process of guided reading is best carried out.[28]

To the untrained eye, guided reading may look like many other reading groups found in primary classrooms. When this practice is well executed, however, it is distinct and specific. Absent an explicit system of standard work processes to support reading group instruction, great variability in outcomes results.[29] This hidden complexity is a contributing factor as to why so many U.S. students fail to learn to read well.

The "DeJean Conversation"

The concept of standard work also creates a powerful lens for sharpening how we look at everyday practices in classrooms and schools. It directs us to further consider what many educators tacitly assume to be a craft activity. It invites us to question: "Might this be done more successfully if it were detailed as a standard work process?"

Early on in initiating our second NIC on enhancing the effectiveness of new teachers, we had an opportunity to observe a faculty team meeting in a New York City high school affiliated with New Visions for Public Schools. The school was in its second year of operation, and most of the staff were either first- or second-year teachers. It was mid-year, and the team was reviewing data on student progress. Students at risk for failure were identified and briefly discussed one by one. As the meeting was drawing to a close, each identified student was assigned to a teacher for individual mentoring. At this point, a first-year teacher, sitting toward the back of a two-ringed semicircle, timidly raised her hand and asked: "Well, how do I talk to DeJean? I know that I have to press him to work harder, but I also want him to know that I am on his side, that I am there to support him through all of this. I really care about him. How do I have this conversation?"

Suddenly, another high-leverage process had come into view. Such teacher–student conversations occur now with great frequency in many schools. Individual mentoring of at-risk students consumes considerable teacher time, and if done well, it can pay off in a big way. But for the most part, as with DeJean's assigned mentor, teachers must figure out how to do this largely on their own. Again, when a key activity like this lacks standard guidance, variability is likely to occur—both in how the process is carried out and in the outcomes achieved. Some teachers will clearly do better than others. Tragically, the field of education has no means to identify this expertise, detail what it consists of, and then test and refine it to advance the performance of the broader profession.

To reiterate, we recognize that each teacher–student interaction is highly particular. Each teacher must still forge a personal relationship with "her DeJean." Regardless, some common patterns surely remain embedded. If these can be explicated, if a provisional definition of quality enactment can be specified and then iteratively tested and refined under diverse conditions, an effective standard work protocol can emerge. (In chapter 5, we detail how Plan-Do-Study-Act cycles are designed and carried out toward this end.) Such a protocol would better support new teachers, such as those that we met at New Visions, as they take on these high-leverage tasks. Moreover, when some of the work complexity embedded in this important and sensitive process is reduced, it holds promise to improve quality more generally across classrooms and schools. Most significant, framing it as a standard work process opens up possibilities for systematic learning to improve it further.

LEARNING FROM VARIATION IN PERFORMANCE

It is common across many fields to find variability in performance that resembles the familiar bell-shaped curve, illustrated in the left panel of figure 2.3.[30] Improvement research seeks to reshape this distribution, moving overall performance to the right while dramatically reducing the frequency of negative outcomes. This is illustrated in the right panel of figure 2.3. Developing standard work processes is a key means of accomplishing this goal.

Interestingly, the starting point for developing effective work practices often already exists in practice. Surely some teachers, for example, are already very good at the "DeJean conversation," although we may not know who they are or exactly what it is that they are doing. That is, within the naturally existing variation seen in the left panel of figure 2.3 are opportunities for learning to improve. While it may not be a matter of "do exactly as I do," the practices of these teachers provide a starting point for systematic learning about how to get better.

Figure 2.3   Variation in performance: what we typically have and what we would like to see

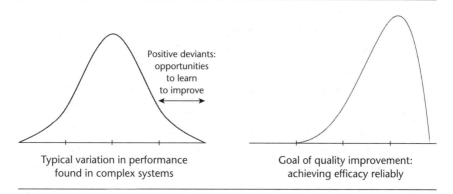

Typical variation in performance found in complex systems

Goal of quality improvement: achieving efficacy reliably

A marvelous little book called the *Power of Positive Deviance* introduces us to public health innovators Jerry and Monique Sternin. The Sternins' work took them into desperately poor villages in Vietnam.[31] They noticed that, even in the presence of dire childhood malnutrition, some children remained healthy. In public health lingo, these children were "positive deviants"—they deviated from the norm in a good way. The discovery of these families launched the Sternins on a journey of learning to improve. Specifically, they wanted to know what these families were doing differently that led them to have relatively healthy children when most children were not?

The Sternins found, among other things, that these families were feeding their children nutritious greens that were readily available but not normally part of the village diet. The families also fed their weakest children smaller quantities of food, but they fed them more often. They learned that children who ate more frequently built up strength. The Sternins were able to translate their observations into explicit nutrition guidance and then worked with the community to establish it as standard practice. Most of the villagers adopted these new practices, and the incidence of childhood malnutrition dropped by more than two-thirds.

Atul Gawande offers a similar lesson in an intriguing story about efforts to improve treatment of cystic fibrosis.[32] Some medical centers do significantly better than others in treating this deadly disease. By all accounts, Fairview-University Children's Hospital in Minneapolis is a positive deviant, outperforming its peers for decades. At a time when most hospitals expected CF patients to survive only to age ten, Fairview patients survived to age twenty-one. When the national survival age gradually rose to thirty-five years, at Fairview it had jumped to forty-six. Interestingly, all of the major treatment centers for cystic fibrosis follow exactly the same research-based protocol, and all staff members at these centers have been highly trained in its use. Regardless, outcomes still varied widely. What made Fairview a positive deviant? Gawande points to the hospital's relentless attention to detail. Fairview aggressively scrutinizes every aspect of the treatment process and seeks continuously to improve it. This laser-like focus on process quality became the model for others.

Next, we begin to dig deeper into the details of how the systematic work of improvement, illustrated in the Cincinnati Children's Hospital, Literacy Collaborative, Vietnam nutrition, and cystic fibrosis cases, is actually accomplished.

3

See the System That Produces the Current Outcomes

Making systems work is the great task of my generation of physicians and scientists. But I would go further and say that making systems work—whether in health care, education, climate change, making a pathway out of poverty—is the great task of our generation as a whole.

—ATUL GAWANDE[1]

WE SAW IN CHAPTER 2 how Mona Mansour and Jeffrey Simmons were troubled by the variable quality of outcomes among young asthma patients at Cincinnati Children's Hospital. So they set out to learn to improve. Their team scrutinized data on how the hospital provided care to these patients and then, based on what they learned, targeted and refined a set of changes to make the system work better for all children. This chapter introduces a set of tools and processes to assist in these tasks of understanding systems and organizing efforts to improve them. As context, we first need to examine a bit deeper the idea of a system, how complexity characterizes the functioning of modern-day social systems, and the important implications this has for efforts to improve them.

The word *system* is readily recognizable to educators as we regularly talk about *school systems*. But familiarity with the term also encourages casual use that obscures its significance for improving outcomes. Most educational reforms reflect at best a partial understanding of system dynamics, and some seem almost oblivious to the fundamental character of the phenomena they seek to change.

In general, the performance of any social system, whether a hospital, a school, or any other organization, is the product of interactions among the people engaged with it, the tools and materials they have at their disposal, and the processes through which these people and resources come together to do work. In simple systems, these interactions are few, and the resulting outcomes may be easily traced. In contrast, in most modern-day institutions the interactions are many in number and densely interconnected. Formally, these are called *complex systems*. Such systems can manifest behaviors that no one intentionally designed, and often it is hard to predict fully the outcomes that may ensue from attempts to change them.[2] This organizational fact transforms efforts to improve into *problems of learning to improve*. It directs us toward a *design-development orientation*, in which we try out change ideas quickly, analyze what happens, modify the ideas based on what we think we have learned, retry, and continue this learning cycle toward system improvement.

The third improvement principle, *seeing the system,* is essential to achieving quality outcomes reliably at scale. To tee up our discussion about this principle, we briefly review the commentary offered by Atul Gawande that led him to the conclusion quoted at the top of this chapter. Although he speaks from his experience in health care, the forces he describes also have salience for education.

Gawande begins his TED talk with a history lesson. He reminds us that medicine was once cheap and relatively simple. In the late 1930s, for instance, there were only a few conditions that doctors could actually treat. A stay in a hospital might offer warmth, food, and the caring attention of a nurse, but often not much more. The expectations for what health care could achieve were quite modest.

Today, of course, the practice of medicine is far different. A well-funded research and development infrastructure has dramatically altered what medical practitioners can do. There are now over ten thousand known human conditions and some four thousand medical and surgical procedures and six thousand drugs to treat them. Over twenty-seven thousand clinical trials were reported in just 2010 alone.[3]

Yet with progress has come problems. Far too often, a wide gap exists between what the profession believes it should be able to accomplish and what actually occurs.[4] Each day patients receive incomplete or inappropriate care. Each year over two million hospitalized individuals contract new infections. Many of these infections prove fatal. And all of this happens as the cost of care continues to escalate well above the rate of inflation year after year.

For decades, Gawande notes, medicine has developed extraordinary technologies and life-saving drugs, and prepared the best specialists. Medical professionals are smart, hard-working, and dedicated. Regarding his own specialization, Gawande says: "In surgery, you couldn't have people who are more specialized, and you couldn't have people who are better trained. Yet we still see unconscionable levels of death and disability that could be avoided." Pondering this conundrum, he suggests an intriguing thought experiment:

> What if you built a car from the very best car parts? Well it would lead you to put in Porsche brakes, a Ferrari engine, a Volvo body, a BMW chassis. And you put it all together and what do you get? A very expensive pile of junk that does not go anywhere. And that is what medical practice can feel like today.[5]

His conclusion is straightforward: adding more parts (meaning any combination of people, tools, and material resources)—even great parts—does not assure a quality result. Rather, we must attend to how all of this joins productively together for the people charged with carrying out this work and for those that they seek to serve. In short, we must make systems work better.

Undergirding Gawande's account is a common dynamic operating across all professions and fields. An explosion of knowledge is driving increased specialization. The tasks that individuals undertake now are much more complex than they once were.[6] Organizations have also become more complex as they try to orchestrate operations across this expanse of specialized work. With so many parts needing to interact well with one another to achieve success, breakdowns can easily occur in one place or another, and wide variation in outcomes is the natural end result.[7]

Assuring good outcomes reliably under these conditions—complex tasks performed within complex systems—raises distinct issues. As we discussed in chapter 2, developing well-honed routines is a key to achieving quality more reliably in the execution of complex tasks. At the same time, addressing organizational complexity requires solving problems of coordination, communication, and system sensing (i.e., having good data about what is actually going on). Not surprisingly, the Asthma Control Team at Cincinnati Children's confronted both types of complexity when they sought ways to improve outcomes for their patients.

MAKING THE CONNECTION TO SCHOOL IMPROVEMENT

The quality chasm in medicine is instructive for educators. As noted previously, medicine benefits from great science, it invests heavily in developing its people, and it supports them with extraordinary technology that enhances their efficacy. Not surprisingly, educational reformers see all three of these factors as critical to improving the U.S. educational system. And they are right; we do need a stronger knowledge base, better professional education programs, and more effective use of technology to advance student learning. Yet, as in medicine, developments along any one of these lines alone is not likely to redress the unsatisfactory student outcomes we now see. And, they may even increase inequities in the years ahead.[8]

Slowed only by the 2008 recession, spending on education, like spending on health care, has been rising for decades. And what the best of U.S. education achieves today is remarkable.[9] Yet at the same time, we have a disturbing number of young adults who struggle to comprehend a simple text, perform basic arithmetic, or write a coherent sentence.[10]

It is hard to reconcile, in a nation that spends as much as we do on public education, that some students predictably will fail, regardless of the resources and attention directed to them.[11] We need ways to explain what seems inexplicable. So we narrate a story. We say that the causes of this harm—the recurring failures that educators cannot seem to redress—lie in various people's venality, incompetence, or insensitivity. We castigate school leaders as unresponsive. Superintendents in turn often see their school principals as the problem and make rapid changes in these positions. When the next new superintendent enters the same district a few years later, similar words are heard and more principal turnover occurs.[12] More recently, individual classroom teachers are seen as the culprits who should be fired.[13]

To be sure, some educators do not belong in front of a classroom or leading a school or a school district. But individual personnel issues, as Tom Nolan, a world-renowned organizational improvement specialist, has noted, are a "six percent problem."[14] Nolan's point is that problematic personnel typically account for only a small percentage of an organization's overall performance problems. The predominant causes of failure lie elsewhere—in how we organize the work that we ask people to carry out.

Operating here is a well-known organizational phenomenon called *attribution error*.[15] When we see unsatisfactory results, we tend to blame the individuals most immediately connected to those results, not recognizing the full causes.[16] The evidence from over a half century of effort across numerous sectors and industries is clear: improving productivity in complex systems is not principally about incentivizing more individual effort, preaching about better intentions, or even enhancing individual competence.[17] Rather, it is about designing better processes for carrying out common work problems and creating more agile mechanisms for sensing and reacting to novel situations.[18] In high-performing organizations, failures are seen not principally as a reason to cast blame, but as occasions to learn. Data are not blunt instruments for imposing sanctions and offering rewards; they are resources used to deepen understanding of current operations and to generate insights about where to focus efforts to improve.[19]

SEEING COMPLEXITY IN OUR EDUCATIONAL SYSTEMS

The one-room schoolhouse is education's equivalent to health care before the knowledge explosion. It was a simple enterprise: a teacher instructing children of mixed ages, perhaps with chalkboards and simple texts. Aspirations were modest: basic reading skills, some competency in arithmetic, and the ability to write one's name.

Now we expect students to master much more content than ever before. Literature texts, previously taught in college courses, have been pushed down into the high school grades. Introductory statistics, once primarily a graduate school course, is now often taught in middle schools. High school science textbooks are far more sophisticated. And students must engage with much more specialized knowledge than ever before. We aspire that all students command not just a basic core of knowledge and skills, but engage in deeper learning about the big ideas that organize our exploding knowledge universe.[20] These ever-expanding expectations greatly increase demands on teachers, both on their knowledge and their capabilities to teach.

Teachers' work has also become more complex. Teachers now include in their classrooms students who were once segregated out in special programs, if they were educated at all. We expect all teachers, regardless of the subject taught, to be responsive to student cultures and languages different from their own. And reformers have advanced still other initiatives that make classrooms more heterogeneous in terms of students' background, abilities, and prior knowledge. The task of managing heterogeneous classrooms is a key teaching problem, and classrooms have clearly become more complex environments in this regard.[21]

Likewise, teachers, principals, and other local school leaders now interact with staff from a vast array of external service organizations. In seeking to close gaps in student achievement, many supplemental programs have sprung up, including individual tutoring, various forms of small group response to intervention, and after-school and summer-school programs. Instructional coaches specializing in areas such as mathematics, science, literacy, and student-data analysis increasingly populate school buildings. Perhaps most demanding of all are the activities associated with the individual educational plans required by state and federal special education initiatives. The latter has brought an increasing array of specialists into schools—speech, hearing, learning disabilities, behavioral counselors, and so on. In principle, all of these efforts aim to support students to learn better, but integrating them well poses a host of often-unaddressed issues.

Most significant, the density of this activity is greatest in our nations' most disadvantaged schools. These schools are doubly challenged in confronting the vast human needs of their student and family populations while at the same time having to manage a huge array of specialists, programs, and external connections targeting these students. These schools are chronically stressed work environments. Even when successful for a period of time, they remain ever vulnerable to future failure.[22]

Finally, education has its own version of a knowledge explosion. Today educators are told to attend to multiple forms of intelligence; differences in student learning styles; the salience of indigenous culture and local communities; findings from cognitive science about how people learn; and social-psychological research on the importance of concepts such as resilience, grit, persistence, and student mindsets. This list of new ideas continues to grow at an accelerating pace. While most of this is not in the form of clinical trial evidence as in health care, regardless, the rapid expansion of reform ideas poses analogous problems for educators.

In sum, a number of forces have made everything about schooling more complex—its goals, as well as the ideas, tools, and technologies that guide its work. As in health care, few professionals can absorb and effectively respond to all of this complexity in their daily work. So it is not surprising that a chasm exists between what we seek to accomplish and what we actually achieve.

FRAMING EDUCATIONAL
IMPROVEMENT AS A SYSTEMS PROBLEM

This systems view drives home a clear but often ignored point: the causes of students' successes and failures are not simple. Educational outcomes emerge from multiple processes that interact in classrooms, schools, and districts and in families, community organizations, and public social services.[23] Moreover, every few years a new set of reforms is enacted on top of previous changes and those on top of more distal changes. This ever-increasing complexity continues to generate new vexing problems to solve.[24] This is hardly a new insight, but its implications for practice and policy regularly go unattended.

For an illustration, we return to the case of the Baltimore Public Schools from chapter 1. Recall that Baltimore, like other school districts, was introducing more rigorous processes for evaluating teachers. Common to many of these systems are standard observation protocols for principals to observe and rate the effectiveness of each teacher. These instruments are principally designed to generate data to inform personnel decisions (renew a contract or not, grant tenure or not), but the district also wants to use the data to improve teaching. (For the moment, we ignore concerns about the use of measures originally designed for one purpose and then subsequently appropriated for some other use.)

In standard district practice, a central office team, perhaps with an outside consultant, would develop a standard procedure for principals to provide feedback that identifies priorities for a teacher's improvement. The district would conduct a training session on the use of the protocol, perhaps a half day or longer, and principals would immediately begin implementing it, several times a year, with each teacher. This course of action seems eminently reasonable, except for one key fact: the new protocol will now be layered on top of a number of other feedback processes already in place. The end result is the multiple, uncoordinated, and sometimes conflicting guidance previously illustrated in figure 1.1.

How does this happen? Clearly, it is not intentional. Rather, it is the natural result of separate reform activities introduced over time by different institutional actors.[25] For example, some time ago, the state of Maryland introduced an induction program in which mentors regularly visit new teachers' classrooms. If the new teacher happens to be a Teach For America (TFA) corps member, that teacher will also see a TFA coach every two weeks. (Other alternative teacher preparation programs and some colleges of education may also provide similar support.) This mentoring is layered on top of earlier reforms by the district's Office of Instruction, which introduced instructional coaches in literacy, math, and other subjects. These coaches also critique and advise new teachers. The English

Language Learner Office and the Special Education department provide still more guidance. More recently, the Office of Instruction introduced school-based professional learning cycles in which teachers are directed to immediate-term improvement targets based on interim student test scores.[26] Many new teachers may also have an informal colleague or mentor. And all of this is in addition to the teachers' guides that accompany the district's textbook series. The latter can literally be a foot-high stack of materials. Adding further to this mix is a vast array of professional support resources available through the district's online teacher portal and more generally across the Internet.

Again, all of these supports were introduced with good intentions—to help teachers improve. But when we look at them through the experiences of the teachers themselves—that is, when we follow the first improvement principle of being user-centered—one lesson jumps out. As was readily apparent to Jarrod Bolte and his improvement team in Baltimore, no one is seeing the overall work system that has been created here. At a minimum, there are significant and unaddressed problems of coordination and communication, as well as missed opportunities to enhance efficiency and effectiveness. Surely, the last thing one would want to do in this case is add still another process.

Problems of this sort are not unique to education. For over sixty years, they have been grist for quality improvement efforts in many other fields. There are good reasons to believe that the same sound principles and tools that have assisted others to improve can help educators do the same.

LEARNING HOW TO SEE THE SYSTEM

A variety of tools and processes scaffold effective ways of thinking and acting on complex systems. They help make visible the actual organizational structures and policies at work.[27] Understanding this is essential context for identifying promising changes and testing specific courses of action aimed at sustained, meaningful improvement.[28]

We first present a protocol, *causal system analysis,* for examining the sources of the unsatisfactory outcomes our educational systems now produce. We then explain how a networked improvement community develops a *working theory of practice improvement*. Along the way, we introduce three tools that can help a network represent its current understanding of a problem and identify key levers for change. When these tools and processes are used, knowledge held by different individuals can be unearthed, explicated, and the warrants for each examined. Along the way collective commitments form to guide the work ahead.

Causal System Analysis

Organizing a NIC begins with an analysis of root causes: "Why do we get the outcomes that we currently do?" In working through this analysis, participants develop a common understanding of the specific problem or problems they are trying to solve. The process also serves as a first test of whether a team can engage productively as a focused improvement community.

As these conversations begin, it is natural for participants to see current operations through the lens of their own particular work and to interpret events based on personal experiences and beliefs. Each individual offers important insights, but typically each provides only a partial view. Engaging diverse perspectives and discerning the connections among them are key to fully seeing the system.

Identifying the Specific Problem to Be Addressed. The first step in carrying out a causal systems analysis is to detail the particular problem to address. Recall that this step is central to the first improvement principle. There is a natural propensity to describe the problem initially in very broad terms; for example, as in the need to reduce the minority gap in achievement or to better prepare mathematics and science teachers. These are highly valued goals. But, framed in this fashion, they are simply too broad to attack as improvement problems. They are the aggregation of countless processes over extended periods of time and multiple contexts. To move improvement requires identifying a specific target.

This phenomenon played out during the initiation phase of Carnegie's Community College Pathways NIC. Early conversations focused on the low graduation rates in community colleges. As these discussions proceeded, it quickly became clear that these outcomes are a collective consequence of numerous processes embedded in advising systems, course requirements, scheduling, teaching methods, student support services, financial aid rules, institutional financing, and many other factors. At this macro level, the problem appears so large as to be overwhelming.

Following the first improvement principle demands strategic thinking to identify specific, high-leverage targets to attack. (See the discussion in chapter 2 about the properties characterizing high-leverage problems.) Gradually, a target problem came into view: the very low success rates in developmental mathematics courses. In many colleges, upwards of 70 percent of new students are tracked into developmental math. And even after three years, the vast majority of these students fail to acquire college-level math credit. Without it, they cannot transfer to a four-year institution or earn admission to many occupational preparation programs. In short, achieving college mathematics credit is a huge roadblock to opportunity for many community college students.[29] Thus, a critical problem to solve. And there were good reasons to believe that much better outcomes were attainable.

Asking the "Why" Questions. The next step is a brainstorming activity among network participants. Over and over, we ask, "Why do we get the results observed?" Initial explanations are offered, and the cycle repeats, probing deeper: "Well, why does that occur?" Depending on the particulars of the issue being considered, this probing may go on for several rounds.

When we started the Community College Pathways NIC, for example, we were told that instructors lack the skills and beliefs to help developmental math students succeed. We asked why. Probing deeper, we heard that community college instructors have no formal pedagogical instruction. We also discovered that adjunct faculty teach most of these courses. We then asked, "Why does that matter?" We learned that adjunct faculty may have limited access to on-campus professional development. We then asked, "Well, why is that?" This question took us into a discussion of the work lives of itinerant faculty. Trying to cobble together something like full-time employment, adjuncts typically pick up assignments at multiple colleges. Given their fractured schedules and the time they spend traveling between campuses, they are often unable to take advantage of professional development opportunities, which cater to the schedules of full-time faculty.

The Fishbone Diagram. A tool called a *fishbone diagram* assists in working through this problem analysis and visually representing the product of these discussions.[30] Each major bone represents a key factor thought to contribute to the unsatisfactory outcomes. The smaller bones capture the details that emerge from conversations about these factors. Typically, five or six primary factors—"major bones"—may be identified, with multiple contributing factors under each. Figure 3.1 illustrates the fishbone diagram that resulted from the analysis of student failures in developmental math.[31] Two "bones" capture observations about students' backgrounds, such as weak academic skills, doubts about their ability to learn math, and questions about the relevance of math in their lives. Not unexpectedly, these student-centered reasons were among the first that the participants raised. A fuller picture emerged, however, when participants were pressed to offer additional explanations. Some mentioned the relevance and accessibility of the instructional materials; the abstractness of the topics and the manner of presentation (e.g., "memorize the algorithm for solving simultaneous quadratic equations") also gave students little motivation to learn. A fourth line of conversation drew attention to institutional processes that impede student progress. A host of issues were raised here, including problems with placement tests, flaws in the advising process that channeled students into different classes, and limited access to required courses. Another major factor captured concerns about the qualifications, pedagogical skills, and commitments of faculty. The sixth, and last, major bone organizes a set of reasons having to do with how state funding policies and transfer requirements create barriers to student success.

While one might contest any given reason shown in the fishbone diagram, one fact clearly stands out: no single person, process, or resource is to blame.

Figure 3.1 Fishbone diagram for low success rates in developmental mathematics

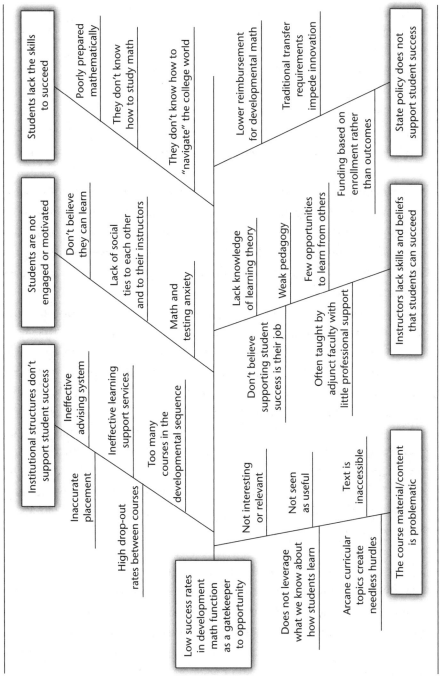

We note that the discussions entailed in a rigorous causal system analysis can make some participants uneasy, as it requires them to be brutally
honest about how and why unsatisfactory outcomes continue to occur.
Because this collective self-reflection can be painful, participants may find
it easier to skip the analysis and jump to the happier task of brainstorming
about solutions. But short-circuiting the discussion of root causes—another manifestation of solutionitis—is a mistake. Although the analysis
can be trying, it is a critical prelude to tactical action.

The System Improvement Map. The causal system analysis also generates useful information for developing a *system improvement map.*
Whereas the fishbone diagram facilitates brainstorming, the system improvement map is an analytic tool. It represents what we learn through
these discussions about how the institution is organized to carry out work
in a particular area.

In general terms, the formal organizations of an institution can be
thought of as a set of interacting subsystems that operate at multiple levels. For educational institutions such as school districts and colleges, the
subsystems most germane for student success consist of an instructional
core (i.e., courses, programs of study, and various materials and technologies to support this); a human resources subsystem that provides staff to
teach and support this core; an information infrastructure that collects
and organizes data to guide and manage institutional activity; a vast array of academic, social-behavioral, and psychological support services
for students and their families; and institutional governance, including
budgeting, financial aid, internal policy making, and external relations.[32]
Mapping these subsystems provides one conceptual organizer for the system improvement map.

The map also parses the organization of schooling into levels at which
educational activity occurs. To guide the community college NIC, distinguishing among three levels seemed important. First is the classroom,
where students encounter teachers around subject matter. Second is the
internal organization of the college, consisting of subunits including academic departments, schools, and divisions. Third is an array of external

Figure 3.2 Illustrative system improvement map

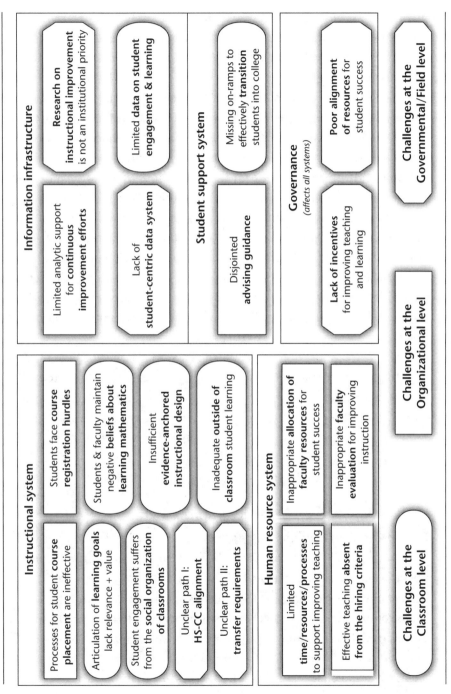

Instructional system

Processes for student course placement are ineffective

Students face course registration hurdles

Articulation of learning goals lack relevance + value

Students & faculty maintain negative beliefs about learning mathematics

Student engagement suffers from the social organization of classrooms

Insufficient evidence-anchored instructional design

Unclear path I: HS-CC alignment

Unclear path II: transfer requirements

Inadequate outside of classroom student learning

Information infrastructure

Limited analytic support for continuous improvement efforts

Research on instructional improvement is not an institutional priority

Lack of student-centric data system

Limited data on student engagement & learning

Student support system

Disjointed advising guidance

Missing on-ramps to effectively transition students into college

Human resource system

Limited time/resources/processes to support improving teaching

Inappropriate allocation of faculty resources for student success

Effective teaching absent from the hiring criteria

Inappropriate faculty evaluation for improving instruction

Governance
(affects all systems)

Lack of incentives for improving teaching and learning

Poor alignment of resources for student success

Challenges at the Classroom level

Challenges at the Organizational level

Challenges at the Governmental/Field level

institutions and professional fields. This third level includes governmental entities such as state legislatures and state boards of higher education, and professional bodies such as the American Mathematical Association of Two-Year Colleges.

The goal of a system improvement map is not to detail every nook and cranny of the organization. Nor is it to completely detail the entire system. Rather, the aim is to map the essential organizational features that are most likely to manifest themselves as improvement work proceeds. To guide us in this work, we return to the first improvement principle about being user-centered. In the case of developmental math, it means seeing the system as students experience it. They arrive at the college doorstep, take placement exams, and are advised to take certain courses of study. They then have distinct learning experiences, depending in large measure on the faculty assigned to teach them. These teaching assignments in turn depend on on how much teaching developmental courses well is valued by the institution. So by starting with the student, we can chart points of intersection where breakdowns might occur.

Figure 3.2 (see previous page) illustrates a simplified version of the system improvement map for the Community College Pathways NIC.[33] The map locates where and how various root causes manifest in the formal organization of community colleges. It directs attention to various roles, processes, policies, and contexts as possible targets for improvement. In this regard, it provides a conceptual bridge for moving from the study of root causes to identifying tactical starting points for change.

A Working Theory of Practice Improvement

As the causal system analysis proceeds and these understandings continue to be refined, a second process begins that aims to identify a working theory of practice improvement. Prompted by the fishbone diagram and the system improvement map as contexts to challenge our thinking, a conversation initiates about where and how productive changes might best be introduced. From a purely logistical perspective, one cannot attack every box in the map at once. Even if time and resources were no object, it would be nearly impossible to know at the outset how a vast ensemble of changes should fit together. Rather, we seek to identify a small but powerful set of drivers to initiate improvement. At the same time, we remain aware that elements left in the background may subsequently move to the foreground as improvement activity proceeds.

Building a working theory of practice improvement is neither straightforward nor obvious. It requires blending observations from the causal systems analysis with relevant research and wise judgments from expert educators. The most compelling improvement hypotheses often exist at the intersection of these "three voices"—how does the system appear to work; what does relevant theory and empirical research suggest about promising changes; and what seems plausible to educators who might try out these changes in their classrooms, schools, and colleges?

The Driver Diagram. A third tool, called a *driver diagram*, organizes the various changes the network is trying out. It gives participants a common language as they build toward a solution to a shared problem. The diagram focuses on a small set of hypotheses about key levers for improvement, specific changes that might be attempted for each, and the interconnections that may exist among them. Although each step in building a driver diagram is quite logical, the final product can be quite complex, depending on the scope of the proposed changes. Here, we introduce a part of the driver diagram used by the Community College Pathways NIC.

The first step is to specify a *measureable improvement aim.* In this case, the initiating team for the NIC established a target of increasing from 5 to 50 percent the proportion of students achieving college math credits in one year of continuous enrollment.[34] Next, the NIC initiating team decided to focus on improving teaching and learning in community college classrooms (the classroom-level boxes in figure 3.2). This was a strategic decision in several regards. First, K–12 research documents great variability in student outcomes among classes within the same schools, and there are good reasons to believe that this variability also characterizes community colleges.[35] Second is a market niche consideration. Many proposed solutions were emerging for improving outcomes in community colleges, but few focused on the core work of classroom teaching and learning. So here was a place a NIC could add real value. Third, classroom instruction is the single costliest item in a college's budget. So improvements here are also high leverage; they can make for much more effective and efficient use of resources.

Identifying a small set of key improvement hypotheses, called *primary drivers*, came next. In essence, the primary drivers are a network's best initial bets about what to target in the context of the causal system analysis. Each driver represents a hypothesis about a change essential to improving student outcomes. The first of the Pathways primary drivers (seen in figure 3.3) focuses on changes in the instructional system. The NIC aims to vitalize ambitious learning goals that truly matter for students' work, personal, and civic lives. This driver is anchored in core findings from cognitive science on the role of struggle in developing deep conceptual understanding, in findings from cross-national comparative studies on effective mathematics teaching and learning, and in results from a small pilot study with community college students carried out while the driver diagram was being developed.[36]

The initiating team also knew that students' prior educational experiences often don't position them well to succeed in college. These experiences have fostered beliefs among many students that they aren't good in math and that it isn't relevant to their lives. Hence, a second primary driver, called "productive persistence," focuses on increasing student motivation, tenacity, and skills for success. Research experiments in social psychology document that these mindsets are amenable to change. The practical issue to address was whether the NIC could translate this research into activities that would work effectively with varied groups of students and across diverse classrooms and colleges.[37]

Third, the NIC recognized that many students struggled with the literacy demands embedded in instructional materials and methods. Studying mathematics is akin to learning a new language. Many community college students come from families whose primary language is something other than English. On occasion this is true for faculty too, although their first language may be different from that of their students. Because classes, of course, are taught in English, sometimes four or more languages come

Figure 3.3   Overview driver diagram for Community College Pathways NIC

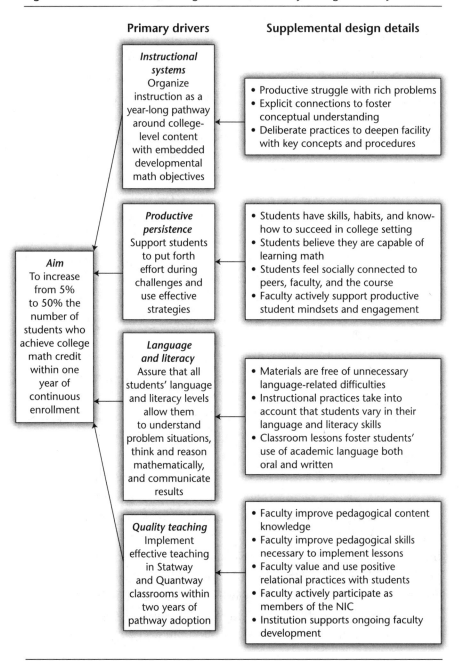

into play. Breaking down these barriers to learning marks out another high-leverage hypothesis for change.[38]

Fourth, and finally, is the "quality teaching" driver. This driver focuses on what is likely the single biggest source of variability in student outcomes: differences in how instruction is organized and carried out. Changes in this area aim to ensure that all instructors have the resources necessary to achieve success as they begin to use the Pathways instructional system and to enhance their expertise further over time.

Taken together, the four primary drivers, displayed in figure 3.3 offer an overview of the landscape for change. Associated with each driver is extensive definition detail as to what the driver means. These definitions are anchored in relevant research and function as *design principles* to guide improvement efforts on each particular driver. We note that the corpus of material grounding these design principles can be quite expansive. The brief statements about supplementary design detail should be read as hyperlinks to a larger document base. If we could see all of this in three dimensions, these supplemental details would appear as standing behind each primary driver.

Even with this elaboration, the primary drivers are still too general to direct change efforts. We need to further specify a set of subhypotheses to activate each driver. These are called *secondary drivers*. Again, the aim in developing a working theory of practice improvement is not to be exhaustive; it is to carefully choose a few secondary drivers that we believe might function as key levers for productive change.

Finally, building off each secondary driver, and moving into finer detail, are the actual change ideas to be developed, tested, and refined.[39] At this point, the theory of practice improvement considers new work processes that may be added, existing processes that may be changed, new tools that may need to be designed and tested, and new norms required to sustain productive change. Since variability in performance often starts here, this is a place to consider opportunities for introducing standard work.

We now illustrate this logic of secondary drivers and specific change ideas for one of the primary drivers of the Community College Pathways

NIC. Figure 3.4 depicts five secondary drivers believed to contribute to productive persistence. We detail one of these—a focus on a strong start for students during their first few weeks. The rationale for this secondary driver comes from reports that many students disengage early in the academic semester.[40] If there is any chance of increasing students' attainment of college math credit within one year, we need to disrupt the forces that foster this disengagement. The aim is to better support students' initiation into the course so that they will experience early success and solidify personal ties to the classroom community. Six change ideas are explications for this particular secondary driver. The first calls for improving the opening lessons. (Note that this idea also connects with the instructional system primary driver.) The second focuses on direct interventions with students. The third calls for a change in the information infrastructure noted in the system improvement map in figure 3.2. Faculty need quicker access to emerging evidence about students most at risk for failure. The fourth and fifth focus on classroom routines that create a sense of community, student belonging, and support for learning. And the last change idea considers implications for faculty professional development. (Note that this also connects with other change activities occurring under the primary driver for quality teaching.)

The preceding account illustrates one complete strand of theory development from a primary driver all the way out to specific change ideas. Clearly, even with only a small set of primary drivers and associated secondary drivers, the ideas for change can quickly grow. At each step in the process, a dynamic interplay occurs among the understandings generated through the causal system analysis, consideration of relevant research findings, and analytical thinking about assumed causes and effects. We must constantly challenge ourselves and our colleagues: "Why would we do this? What do we expect should occur?" Constantly examining the network of connections assumed in the driver diagram is key to orchestrating an integrated working theory of improvement. If we don't, the same forces that produced the cacophony for the new teachers in Baltimore could easily emerge here, too.

Figure 3.4 Detailing the driver for productive persistence

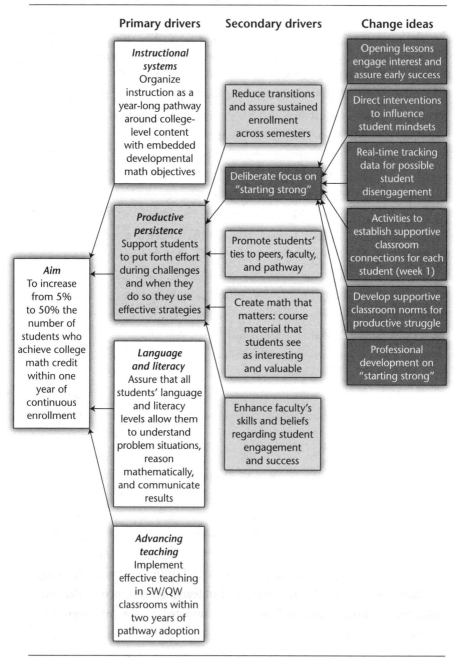

Broad organizational benefits accrue to a NIC through developing a driver diagram. Participants can now see where their particular ideas, interests, and expertise fit within the larger mosaic. Making this complexity visible—showing all the pieces and how they are thought to fit together—helps to break down the siloed reasoning that is characteristic of so much educational reform. In addition, parsing the overall scope of activities into smaller and discrete pieces allows even the busiest professionals to find a place where they might contribute to the improvement efforts of the larger community. Lastly, the diagram operates as an organizer for managing and making accessible the practical knowledge that is created as improvement efforts proceed across the network. So in multiple ways, the driver diagram is truly a "working" theory of practice improvement.

The empirical methods, introduced in the next two chapters, are used to test the change ideas represented in a driver diagram. As these tests accumulate, evidence builds about possible linkages among change ideas, and secondary and primary drivers. Results from these tests may raise challenges regarding the adequacy of some aspects of the framework. If, for example, measurable changes occur in the primary drivers, but the target outcomes do not improve, something important is missing. So when evidence about what works under varied conditions is gathered, the working theory of improvement evolves. This reflects a simple fact about systems: one's understanding of a system continues to deepen through efforts to change it. It is learning by doing.

Finally, engaging in such work fosters a sense of humility about what one actually knows. Even with all the activity that goes into developing the initial version of the working theory of practice improvement, the theory remains provisional. It offers guidance on how to proceed, even as network participants engage it in the spirit of *"possibly wrong and definitely incomplete."* As the network attends to emerging evidence as to what is and is not working, oversights and initial errors in thinking are likely to surface. This is at the heart of learning to improve. Periodically, the working theory will need to be updated. In the interregnums, it guides work.

FORMULATING SOLUTIONS AS SYSTEMS, ADAPTIVE INTEGRATION AS THE GOAL

So far we have focused on tools and processes that can help teams develop deeper understandings about the organizations they seek to improve and detail possible changes to accomplish this goal. We note an important distinction in the nature of driver diagrams, depending on the application. In some cases, the primary drivers operate largely independent of one another. Hence, we would expect significant outcomes to accrue from improvements within even a single driver. And as a corollary, the more drivers an organization addresses, the larger the improvements should be. This is a natural consequence of what "independent" means. In other cases, and more typical in education, the drivers and related change ideas function as a package of activities that must mesh well. These change packages take the character of systems; they are in essence *solution systems*. For positive effects to accrue reliably in these situations, we must coordinate improvements across all of the drivers. A material weakness in any one driver can undermine the efficacy of the overall solution.[41] The driver diagram for the Community College Pathways NIC is of this form.

In addition, any proposed change, whether it focuses on just one driver or a full solution system, must be integrated into the existing organization of a classroom, school, or district. Each of these already exists as a complex system before any interventionist arrives at the door. Unlike traditional policy research and evaluation studies that tend to treat aspects of local context as random externalities, improvement research directly engages concerns about how local conditions shape the take-up and use of a set of change ideas. Addressing these issues is key to achieving the ultimate improvement goal: quality performance reliably at scale.

Key here is the notion of *adaptive integration*. Improvement research focuses on learning how to make things work under a variety of different organizational conditions. This may entail some adaptations to the intervention itself, and it may also require addressing some site-specific problems, necessary to solve, for the intervention to be integrated well. This stands as a strong counterpoint to prevailing beliefs that innovation diffusion is simply a matter of adopting proven programs and then implementing them with fidelity.[42] Failing to appreciate fully the significance of context has often led good reform ideas to fail.[43]

We offer next an example of a solution system and how differences in context created a problem-solving agenda for achieving effective local adaptation.

Example: The Introduction of Instructional Coaches

We return to the discussion of school-based instructional coaches introduced in chapter 2. Late in the summer of 2000, the Los Angeles Unified School District latched onto this reform idea and proceeded to hire hundreds of coaches in a few short weeks.[44] Numerous labor agreements had to be worked through, and prospective coaches had to be identified, recruited, and transferred into their new roles. Much activity went into rolling out coaching systemwide. Although some training was offered, the tacit assumption was that, if qualified teachers were given coaching responsibilities, they would largely know what to do to improve instruction.[45]

A Solution System. In essence, Los Angeles Unified School District leaders sought to use coaching to improve the quality of instruction, which they believed would ultimately lead to improvements in student learning. Represented at the center of a conventional logic model (see figure 3.5), the district defined several key components as essential to quality teaching: teachers' content and pedagogical knowledge, content coverage that aligns with district learning goals, and classroom environments supportive of student engagement. In the context of a driver diagram, these would appear as substantive elaboration standing behind the instructional quality box. It represents district guidance as to what coaches should seek to develop in every classroom. So far, so good.

The actual work of instructional coaching, however, was left largely as a black box in the logic model. The district solved the bureaucratic details of hiring and placing coaches into schools, specified the dimensions of instructional quality they sought to improve, and then good things were supposed to happen to transform teaching and learning. But exactly what

Figure 3.5   The coaching "black box" logic model

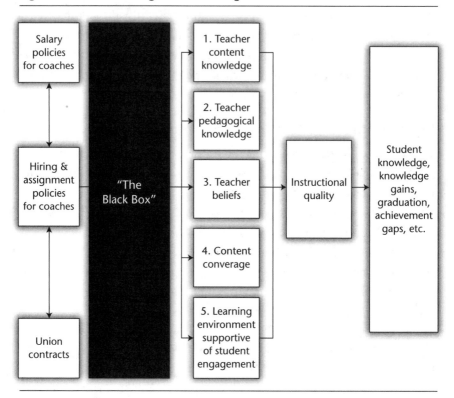

this was and how it was to be done remained unclear. Not surprisingly, results disappointed.

Stepping out of the specifics of Los Angeles, if we were to open the black box, we would quickly see that instructional coaching is a solution system consisting of several interrelated new processes, tools, and work relationships. The list includes

- *Coach assignment process.* Who might make for a good coach at each specific school? What aspects of local context, including relationship histories, are especially important to attend to?
- *Coaching allocation process.* The coach's time is a scarce resource. How should coaches focus their time? Which teachers should get how much time on what teaching practices?

- *Coach–principal instructional leadership process.* Relational trust in this leadership dynamic is essential. How should the school principal and coach work together to advance instructional improvement? How is trust between them nurtured and sustained?
- *The observation-feedback process.* This is the core work activity in coaching. What does good coaching actually look like, and what tools are necessary to support it? What should coaches observe, how should they interpret what they see, and how best can they provide feedback?
- *Derivative process: professional development of coaches.* Coaching is a new professional role. How will coaches learn to do this new work? And how can a district best develop coaching expertise?

In the context of a driver diagram, these five processes would appear as primary drivers.

In short, behind the deceptively simple title of "instructional coaching" stands a complex solution system needing to be developed. And we note that for at least one of the primary drivers, the professional development of coaches, this involves detailing a whole other solution system unto itself. That is, the professional development of coaches driver, which stands in support of improving the quality of teaching to improve the quality of student learning, would need expansion out into its own driver diagram that articulates how quality coaches will be developed and supported.

Adaptive Integration. As noted earlier, coaching is not a generic activity. While districts may share a common label for it, quality enactment depends in large measure on local context. Most of the processes described in the preceding section, for example, would need to be tailored, in some cases substantially, to district-specific curricula and pedagogies.[46] Appropriate design also depends on the local purposes coaching is supposed to serve. Is coaching formative—intended to help teachers improve? Is it something districts use to monitor teachers—to see if they are covering the material in accord with district guidelines? Is it to be used to make personnel decisions? Or is it intended to do all of the above?

In addition, successfully integrating a coaching initiative into a school's current operations must take into account other improvement processes that may be occurring at the same time. For example, teachers' responses to a coaching intervention are likely to be very different if accompanied by a high-stakes system for individual accountability. Coaching encourages teachers to expose problems in their instruction and to experiment with new practices that might not at first work. Success here places a premium on reducing teachers' sense of risk, as this functions as a barrier for learning to improve. In contrast, high-stakes accountability elevates risk and may discourage teachers from revealing weaknesses or embracing change.

More generally, many of the educational reforms that we now seek to introduce into schools reach deeply into the day-to-day work lives of teachers, principals, and other educators. It is natural for them to feel vulnerable when they are asked to change how they do their jobs and relate to one another.[47] Not surprisingly, successfully introducing change depends significantly on the trust that exists among teachers and with their principals. A range of professional norms may also come into play, including whether teachers feel comfortable opening their classrooms to others.[48] Consequently, effectively integrating an intervention such as coaching will be tougher in some places than others. Unless critical questions are addressed—Is this context conducive to the changes? What will it take to make it work here?—wide variability in effects will continue to occur over and over again.

For all these reasons and more, issues of adaptive integration loom large in education and deserve a major place on the improvement research agenda.

CONCLUDING OBSERVATIONS

A third quality improvement principle—seeing the system—has now come fully into view. It is hard to improve outcomes when we do not fully appreciate how our educational systems operate to produce the results we currently observe. Improvement science directs explicit attention to a detailed analysis of the problems we aim to fix. Unfortunately, educational reformers too often jump over this step in their eagerness to bring about change.

This need for systems thinking is equally important in the design of improvement efforts. The latter is essentially a collection of hypotheses about change in some set of work processes. The logic theorized to operate among a set of changes often takes the form of a solution system. How this set of changes work individually and productively mesh with one another becomes the target for improvement research. And then, there is the issue of adaptive integration. Much needs to be understood in order to effectively integrate any set of promising changes into the varied contexts that are our nation's schools and colleges.

Tools such as fishbone diagrams, program improvement maps, and driver diagrams help illume these dynamics. They assist in clarifying current problems and in inviting new thinking about possible solutions. These frameworks organize the practical efforts of a NIC, affording insights about where and how network participants might contribute toward meaningful change.

Now, we move on to consider how to determine whether the changes we pursue in each of these regards are actually improvements.

4

We Cannot Improve at Scale What We Cannot Measure

I am a kind of burr; I shall stick.

—WILLIAM SHAKESPEARE, *MEASURE FOR MEASURE*[1]

IN HER BOOK *Relentless Pursuit,* Donna Foote writes about Teach For America (TFA) corps member Dave Buerhle.[2] Like many TFA members, Dave was a top student recruited out of a selective undergraduate institution. Bypassing conventional teacher preparation, Dave participated in a six-week TFA training program and then started teaching in a very disadvantaged urban school. He had aced the TFA application and interview processes, placing him among a very select group, so his potential was high. Yet by December of his first year, Dave had decided to quit the program. In many large urban districts, his resignation might have received little notice—just one more new teacher leaving a low-performing school. For TFA, however, Dave's decision, and those of others like him, signaled an organizational failure—and an important opportunity to learn to improve.

We recognize that TFA is a lightning rod on today's education scene. Many find its strategy highly compelling; others are strongly critical.

Ours is not a story about the TFA strategy. Rather, we look inside the organization at how it uses measurement to continuously get better at what it does. Whether a TFA supporter or a detractor, all can learn from it on this account.

Today over 85 percent of TFA corps members complete their full two-year commitment—a worthy accomplishment given the historically high teacher turnover rate in the types of schools where TFA members are typically placed.[3] Impressive student learning gains also occur in many of their classrooms. And TFA has managed to sustain its effectiveness even as it has rapidly grown. (As business executives know well, fast expansion often creates challenges for maintaining quality.[4]) In short, TFA has made noteworthy progress on the central goal of improvement—achieving quality in what it does reliably at scale.

Unlike school districts, TFA cannot control the placement of its teachers or the support they receive from school site staff. The latter matters a great deal because research shows that support, both from principals and fellow teachers, plays an important role in the retention and effectiveness of new teachers.[5] Instead, TFA focused on one of the key levers it *could* control: improving the selection process.[6] To do so, TFA leaders recognized that they needed evidence about how well the selection processes were actually working. In gathering this evidence, TFA embraced the fourth improvement principle: the importance of measurement in advancing quality reliably at scale.

TFA confronted a formidable problem as it began its efforts to improve back in 2001. At the time, few knew much about how to select effective teachers, and some doubted it was even possible. Several years later in a much-quoted article in the *New Yorker*, Malcom Gladwell wrote that it was nearly impossible to recognize teaching potential at the moment that a teacher is hired. Gladwell suggested that choosing teachers was akin to selecting the next great NFL quarterback. "There are certain jobs," he wrote, "where almost nothing you can learn about candidates before they start predicts how they'll do once they're hired."[7] Research by economists Doug Staigler and Jonah Rockoff supports this view.[8] They conclude that districts might be better off by just opening their doors to a much broader group of teacher candidates and then fire as many as 80 percent of them after seeing how well they did in their first year of teaching.

Despite these sobering accounts, the TFA team thought they could and should be able to do better. The team began by scouring the limited existing research on the topic and by gathering insights from respected principals. After many long debates, they settled on twelve important attributes that they thought mattered in selecting teachers.[9] The list determined the information TFA sought from candidates in the initial application. It also informed the interviews conducted and the design of a teaching activity that candidates were asked to perform. TFA aligned scoring rubrics to the twelve attributes and used them to inform final selections.

The departure of Dave Buerhle and others like him triggered a re-evaluation by TFA of the processes it used and the data generated. The TFA team conducted statistical analyses to examine the relationships between rubric data and the outcomes they sought. They examined individual records of departing corps members for clues. They also studied their most successful teachers and interviewed mentors and principals. Data on some characteristics that TFA at first sought to assess—such as being reflective—told them little about how well corps members actually did. So they dropped it from their rubrics. Along the way, TFA also identified new criteria, such as the teacher's ability to motivate others. These refinements led TFA to make changes in its application and selection processes and in the scoring rubrics associated with each component.

In carrying out this work, TFA drew on the two important resources discussed in chapters 2 and 3: a commitment to refining a *standard process* for candidate application and selection and a *working theory* about key candidate characteristics that TFA thought essential to its success. Then, the TFA team added data to fuel their efforts at learning to improve. Said Steven Farr, TFA's chief academic officer: "Measurement turned the lights on."[10] Key was their ability to link the data generated through their standard application and selection process (i.e., rubric scores on candidates' attributes) to the outcomes they cared about: teacher retention and success in the classroom. Each new applicant cohort became a "learning loop" that generated new data and provoked new challenges. Each year brought a chance to tweak the process, try something new, and see whether better outcomes resulted. TFA's measures were admittedly imperfect at first, but they still provided useful feedback. As Farr explained, "We don't need highly precise measures to guide process improvement. There could be 10–20 percent error but the data are still valuable."[11] TFA's working theory of practice (how best to select new corps members) continued to evolve, and team members grew smarter over time about how best to carry out their core work.

TFA's effort to improve its selection process illustrates the fundamental dynamic that undergirds improvement science. Theory, measurement, and standard work processes are constitutive and interrelated elements for improvement. TFA began by putting stakes in the ground on each of these matters even as the team acknowledged the provisional nature of their understanding about each. Key to improvement, as they analyzed emerging evidence, they remained open to change. As any one element in figure 4.1 was refined, it often pressed on the other two, triggering changes there also. For example, when the data on candidate "reflectiveness" did not predict outcomes, the application and interview processes were also modified. When qualitative judgments from interviews did

Figure 4.1 The learning loop for quality improvement

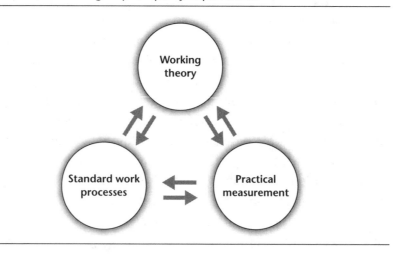

not align with rubric scores, this pressed the team to reexamine whether the rubric was working as intended and also to reconsider whether the selection attributions needed to be further refined. This systematic interplay of practical insight, theory, and evidence is a characteristic of disciplined inquiry across diverse scientific fields.[12] In TFA's case—and in improvement science generally—this interplay now focuses on the very practical considerations affecting the quality of an organization's day-to-day operations.

USING DIFFERENT TYPES OF MEASURES FOR DIFFERENT PURPOSES

School systems now collect more data than ever. The No Child Left Behind Act of 2001 instituted annual measurement of student performance and created new reporting requirements, including separate metrics on the progress of different student subgroups. More recently, Race to the Top, the Investing in Innovation Fund, and the Teacher Incentive Fund have pressed states and districts to develop new measures of teacher effectiveness that identify teachers for actions ranging from financial rewards and promotion to termination. Securing comparable performance data is essential to making these accountability measures work. This data requirement leads to the design of measures that can be applied broadly across different schools, grades, subjects, and students. However, this generic quality also exacts a price: while the measures can signal where improvements are needed, they rarely provide the detail needed to help teachers and schools actually improve.

The operations at TFA also offer insights on this point. The organization regularly uses conventional indicators such as students' standardized tests scores and teacher performance measures (including value-added scores) when analyzing its overall performance. As with all their work, these measures are continuously evolving as the organization learns how to better measure what it cares about. To guide its efforts at organizational change, TFA also invests in data more closely tied to the specific work processes it seeks to improve. The importance of using different types of data for different purposes has been one of TFA's key lessons. According to Senior Vice President Ted Quinn,

> In a world where good data is hard to come by for various reasons, it's especially important to be smart and scrappy and opportunistic about what kinds of data you truly need for each purpose *because you are never going to have one data source that works for all purposes.*[13] [emphasis added]

Quinn's connection between the purpose of measurement and the kind of data that are needed reflects a long-standing measurement principle.[14] In brief, the validity of a measure is established for some specific set of uses (or consequences); measures do not have the property of being valid in general. This is an important but often overlooked distinction in contemporary conversations about data-driven change. Much of educational policy tacitly assumes that data are data, and that if we build a measurement system for one purpose, we can repurpose it later for other uses. For example, policy leaders now call for teacher evaluation data to be used to improve teaching, but these data systems were not designed with this purpose principally in mind. What serves to meet accountability goals may come up short for informing improvement.

In the following sections, we contrast the characteristics of measures that are useful for improvement with measures that are designed for accountability and with measures that are typically used in academic research. Each purpose demands data of a different sort.[15]

Measurement for Improvement and Measurement for Accountability

The purpose of *measurement for improvement* is to inform efforts to change. These measures are tied explicitly to a working theory of practice improvement, such as that captured in the driver diagram introduced in chapter 3. The goal is to provide useful information for improving the specific process or processes represented in this working theory. This purpose imposes requirements on what is measured, how it is measured, and on the social processes shaping data use. To illustrate these features, we look at two efforts to assess teaching: the Developing Language and Literacy

Teaching (DLLT) observation system, which is explicitly designed as a tool to help teachers improve; and the Charlotte Danielson Framework for Teaching, which is commonly employed to evaluate teachers.

A Comparison of Two Observation Rubrics. The DLLT observation system was designed to align with comprehensive literacy instruction in kindergarten through second grade.[16] As noted in chapter 2, such instruction is typically organized around six specific activities or "macro processes" (interactive read aloud, shared reading, guided reading, interactive writing, writing workshop, and word study). Each macro process consists of a sequenced set of micro processes. A separate set of rubrics exists for each macro process; the components in each rubric set correspond with the specific micro processes that form the activity. Guided reading, for example, consists of the six distinct micro processes illustrated in figure 4.2. Correspondingly, the DLLT rubric set for guided reading consists of six elements, one for each micro process.

Equally important, all of the rubric elements in the DLLT reflect a working theory of how teachers' practice tends to develop over time. This theory is anchored in both the clinical experiences of literacy coaches and more general academic research on expertise development. Consistent

Figure 4.2 The six micro processes defining standard work for guided reading

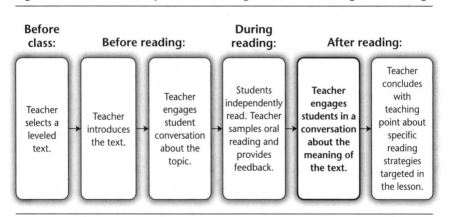

Before class:	Before reading:		During reading:	After reading:	
Teacher selects a leveled text.	Teacher introduces the text.	Teacher engages student conversation about the topic.	Students independently read. Teacher samples oral reading and provides feedback.	Teacher engages students in a conversation about the meaning of the text.	Teacher concludes with teaching point about specific reading strategies targeted in the lesson.

with this developmental perspective, four descriptors exist for each observational element. These descriptors traverse from simply attempting a micro process at one end to expert practice at the other. Teachers new to comprehensive literacy are just learning the procedural routines for the first time. Most of their lessons will typically reflect a rather mechanical enactment of these basic routines. These teachers are less skilled, for example, in using student responses during the lesson to scaffold subsequent instruction. Consequently, their lessons may look quite similar regardless of the particular needs of students. In contrast, the procedural aspects of comprehensive literacy instruction have become routine for more expert teachers. These teachers have more practical experiences to draw upon in interpreting students' work and, having mastered the basic routines, can direct more of their attention to in-the-moment decision making.[17] Consequently, they are more likely to successfully tailor their actions to the targeted objectives in a given lesson and for a specific group of students.

We illustrate in figure 4.3 these properties of the DLLT for the rubric element that aligns with the fifth micro process in guided reading—the conversation that a teacher has with children after they read a text. In a novice teacher's lesson, students may engage in a discussion of the text just read, but their responses are often only peripherally related to the actual text because the teacher will be less skilled in drawing them into the meta-cognitive activity envisioned for this micro process. They may retell parts of the story, but any analysis and interpretation are unlikely. This lesson would align with a score of 1 or 2 on the rubric descriptors. By contrast, in a skillfully executed lesson, the teacher extends students' conversations along lines captured by descriptors 3 and 4. The lesson now engages students in a discussion of important concepts embedded in the text. The conversation might analyze causes and effects, individual motives, and possible alternative explanations for events. A teacher might ask students why they think a key event happened and encourage them to use evidence from the text to explain their reasoning.

The principal purpose of a rubric such as the DLLT is formative. The descriptors closely align with the actual work being done by teachers and students. They point to specific micro processes that might benefit from

Figure 4.3   Illustration of a rating element from the DLLT rubric

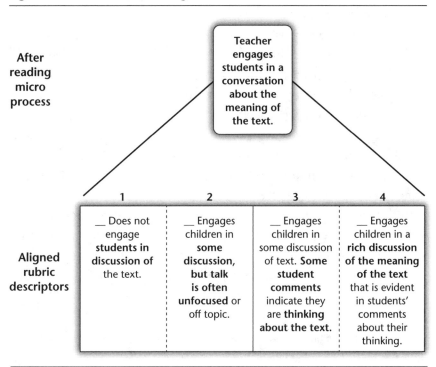

improvement, and they signal what quality literacy teaching actually looks like. With this information, teachers, perhaps working with a literacy mentor, can target specific aspects of their teaching for change.

By contrast, the Charlotte Danielson Framework for Teaching is primarily used as an accountability instrument. Rather than being organized around specific instructional activities and micro processes, the Danielson framework is organized around a more general set of teaching standards for lesson planning, classroom environment, the conduct of instruction, and out-of-class professional responsibilities. The rubric is purposely agnostic about instructional model, subject matter, and grade level. Its generic nature makes the Danielson framework much more broadly applicable than the DLLT. In particular, it allows for evaluations that are able to rank the effectiveness of all teachers in a district on a single measure. The trade-off, however, is that it provides less detailed information for improvement.[18]

It is instructive to consider how the Danielson framework assesses the nature of a teacher's feedback to students. Figure 4.4 displays the associated elements of the rubric. The four-point rating scales were constructed to distinguish levels of performance, as this is central to *measurement for accountability*. The descriptors distinguish teachers by the timeliness and quality of their feedback to students, but provide little detail about what proficient feedback actually looks like. They also offer little guidance as to how one might improve beyond a general nostrum of "provide more timely and higher quality feedback."

While both instruments provide valuable information about effective teaching, the different purposes that they are designed to serve lead to the observed differences in the measures.[19] These different purposes also shape how the data from the instruments are used and by whom. The Danielson

Figure 4.4 Illustration of rating elements from the Danielson rubric on providing feedback to students

	1	2	3	4
	Unsatisfactory	**Basic**	**Proficient**	**Distinguished**
Quality: Accurate, Substantive, Constructive and Specific	__ Feedback is either not provided or is of uniformly poor quality.	__ Feedback is inconsistent in quality; some elements of high quality are present; others are not.	__ Feedback is consistently high quality.	__ Feedback is consistently high quality. Provision is made for students to use feedback in their learning.
Timeliness	__ Feedback is not provided in a timely manner.	__ Timeliness of feedback is inconsistent.	__ Feedback is consistently provided in a timely manner.	__ Feedback is consistently provided in a timely manner. Students make prompt use of the feedback in their learning.

framework is used in the context of teacher accountability. To ensure neutrality, many argue that the ideal evaluator should be someone outside the school with whom the teacher has no prior relationship. In some systems, classroom videos are collected rather than live observations, and nonprofessionals are used to score them. This scoring process places a premium on devising rubrics that focus on easily observable classroom behaviors that can be reliably marked by many different individuals with only modest training. While Danielson observations may occur several times in a year, the results are typically aggregated at the end of the year to derive an overall score for each teacher. The observation scores are then combined with other measures of performance (e.g., value-added scores, principal reports, and student surveys) to place teachers, typically, into one of four or five categories.

In contrast, professional knowledge about literacy instruction is necessary to use an observational protocol such as the DLLT. In the Literacy Collaborative, where the DLLT was originally developed, a trained literacy coach might use the instrument to guide work with a teacher over the course of an academic year or longer.[20] The coach takes great pains to establish a low-stakes trusting environment in which the teacher feels safe trying new practices and getting feedback. Teachers are observed frequently, and the timeliness of feedback is important. At any point, the coach might attend to only one or two of the micro processes in guiding the teacher toward new instructional moves. The value of the rubric is largely in the conversations that it helps to scaffold about what quality looks like in terms of the actual instructional activities that teachers are attempting each day in their classrooms. While these data can be aggregated over time into a summary measure, it is the specificity and detail that make the DLLT especially useful for teaching improvement.

Our intent in contrasting the DLLT and the Danielson framework is simply to illustrate how the purpose of measurement shapes an instrument's design and use. Evaluation systems that aim to sort teachers into performance categories naturally lead to broad, general measures of teaching such as the Danielson framework. This helps identify high and low performers, and it promotes a sense of fairness because everyone is being judged against the same standard. It also formalizes the measurement process and places primacy on the reliability of the final scores, important since individuals' livelihoods are at stake and potential lawsuits loom. These requirements tend to add significantly to the time needed to carry out these evaluation protocols.

In contrast, informing improvement places primacy on evidence that directly links to the specific work processes that are the object of change. It seeks formative data that helps teachers, and those mentoring them, to decide what to work on next. Frequent and timely information, shared in a safe environment, creates conditions necessary for learning to improve.

Finally, it is worth noting that the Literacy Collaborative, like TFA, had two important resources at its disposal as it developed the DLLT. It had a detailed working theory about students' literacy learning and a set of standard work processes deliberately designed to advance this learning (i.e., the six core practices that form comprehensive literacy instruction). Both are critical for developing improvement measures. And as noted earlier, once measurement is introduced, a system of continuous learning can ensue. Data can challenge possible weaknesses in either the theoretical conceptions about student learning or in specific details of how standard work processes might best advance it. In a complementary fashion, qualitative observations gleaned directly from coaching teachers can raise questions about the adequacy of the measurement protocols when rubric data seem discrepant with professional judgments. This reciprocal dynamic, as previously illustrated in figure 4.1, stimulates the ongoing cycles of testing and refinement that are key to achieving quality outcomes more reliably at scale.

Next, we contrast improvement measures with those developed to test theoretical hypotheses in academic research. Here, too, there are differences in what is measured, how it is measured, and how the data are subsequently used.

Measurement for Research and Measurement for Improvement

Improvement research has a special relationship with academic research in the social sciences.[21] The designs of educational interventions are often rooted in insights from multiple disciplines, including cognitive science, psychology, anthropology, economics, and sociology. For example, the efforts of the Community College Pathways NIC have been strongly influenced by basic research on human cognition, motivation, and work performance. Academic research and improvement research share common DNA in that both develop theory and use measures to test these theories. But the kind of knowledge pursued in these two domains is quite different: they entail different kinds of theories, and so they require different types of measures.

The goal of basic social science research is to create general theories applicable to a wide range of human conditions. These theories typically consist of an interrelated set of propositions that aim to provide a coherent explanation for some general social and behavioral phenomena. Discerning how these general concepts might be put into practice reliably, with different contexts and student populations, entails a distinctly different form of inquiry.[22] At base here is the difference between the generality that is valued in academic research and the specificity that is needed to guide practice improvement.

Disciplinary researchers value novelty in conceptualization, counter-intuitiveness, and the explication of fine distinctions among closely related ideas. These features, however, often do not map easily onto student experiences and behaviors that practitioners are able to discern and act upon.[23] For example, as the Community College Pathways NIC team began to detail its work, they identified some forty different subconcepts in the social-psychological literature under related topics such as "motivation," "grit," "resilience," "mastery orientation," and "internal locus of control." But no practitioner can or should try to juggle forty different ideas to analyze what may be transpiring at a given moment with students. Quite simply, the sort of conceptual detail that is the grist for academic researchers (and often the most valued in considerations for promotion and tenure) creates a problem for practitioners who seek to ground their actions in the best of what is actually known.

In contrast, a theory for practice improvement does not seek to document every novel feature of human psychology or social structures that may shape the ways people think or behave. The goal is to focus on a relatively small number of impactful concepts that can be used reliably to guide action. Such a theory requires a blending of the clinical knowledge held by expert educators with a synthesis of core empirically grounded insights from academic research. In essence, a theory of practice improvement speaks simultaneously to two very different audiences. It needs to represent well the core findings from the relevant academic disciplines, and practitioners need to find these concepts informative for action. When so structured, this theory forms a viable language for organizing work across a networked improvement community.

Differences between academic research and improvement science are also manifest in the nature and uses of measurement. Academic research focuses on testing relational propositions among key constructs that form a theory. Researchers develop long, detailed measures in an effort to achieve high reliability in measuring each construct and thereby to improve precision for testing hypotheses among them. This goal encourages researchers to include redundant items (i.e., asking the same question in slightly different ways) in their data collection instruments. This *measurement for research* logic works for specialized studies that may be done only a few times and when participants may even be paid. In contrast, such time-intensive data collection processes are a nonstarter for measures that must be routinely collected in practice to inform its improvement.

We now come to another distinctive feature of improvement research. It demands *practical measurement*. For both teachers and students, time is a highly limited resource, and data collection needs to fit in this space. That means measures to inform improvement must be embedded in the regular work of teaching and learning. Since the intent of the data collection is to advance continuous improvement, data need to be collected frequently to identify opportunities for change and to assess whether positive changes are in fact occurring. Rather than measure constructs, the goal is to predict important future consequences before they occur so that productive actions can be taken. And since improvement focuses on specific student populations and contexts (e.g., developmental math learning for students in community colleges), the language used in interview questions and in survey items should be natural and comprehensible to those asked to answer them.

Summing Up

By contrasting the uses of different measures, we are now able to see the distinctive features and conditions of measurement for improvement. Figure 4.5 summarizes what we have learned. Improvement requires measures that (a) operationalize a working theory of improvement; (b) are specific to the work processes that are the object of change; (c) have formative value signaling subsequent action useful to consider; (d) are framed in a language that is meaningful to those engaged in the work; (e) produce data accessible in a timely manner; and (f) are embedded in social routines that secure the trust and openness necessary to sustain meaningful change efforts.

On balance, it is important to recognize that improvement research relies in key ways on both accountability and research measures. Improvement research will often draw, for example, on accountability measures in framing the overall targets that organize improvement. For example, the Community College Pathways NIC aimed to increase the percentage of developmental math students who were awarded college math credit within one year of continuous enrollment. Such credit attainment is a basic accountability indicator in postsecondary institutions. Likewise, measures developed in academic research provide a good foundation for developing the practical measures necessary for improvement. We illustrate this below.

Lastly, we note that the absence of practical measures is one of the most significant differences between education and health care. Vast amounts of clinical data are routinely collected in health care, and much of it now is finding its way into electronic record systems. These data are a key resource for much of the improvement research in the health-care field.[24] In education, comparable clinical records typically don't exist, either in the form of handwritten notes or online systems. Fortunately, the education field is now poised for transformation. As digital platforms become more common in classrooms, the data recorded in these systems open up

Figure 4.5   Differences in measurement for accountability, improvement, and academic research

	Measurement for Accountability	Measurement for Improvement	Measurement for Research
Purpose	• Identifying exemplary or problematic individual teachers, schools, or districts.	• Determining whether an educational change is an improvement.	• Test or develop a theory regarding the relations among two or more conceptual variables.
Sample Question	• "Which teachers should be placed on a corrective action plan?"	• "If I do X in my classroom, will it create a sense of belonging for my most marginalized students?"	• "Are students' sense of self efficacy and mindset about mathematics related?"
What do you measure?	• End of the line outcomes.	• Work processes that are the object of change.	• Latent variables.
How often do you measure it?	• Typically reported out once a year (at the end).	• Frequently	• Typically once or twice per study.
Key technical considerations	• Inter-rater reliability and temporal stability. • Instruments designed so that raters can be easily trained.	• Sensitivity to change • Predictive validity • Requires considerable professional knowledge to use well. • Easily embedded in day to day work (ideal is unobtrusive measures).	• Careful, detailed representation of latent construct. • Instrument reliability
Most important qualities of the measures	• Summative, global measures of performance applicable to all.	• Formative value; signals actionable changes	• Construct validity
Social conditions for use	• Process formality to assure appearances of neutrality and objectivity. • School and district leaders are primary users.	• Data shared in a low-stakes, safe environment conducive to change. • Educators, coaches/mentors are primary users.	• Meets scientific standards in the discipline. • Usefulness to study participants is generally not a key concern.
Limitation for improving practice	• Causes of any observed differences are opaque as data are not tied to specific practices. Limited formative value as results are typically reported after the school year has concluded.	• Premium on practicality poses challenges for the efficient collection and rapidly reporting on data.	• Impractical to administer as a part of standard practice in classrooms. Not specifically designed to detect the effect of changes in practice, and so less informative for iterative improvement efforts.

extraordinary possibilities for accelerating learning to improve. Protecting the integrity of how these data are used, however, is critical to realizing these possibilities. A key to transforming educational organizations into the continuous learning organizations described in this book is to avoid the temptation to use these more detailed data in an attempt to micromanage workers from afar. The latter approach runs contrary to best practice evidence about the conditions necessary for quality improvement in complex organizations.[25]

ILLUSTRATING MEASUREMENT FOR IMPROVEMENT

A measurement system for improvement must align with a network's working theory of practice improvement. This means that we must develop measures for the network's aims, its primary drivers, and for all of the specific changes that are being introduced and tested. Such an information system is necessary in order to discern whether the changes introduced are actually improvements, and for whom and under what circumstances.

Measuring Targeted Outcomes

The first role of measurement is to clarify what the networked improvement community is actually trying to accomplish. *Outcome measures* operationalize the aim statement in the driver diagram. These data provide a way of assessing whether progress is being made on the specific problem to be solved; they serve as the NIC's "north star." In the case of the Community College Pathways NIC, all colleges use the same measure: the percentage of students assigned to developmental math who officially enroll in the year-long program and who proceed to pass both semesters with a C or better.[26] In addition, NIC faculty members agreed to administer common end-of-course exams to provide more detailed data to guide their instructional improvement efforts.

A specific, shared definition of this sort is vital to the success of a NIC. It is not enough for network participants to assert that they are working together toward some general goal. Precisely defining a common outcome measure and aim forces the community to have explicit conversations about what they seek to achieve by when and for whom. As program implementation proceeds, these outcome data provide ongoing feedback as to where the NIC is succeeding and where it is not. This in turn drives subsequent deliberations about the next round of networkwide improvement priorities.

Measuring Primary Drivers

Outcome measures can be thought of as the "big-dot" or "end-of-the-line" indicators of the success of an improvement project. To guide immediate and ongoing improvement efforts, NICs also need measures for the major mechanisms hypothesized to promote this improvement. These are the primary drivers. These drivers represent key and more immediate targets en route to achieving the desired big-dot outcomes.

Developing a Measure for Productive Persistence. As noted previously, a set of noncognitive factors was hypothesized as a primary driver for improving student outcomes in the Community College Pathways NIC.[27] As the NIC was forming, no coherent framework existed for which noncognitive factors really mattered. Instead, the NIC confronted a cacophony of academic concepts and practical activities being attempted by colleges to improve student persistence. Researchers often use different names for closely related concepts; practitioners sometimes use the same name for very different student support activities. If the Community College Pathways NIC were to improve success reliably at scale, it would need to define operationally what advancing productive persistence actually meant.[28]

I. *The Concept Framework.* Ultimately, the Pathways NIC settled on a definition of productive persistence illustrated in figure 4.6. It included key knowledge and skills that students need to navigate through college, student mindsets about their ability to learn math, their beliefs about the relevance of math in their lives, the strength of students' social connections to their course of study, and key instructional and relational practices used by faculty to sustain student effort in learning.

Figure 4.6   Concept framework for productive persistence in developmental math

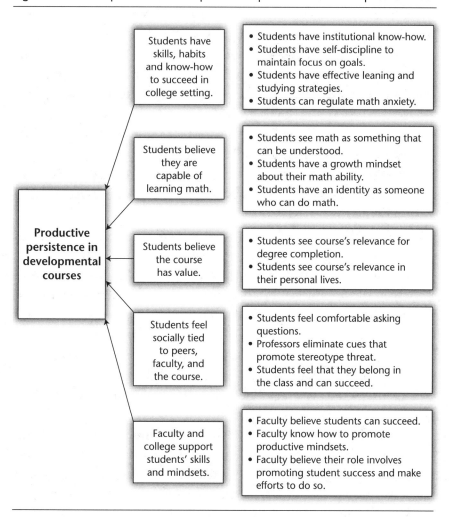

This *concept framework* (aka supplemental design detail introduced in chapter 3) emerged out of an innovation activity, called a ninety-day cycle.[29] The goal of the cycle was to synthesize extant empirical findings on malleable noncognitive factors and then consolidate these findings into a small set of core concepts that might form a coherent, compelling, and practical (albeit also provisional) working theory of improvement. The concept framework emerged through an interactive process in which prototype versions were vetted by academic experts and diverse faculty and institutional leaders. In essence, three distinct activity strands occurred interactively: research synthesis, academic expert review, and professional educator assessments. Evolving ideas from each strand were tested against the other two. The aim was to develop a framework recognizable to both practical and theoretical experts, each of whom deeply understands this domain but through different lenses. This framework then became the basis for the development of practical measures. It also guided the articulation of changes that might be introduced into community college classrooms to advance these intermediate outcomes.

II. *The Development of a Practical Measure.* The development of a practical measure of productive persistence required a second ninety-day cycle. The team began by reviewing the research literature for extant measures related to the concept framework.[30] The most feasible option was an individual student survey. After identifying more than nine hundred possible items, the team confronted the same problem as in the framework development task. Out of this surplus of possibilities, what were the most important questions to ask? Since data collection would be woven into regular classroom instruction, time would be extremely limited. Through consultation with community college faculty, the team concluded that the survey could not take more than three minutes to administer on the first day of class. This practical constraint further refined the overall search: what were the twenty-five best questions to ask? A good answer here demanded clarity about the role of a primary-driver measure.

By virtue of its position as an intermediate target, a good measure for a primary driver should (1) predict the ultimate outcomes of interest (i.e., students' sustained participation and success in learning); (2) be sensitive to process changes that might be introduced (i.e., the productive persistence measure functions as the immediate outcome for interventions aiming to increase it); and (3) provide guidance as to where subsequent improvement efforts might focus (i.e., for whom and where the Pathways are succeeding and not). These criteria shaped a technical review that considerably reduced the overall list of possibilities.[31] Some items were redundant and could easily be eliminated. (Recall that redundant items are often built into academic research measures by design.) Community college faculty judged other items as too abstractly worded to be useful. Some items actually contained two somewhat different questions embedded in them, creating doubts as to what students' responses actually meant. In other cases, the response categories seemed vague and could be improved by shifting to more explicit descriptors (for example, asking how often something happened rather than agreeing or disagreeing that it did).[32]

The surviving list of possible items next went through a review and tests with community college students.[33] As students answered pilot questions and then talked about what they thought each was asking, it became clear that some questions needed to be rewritten in language more relevant to developmental math classrooms and more aligned with the way students actually talked.

Statistical evidence from analyses of pilot items also informed the process. As noted previously, the goal was to come up with the most predictive set of twenty-five items. Interestingly, this led to a different principle for guiding item selection than that typically used in the construction of social-psychological measures. In developing academic research measures, priority is placed on choosing items that are thought best to measure a single construct. This results in a set of items that are highly correlated with each other. In contrast, selecting items for a primary driver directs attention to the predictive power of each item (i.e., whether it distinguishes among students who are more or less likely to succeed subsequently; see the later example). Now each item should predict the "big-dot" outcomes but ideally have little or no relationship to the other items. Such an item set maximizes the predictive utility of the instrument.[34]

Through these multiple processes a three-minute practical measure was eventually born.[35]

III. *Evidence About Sensitivity to Process Changes.* The first few weeks of a class are a critical period for student engagement. If students fear failure or sense they might not belong, they may withhold the effort necessary to succeed.[36] Consequently, the Pathways design included a "Starting Strong change package" that sought to help students experience early success; feel hopeful about their academic futures; and connect them to peers, the course, and its instructor. Routines were introduced to reduce student anxiety, to increase interest in the course, and to form supportive student work groups. Complementing these routines was a growth mindset intervention that drew on pioneering experimental studies in social psychology by Carol Dweck and colleagues.[37] This brief intervention (about thirty minutes) consists of a persuasive reading and writing exercise designed to shift students away from the idea that "I am just not good at math" (i.e., a fixed mindset about math) toward a view that math ability can be grown and developed.

As a first check on the adequacy of the productive persistence measure, the team compared student responses to the survey administered on the first day of class with results when readministered after three weeks of instruction. The evidence, presented in figure 4.7, was encouraging. The team found moderate to large changes in four measured student attitudes after the first three weeks. Students' interest in math had increased, their math anxiety and uncertainty about belonging had decreased, and they were much less likely to hold a fixed mindset about learning math. So on average, the initial attempt at starting stronger had moved these key intermediate outcomes in the right direction. Reciprocally, from the point of view of measure development, the team now had evidence that these survey items were sensitive to change. Confidence increased as results replicated a second year.

IV. *Evidence of Predictive Validity.* The second key characteristic of a measure for a primary driver is that it should predict the outcomes targeted for improvement. The improvement team had developed an "at-riskness" indicator based on student responses to the productive

Figure 4.7   Sensitivity of the productive persistence measure to process changes

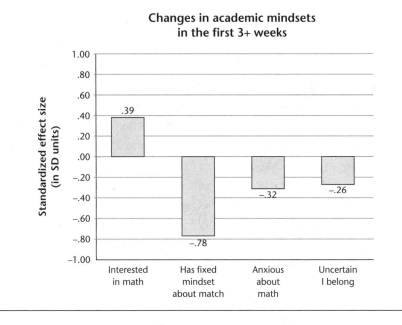

Changes in academic mindsets
in the first 3+ weeks

persistence questions asked on the first day of the course. Students were categorized as high, medium, or low risk depending on the number of different subconcepts on which worrisome responses were reported.[38] As the first end-of-course data became available, predictable patterns emerged. Students judged high risk from the first day of class were twice as likely to fail as their lower-risk classmates. Moreover, these survey responses predicted end-of-course performance even after taking into account differences in students' background mathematical knowledge, demographic characteristics such as race/ethnicity, home language, and number of dependents. So the measure passed a second critical test: it functioned as a leading indicator forecasting ultimate outcomes.

V. *Insights for Continuous Improvement.* The team now dug deeper to examine whether any of the separate components comprising the productive persistence survey might yield guidance about how to further strengthen the Starting Strong change package. They found that one survey item in particular—assessing students' belonging uncertainty—was the single best predictor of whether students dropped the course before the end of the semester (see figure 4.8).[39] Moreover, this item was an especially powerful predictor for African American students. Their likelihood of success varied by a factor of 10 depending on how they responded to the question, "How often, if ever, do you wonder: 'Maybe I don't belong here'?" A clear priority for the next round of improvement had come into focus. Prior academic research had established belonging uncertainty as an important social-psychological phenomenon.[40] However, this research offered little guidance as to how to do better. So the NIC would have to experiment and invent its own solutions. This was a place where rapid small-scale tests of change seemed a promising route toward learning to improve.

Figure 4.8 Belonging uncertainty predicts failure to persist

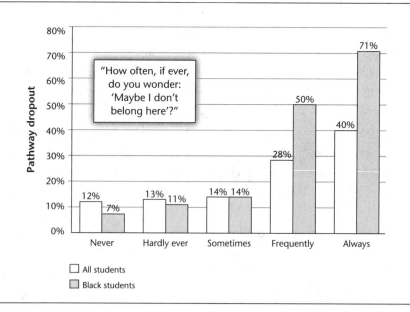

CONCLUDING OBSERVATIONS

This chapter has focused on another key improvement science principle: we cannot improve at scale what we cannot measure. Common measures of outcomes and primary drivers are a key structuring agent for a NIC. These measures operationalize the concepts articulated in the driver diagram and generate data that allows community members to learn from each other and improve together over time. These data become especially important as the scale of work increases. As any improvement initiative spreads, there is the present danger of degradation in quality. In addition, it is no longer easy to see directly what is and is not working. Common data are the key to sensing overall system performance, identifying sources of variation in outcomes, and continuing the processes of learning to improve. Absent such data, quality at scale remains an elusive goal.

Our discussion of measurement continues in the next chapter as we move to the far right-hand side of the driver diagram where an individual process is being changed or perhaps something new is being designed, introduced, tested, and refined. Measures collected at this level allow us to address our most basic improvement questions: "How will we know whether each specific process change is actually an improvement?"

5

Use Disciplined Inquiry
to Drive Improvement

*If you want truly to understand
something, try to change it.*

—KURT LEWIN[1]

BY DEFINITION, IMPROVEMENT requires change. Unfortunately in education, change too often fails to bring improvement—even when smart people are working on the right problems and drawing on cutting-edge ideas. Believing in the power of some new reform proposal and propelled by a sense of urgency, educational leaders often plunge headlong into large-scale implementation. Invariably, outcomes fall far short of expectations. Enthusiasm wanes, and the field moves on to the next idea without ever really understanding why the last one failed. Such is the pattern of change in public education: implement fast, learn slow, and burn good will as you go.

The difficulty of enacting reliable change is simply a fact of life about complex systems. As noted in chapter 3, it is often impossible to predict all the ramifications that some planned change will cause to happen in an organization. While the statistical models of policy analysis and the charting tools of strategic planning are powerful, they can easily seduce us into believing that we understand more than we actually do. Consequently, improvement science takes a very different tack. It approaches change as a *learning-to-improve problem*. Like those advocating large-scale implementation, it too holds as its end goal improving outcomes broadly across classrooms, schools, colleges, districts, or even whole states. It, however, recognizes the complex systems character of productive change, and drawing on Kurt Lewin's inspiration, it embraces an experimenting logic. Introducing change is structured so that participants can learn their way into what it will actually take to enact some new practice reliably with quality at scale. Here we detail the methods that guide such inquiries and introduce tools to assist in carrying out this work.

ASKING THREE IMPROVEMENT QUESTIONS

All activity in improvement science is disciplined by three deceptively simple questions:

1. What specifically are we trying to accomplish?
2. What change might we introduce and why?
3. How will we know that a change is actually an improvement?[2]

As we saw in chapter 3, the first two questions are central to the causal system analysis and the development of a working theory of improvement. The third question underpins our discussion in chapter 4 on the design of practical measurement systems.

In this chapter, we use these same questions to drill down into the actual work of improvement. The three questions scaffold a learning dynamic that involves making hypotheses about change explicit, testing these hypotheses against evidence, revising one's change ideas based on what is learned through such tests, and testing again. Improvement research typically entails cycling through this process multiple times.

To see how these steps all come together, we revisit the case of the Asthma Control Team at Cincinnati Children's Hospital from chapter 2.

IMPROVING WORK PROCESSES TO ACHIEVE TARGETED AIMS

The Asthma Control Team at Cincinnati Children's united around an explicit response to the first improvement question: "What specifically are we trying to accomplish?" Their answer:

> By June 30, 2012, eliminate the disparity between Medicaid and privately insured asthmatic children in their readmissions to Emergency Department and inpatient services. This entails a 20 percent reduction in readmissions and inpatient services for children from poor families.

As we can see, the team went far beyond the vague goal of "improving asthma care." They specified what counted as improvement, how much they sought to achieve, for whom, and by when. There was no doubt about exactly where their efforts were pointed.

Cincinnati Children's set about changing these outcomes by re-engineering key processes in how the team served asthma patients. As noted in chapter 2, the team recognized that environmental conditions in many poor children's homes, such as the presence of mold and cockroaches, could trigger asthma attacks that required hospitalization. They also knew that medications were inconsistently used, especially by children on Medicaid. They hypothesized that these two drivers were primarily responsible for the disparate outcomes they continued to see. At this point, the improvement team could simply have lamented the circumstances in which many of these children lived. Instead, they set out to design a better system to lessen the impact of each of these drivers. Now they were ready to take on the second improvement question: "What change might we introduce and why?"

As it turns out, pursuing its improvement aim would require the hospital to make many changes to several parts of its service system. Mitigating the asthma risks associated with environmental conditions, for example, would require physicians to change their intake protocol to ensure that questions about the possible presence of mold and cockroaches in the home were asked and recorded. The hospital would also need a new process to more reliably trigger referrals to social service agencies. Addressing the inconsistent use of medications would require the hospital to change the discharge process to better inform children and their families about the importance of regular use of medications. Since some families had problems obtaining the medications, the hospital also now saw a need to coordinate with local pharmacies and insurance companies to make sure that patients could get their prescriptions filled. Tackling each specific concern would demand changes in the daily routines of many different individuals.

For example, a new intake protocol required physicians to modify a routine at the heart of their practice—how they talked with their patients. What's more, for the protocol to have the intended impact, it would need to be integrated into the daily activity of one hundred fifty pediatricians working across multiple different hospital units. The team focused on learning fast by starting small, with just one pediatrician and one unit, and then systematically expanded out to others. At each step in the process, the team was building the know-how necessary to work at a larger and larger scale.

Their learning journey was disciplined by the third improvement question: "How will we know that a change is actually an improvement?" For their efforts on improving the intake protocol, the team identified a key performance indicator to track: was information about the possible presence of cockroaches in the home actually recorded in children's files? By pulling past records from June through September 2010, they created a data baseline on practice prior to initiation of the improvement project. The team found that many weeks went by in which only a few cases were adequately documented. It seemed clear that questions about conditions in the home were just not being asked.

By June 2011 the team had conducted a sufficient number of improvement cycles that they felt ready to initiate widespread implementation. To check progress going forward, team members reviewed new patient records every week to count whether appropriate documentation was now being recorded. They tracked the data over time in what is known as a *run chart*.[3] Figure 5.1 displays the percentage of cases with cockroach documentation before and after the new intake protocol was implemented hospitalwide. In the first week of implementation, the percentage of records

Figure 5.1   Using a run chart to test whether a change is a reliable improvement

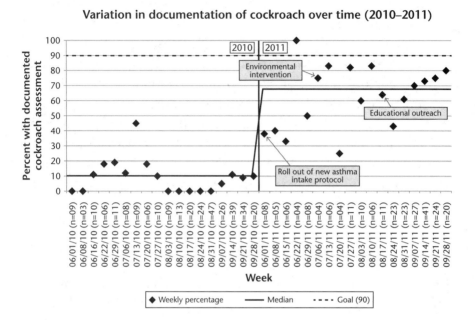

Source: Andrew F. Beck, Hadley S. Sauers, Robert S. Kahn, Connie Yau, Jason Weiser, and Jeffrey Simmons, "Improved Documentation and Care Planning With an Asthma-Specific History and Physical," *Hospital Pediatrics,* 2 (2012): 194–201.

with documented cockroach information jumped from a baseline of 9 percent to 40 percent.

Moving in parallel with improvement cycles on the new intake protocol were efforts to improve referrals to social services. These new routines were ready to go systemwide in July. Given that physicians now saw that their documentation efforts were more likely to result in needed follow-up social services (labeled environmental intervention on the graph), documentation rates jumped further. When it appeared that implementation might be slipping some, the team added a training component for hospital staff in August to reinforce the importance of reliably implementing the new protocol. By September 2011, over 70 percent of the patient records consistently included information about whether cockroaches were present in the home (far right side of figure 5.1). While the team still had more work to do to reach the process target that they had set, 90 percent of all records with appropriate documentation, the changes were clearly moving in the right direction.

Through sustained coordinated actions like these, the Asthma Control Team significantly reduced the readmissions rates for poor children and virtually eliminated the long-standing disparities in care that had triggered their improvement drive. These efforts return us to an important observation discussed in chapter 2: much of the variation in outcomes is linked to how key work processes are carried out. Leaders at Cincinnati Children's didn't blame families, castigate staff, or call for superhuman efforts on the part of pediatricians. Rather, they simply went to work to learn how to change the system so better outcomes would result.

ORGANIZING THE LEARNING JOURNEY

Cincinnati Children's provides an impressive example of how improvement research can advance quality outcomes reliably at scale. By identifying key work processes, gathering data about those processes, and learning their way from small tests of change into large-scale implementation, the Asthma Control Team ultimately met its ambitious aim of eliminating disparities in the hospital readmissions rate. The three improvement questions kept them focused on their destination, the very practical changes necessary to get them there, while also constantly examining data as to whether they were progressing toward the outcomes they cared about.

Now we illustrate how these same methods can be systematically applied in the field of education toward similar ends.

Sizing Up the Context

Developing initiatives that achieve effectiveness reliably at scale begins with a careful analysis of the institutional context for change. Three considerations organize this analysis. First is a critical assessment of available *know-how.* Educators—practitioners, policy makers, and researchers alike—are rarely at a loss for ideas about how to make things better. But they often lack the specific, practical knowledge necessary to get these ideas to actually work. Take the small high school initiative discussed in the introduction. There was an explicit problem to solve and a good idea to pursue. Few educators, however, had ever restructured large dysfunctional high schools into multiple small schools on the timetables set and under the constraints imposed. The field simply lacked the necessary knowledge as to how actually to execute under these conditions.

Second, advancing change at scale makes demands on both *organizational capacity and human capabilities*. Even if a few educators know how to make some set of change ideas come alive, one still needs to assess whether a sufficient number of these people exist and whether the necessary organizational supports are in place to execute at the scale envisioned. Educational leaders too often wave off this concern with the mantra, "We are building the plane as we fly it." Taking this expression a bit more literally would be a good idea. One is not likely to get such a plane off the ground, and even if one did, it would almost certainly be heading toward a fiery crash![4] At base here is a general organizational fact of life. The rate of spread for any effective change is a function of the size of the current expertise base that can teach and mentor others how to do this work. As new change ideas are brought into education, by definition, this expertise base tends to be very limited.

Third is an assessment of the politics of change. Improvement efforts need the *good will and engagement* of the people whose work is the subject of change. How are those most directly affected likely to respond? Change can move quickly when educators are receptive to the ideas being advanced. In contrast, the presence of suspicion and resistance constitutes a major hurdle in navigating a productive improvement journey. It is especially important in these situations to attend carefully to the principle of user-centeredness introduced in chapter 1. Embedded in educator worries and concerns are often critical insights. Taking these into account is essential in truly moving change forward.

How one analyzes an institutional context in terms of these three concerns dictates the most prudent approach to follow. Common practice in education today is to go straight to large-scale implementation—the bottom-right box in figure 5.2. Yet rarely do reformers operate under

Figure 5.2   A framework for analyzing the institutional context for improvement

Sizing up a context		Participants' will		
		Resistant	*Indifferent*	*Ready*
Extant know-how limited	**Limited capacity**	Very small scale	Very small scale	Very small scale
	Good capacity	Small-scale test	Small-scale test	Moderate-Scale test
Substantial know-how exists	**Limited capacity**	Small-scale test	Moderate-scale test	Large-scale test
	Good capacity	Moderate-scale test	Large-scale test	System-wide implementation

conditions where they truly know how to make a new idea work well, where the necessary capacity exists to execute it at scale, and where the workforce is ready to take on a new challenge. So it is hardly surprising that initiatives regularly fail to deliver on the promises made. The conventional way of working also extracts collateral costs. Districts often wind up spending considerable funds and staff energy trying to fix unforeseen problems. Senior leaders must take time and shift attention from other important tasks as they work to shore up the initiative both behind the scenes and in public. Frontline educators are frustrated at being required to do things they know can't work. Throughout it all, trust erodes and a culture of cynicism builds.

There is a better way: starting with small, rapid tests of change and then expanding the initiative out as the improvement team learns. A set of general principles guides the approach: (1) wherever possible, learn quickly and cheaply; (2) be minimally intrusive—some changes will fail, and we want to limit negative consequences on individuals' time and personal lives; and (3) develop empirical evidence at every step to guide subsequent improvement cycles. Doing so simultaneously advances three valued goals. First, through small tests of change, we develop the technical knowledge to turn a good idea into something that can actually be executed effectively. Second, we build capabilities among the individuals involved in the early testing. The practical expertise they develop through working out a set of change ideas becomes an invaluable resource to coach others as they learn to do the same. Third, as early adopters experience heightened efficacy in their day-to-day work, they also now become champions for these changes to be taken up by others. So starting small to learn fast also helps build will for larger-scale change.

To be clear, not every improvement problem must start as a very small test of change. If know-how and capacity already exist, one can begin with a large-scale test, and under the right political conditions, even go directly to full-scale implementation. More often than not, however, an analysis of institutional context will locate educational reforms in the upper-left box of figure 5.2.

The Plan-Do-Study-Act Inquiry Cycle

The faster a network can learn, the faster it can move from small-scale testing to systemwide implementation. The *Plan-Do-Study-Act (PDSA) cycle,* a basic method of inquiry in improvement research, guides this rapid learning. A PDSA cycle follows the logic of systematic experimentation, common in scientific endeavors, now applied to everyday practices. As illustrated in figure 5.3, this cycle consists of four steps carried out repeatedly to answer new questions as the scope of the inquiry expands.[5] The heart of the cycle is articulating hypotheses, based on a working theory of improvement, and then gathering data to test them. Predictions are made about the results expected. When these predictions are compared to what actually happens, gaps in understanding are revealed. Previously unrecognized but critical details about how work is carried out suddenly come into view. Context issues that are key to successful change manifest themselves as well. Especially in the early stages of a change effort, when new practices are being tried, we should expect many of our predictions to be wrong.

Often multiple PDSA cycles are needed to develop a change idea that actually works. Each cycle builds on what was learned in previous cycles until a team has discerned how to effect improvements reliably under

Figure 5.3   Plan-Do-Study-Act cycle[6]

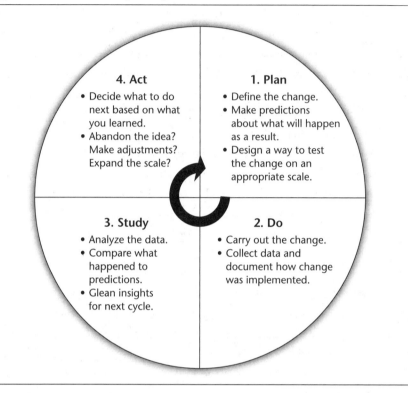

different conditions. One of the advantages of the PDSA cycle is that it is a very flexible tool to guide learning at different stages—from a good idea to a quick prototype to something that may work in a few places and, finally, to a robust large-scale improvement. To illustrate PDSA cycles, we return to the Building a Teaching Effectiveness Network.

A CASE EXAMPLE: IMPROVING FEEDBACK FOR NEW TEACHERS

In the summer of 2011, an improvement team from Austin Independent School District (AISD) gathered for an off-site retreat. Its goal was to strengthen support for new teachers and to create an overall work environment that would encourage them to stay. Almost 20 percent of Austin's teachers had entered the district in the past three years.[7] The team recognized that improvements focused on beginning teachers could have powerful long-term effects on student learning.

Laura Baker, then head of professional development for the district, led the group. Joining her were two colleagues from the district's Educator Quality Department, a representative from the local teachers' union, a well-respected principal, and three new teachers. They gathered around an early version of a driver diagram that had been developed with colleagues from Baltimore and New York City public schools and with the help of several experts on new teacher development, including Susan Moore Johnson from Harvard University, and several staff members from the Carnegie Foundation.[8] This early-stage driver diagram sketched out a preliminary aim statement and five primary levers for change.[9] (See figure 5.4.)

Figure 5.4   Preliminary version of Building a Teaching Effectiveness Network driver diagram (only primary drivers displayed)

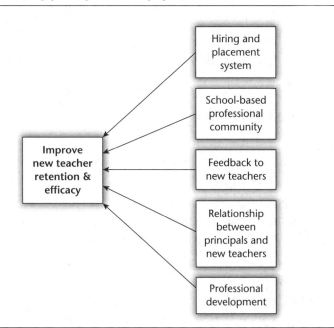

It took the better part of a day for the team to agree on where they should start. They recognized that better hiring and placement of new teachers was important, but improving these processes would likely require changes in union and district policy. A different improvement team with different leadership would need to be formed to take on this task. In contrast, improving the quality of feedback to new teachers and increasing the engagement of principals were challenges they could more readily do something about. A couple of the team members wondered, however, whether this was really necessary. "Don't principals already know how to give feedback to their teachers?" they questioned. Shirley Dean, a second-year teacher on the team, solidified the group's commitment to this problem. She told them: "It sounds like everyone here agrees that principals should talk with new teachers and give them feedback. I can tell you this just does not happen very often. In the two years I have been here, I don't know if I've ever had a real conversation about my teaching with any of my administrators. I've been told that I'm doing fine, but 'fine' just doesn't feel like enough for me. I'd like to know what my principal thinks about my teaching."

The team agreed: all new teachers should get frequent, actionable, and coherent feedback. Exactly how to achieve this was much less clear. Could they actually design a feedback process that would work for every teacher in every school?

Very Small Tests of Change

The team started brainstorming about what a good feedback conversation might look like. Baker jotted down notes about each idea on a large whiteboard. Some team members focused on the content of the conversation. The principal's comments, they said, should prompt the teacher to reflect on his or her practice; the comments should give the teacher a clear idea of what specifically to work on; and the principal and new teacher should come to an agreement about what success would look like. Others attended more to the teacher–principal relationship. The principal, they said, should reinforce what was going well; the teacher should help select a focus area; and the teacher should leave the conversation feeling supported. Few disagreed that these were all worthwhile objectives. Some did doubt, however, whether it was possible for a teacher and a principal to agree on an improvement focus in a single, short conversation. They also wondered whether some new teachers would even know where they needed help.

Rather than spending endless amounts of time worrying about all possible contingencies and trying to perfect a protocol through a series of committee meetings, the AISD team decided to learn their way into a workable solution. David Kauffman, the experienced principal on the team, volunteered to attempt a feedback conversation of this sort right then and there with Shirley Dean.

Kauffman took a couple of minutes to think through how he would incorporate the ideas suggested by the group into a structured conversation. He jotted down six prompts to guide the conversation and shared them with the group. This sketchy protocol would be the first *change idea* to be tested. The goal for this first test was to learn whether a short conversation guided by these six prompts would result in a clear focus area for Dean to work on while also leaving her feeling personally supported.

Kauffman had just met Dean that morning and lacked the knowledge he would normally have from visits to her classroom. So he wondered whether he and Dean would be able to have a meaningful discussion about her teaching. But after a couple of moments of nervous laughter, the two began talking as the rest of the team observed and took notes. The two quickly became engrossed in a conversation about how to carry out a whole class discussion of an engaging mathematics problem. Kauffman's prompts helped Dean think aloud about what was actually happening in her classroom and what a quality class discussion looked like. As the conversation concluded, Kauffman suggested that Dean observe a couple of teachers who were particularly skilled at this practice. While this activity unfolded, team members noted whether Kauffman followed the prompts he had written down; they also attended to the specific language he used and some key moves that he made.

Figure 5.5 summarizes the team's documentation of their change idea and predictions ("Plan"); about what actually happened ("Do"); and their

Figure 5.5 Austin's first PDSA test of change

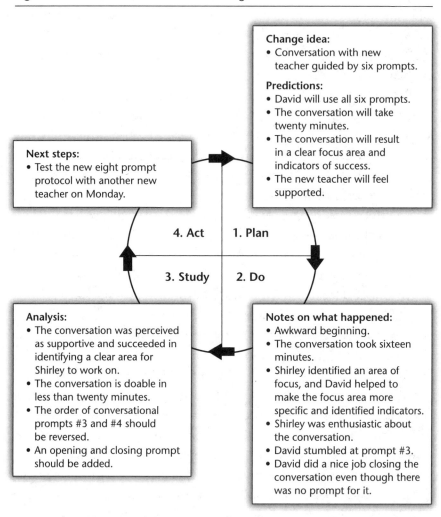

inferences about next steps ("Study"). Enough evidence had been assembled to suggest that a protocol of this sort had potential. The team suggested reordering a couple of prompts in places where the conversation felt awkward. They also added two prompts that Kauffman had improvised to start and then close the conversation. With next steps specified, they were ready to try again ("Act").

David Kauffman volunteered to test the revision with four new teachers in his own school. Laura Baker, the improvement team lead, called Kauffman before each of these conversations to record his predictions for each test. Immediately after each test, Kauffman briefed Baker in an e-mail or a quick phone call. Whenever a conversation deviated from his predictions, they gained insights into how the protocol might be improved.

In the second test, Kauffman tried the conversation without the prompts in front of him. He had encountered a new gym teacher in the hallway and thought he might just jump right into a conversation with him. Kauffman walked away, however, not feeling especially good about this impromptu effort. The conversation felt a bit haphazard; Kauffman surmised that having the protocol in front of him allowed him to concentrate more fully on the teacher's particular concerns. An entirely different problem emerged during the third test. An eager new second grade teacher identified "differentiation strategies within her math class" as her target for improvement. Kauffman knew that she was not ready to work on differentiation because she had not yet established some basic classroom management routines. In the debrief with Baker, they added detail to this aspect of the protocol to indicate how a principal might redirect a feedback conversation were such an event to occur. The fourth test of the protocol went off without a hitch.

Through this first set of tests, Baker and Kauffman had learned about important details necessary for productive feedback sessions. It was time now to test whether what they had learned would work beyond the walls of Kauffman's school. It was also time to think about how to connect the feedback conversation to getting each teacher follow-up support.

Moving Toward Scale: Testing in Multiple Contexts with Diverse Individuals

Baker carefully chose the next five schools to test the feedback protocol. The principals of these schools were close colleagues of Kauffman's; they trusted him, and they already met as a group on a monthly basis. Equally important, the schools provided very different contexts that might well affect how the process could be carried out. One was a comprehensive high school with a large administration. Another was a small elementary school run by only the principal. Some schools had instructional coaches or mentoring programs; others did not. Taken together, these schools represented a good cross-section of the district.

Detailing a Robust Process. All of the principals agreed to try the new conversation protocol. They also began to brainstorm about expanding the process beyond the feedback conversation, to include targeted teacher support and a follow-up classroom observation. In addition, they identified a delivery standard: a complete cycle of this process should occur every two weeks for each new teacher.

As soon as the first tests began in the five schools, a new problem arose. Three of the schools had many more new teachers than Kauffman's. If only the principal observed the teachers and offered them feedback, there was no way the delivery standard could be met. More people would need to be brought into the process.

In response, one school decided to test a "case manager" role. An assistant principal would now serve as the primary feedback provider and orchestrate the two-week cycle. The principal would have an initial conversation with each new teacher to set the stage and then check in with that teacher once every two months. Some schools would eventually need more than one case manager.

Each school also sought to clarify how professional support would be provided. Another new role, "support provider," had to be sketched out, tested, and refined. This prompted several additional sets of PDSA cycles at multiple schools. Here, too, the diversity in organizational contexts manifested itself. At Kauffman's school, instructional coaches could fill this role, but not all of the schools were in the same position. Other schools tried using experienced teachers to mentor and provide support. The improvement team eventually settled on a system that formalized three roles (principal, case manager, support provider), each of which would need to be adapted somewhat based on local resources and constraints. The *process map* in figure 5.6 summarizes how the team now understood that all of this should work.

Figure 5.6 Prototype process map for the feedback-support-observation cycle

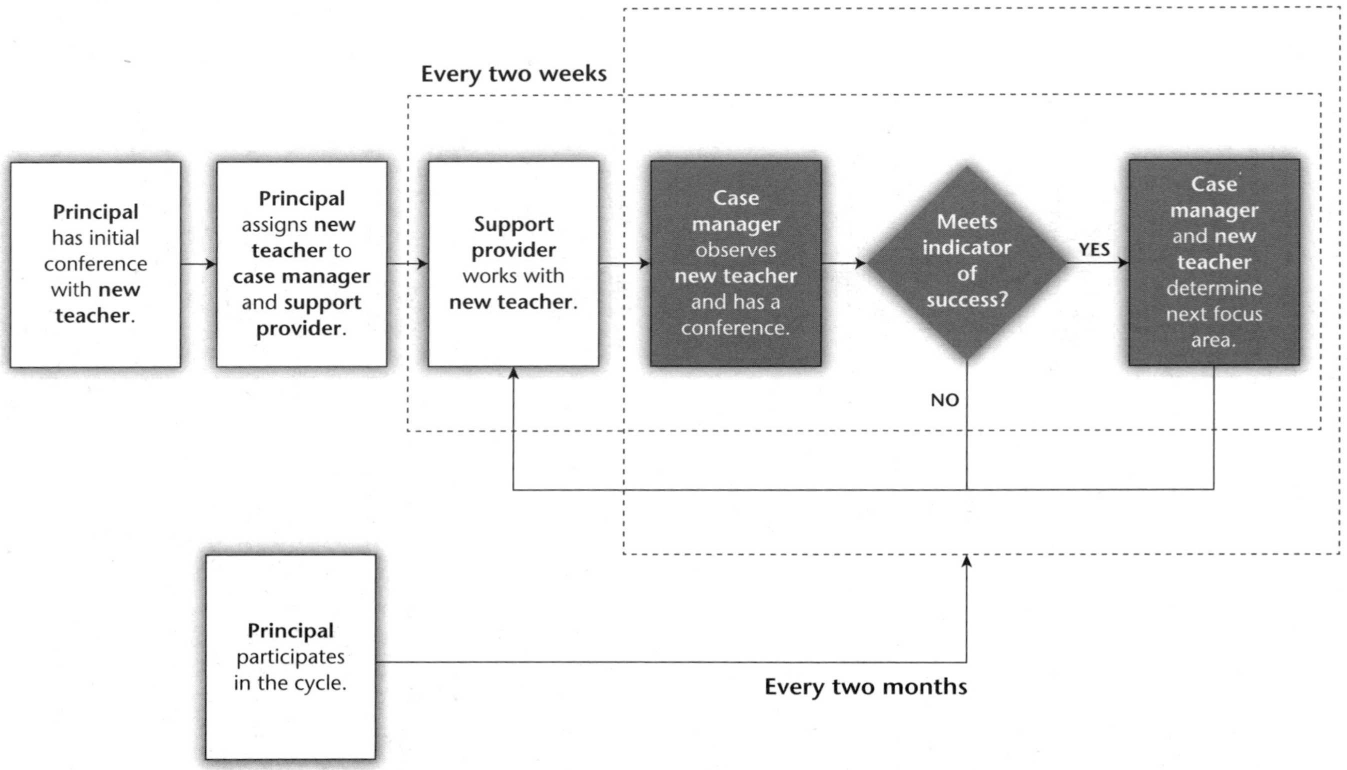

As these PDSA cycles proceeded, Baker and colleagues saw notable improvements in the regularity of feedback and support that new teachers received. However, the work system had also become more complex. It exposed a new although not uncommon problem: how to maintain good communication and coordination among multiple actors seeking to advance a common objective. The feedback-support-observation process now involved "hand-offs" among case managers, support providers, and the school principal. How could the improvement team ensure that all participants were giving consistent messages and pointing their new teachers in the same direction?

Two new change ideas emerged in an attempt to address this issue. One of the schools—a large high school with 175 teachers and 6 administrators—began work on adapting an existing online tool to document the various interactions with each new teacher. The administrative team had already developed a practice of using their iPads to jot down notes as part of their classroom rounds. Baker guided revision of the tool so that the note-taking feature aligned better with the feedback conversation protocol. This change idea then went out to testing in the other four schools.

Meanwhile, another school began work on designing a regular coordination meeting that brought together the principal, case managers, and support providers. In the first attempt, the meeting lasted almost two hours, and they had talked about only half of the schools' new teachers. Other schools soon joined in PDSA cycles on coordination meetings. Improvements occurred more quickly now as schools began learning from each other. The end result was an efficient routine that focused on just the relevant information and individuals. They now had designed a process that could be done well in thirty minutes.

By the end, the improvement team was testing along five ramps, each focused on a different aspect of the overall feedback-support-observation process (see figure 5.7). Taken together, these five elements formed an emerging definition for a standard work process. The need for each element had become visible through early PDSA cycles across multiple different schools. Looking back at the original whiteboard notes, the team could see that much of this had not been anticipated. AISD had learned its way

Figure 5.7   Testing along multiple ramps

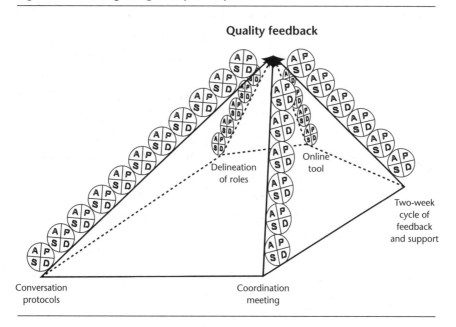

into a more robust design through systematic rapid tests of change. The team members were now ready for further testing in additional schools.

Equally important, new champions for the work emerged as these improvement cycles were unfolding. Daniel Girard, the principal of the large comprehensive high school, was originally skeptical about the need for face-to-face conversations with his new teachers. Wasn't e-mail feedback good enough? Through the work, he came to see the importance of taking the time to meet with new teachers. Even though he had forty novices in his building, he had found a way to make this approach work. His principal colleagues around the district took notice. Laura Baker suddenly found herself in the unusual position of fielding requests from other schools to participate.

Identifying District Infrastructure to Be Developed. The next stage involved spreading the process to thirteen schools. The AISD team now expanded the work into one of the district's vertical teams—the set of elementary and middle schools that fed into a single high school and fell under the authority of a single associate superintendent. Kauffmann and Girard made the pitch to the rest of their colleagues and got every one onboard. All of the schools sought to implement the five elements of the evolving standard work process. The team would now be able to see whether this process was sufficiently detailed to ensure that new teachers received frequent, coherent, and actionable feedback across these thirteen contexts.

Working with an entire vertical team also opened up new challenges. Baker now recognized that district-level actions would be needed to incent and support all of their schools to take on these changes. Providing quality feedback to new teachers would need to be explicitly recognized as part of the principals' and school administrators' jobs, integrated into their job descriptions, and become part of their annual performance reviews. Principals and case managers would need professional development, the focus on new teachers would need to be integrated into the district's mentoring and coaching programs, and the district would need to invest more in its technology resources to facilitate process coordination and communications. The AISD team's learning journey continued to evolve. They were now shifting attention to the specific tools, policies, programs, and training that would soon be needed to support this process as it went districtwide.

Figure 5.8 summarizes AISD's improvement stages in moving from a seemingly simple problem—"How can we get good conversations occurring between new teachers and their principals?"—through to an initiative that was poised to scale. Along the way the AISD team had built the practical knowledge and human capabilities needed, and they had identified the institutional capacities to be developed to get the feedback-support-observation process to work reliably in the hands of many different educators and across varied school contexts. And interestingly, this had evolved into more than just another project—so many of which come and go frequently in school districts. Through their participation in BTEN, AISD now had a base of expertise in quality improvement that had value beyond BTEN. Moreover, additional Austin educators now wanted

Figure 5.8   A developmental continuum for reliable change

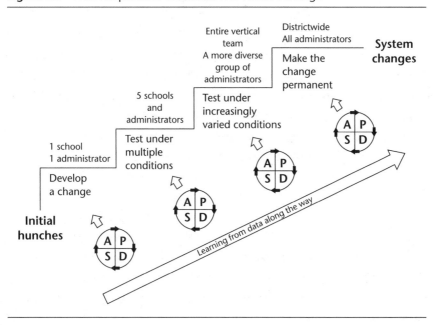

to learn how to do improvement research on a variety of different problems in their schools.[10] So although the quality improvement journey began slowly in Austin, the flywheel was now spinning.

So How Well Are the Changes Actually Performing?

Every step in AISD's improvement journey was determined by evidence gathered in response to the third improvement question: "How do we know this change is an improvement?"

In general, the data needed to take the first steps in a change process can be quite simple. For example, the positive testimony from David Kauffmann and the new teachers in his school was sufficient to warrant further testing of the conversation protocol in a small number of other schools. As the scale of testing increases, gathering common data across sites becomes key to learning how to achieve quality reliably and under more diverse circumstances. This requires the development of practical measures as introduced in chapter 4.

Measuring the Actual Change Processes. The early work in five schools provided insights about what to look for as the change process was being carried out. It also created opportunities to quickly test how process-level data might be gathered most easily. Four *process measures* eventually emerged. Data on frequency of the feedback cycles helped the team to assess whether the two-week delivery standard was being maintained. The online tool provided unobtrusive data about whether administrators were making a record of their conversations with new teachers and how regularly coordination meetings among principals, case managers, and support providers were occurring. Rounding out the set of process measures was a short teacher survey that took less than one minute to complete. It was administered to a sample of teachers, immediately following feedback conversations, to ask about their views of the event. The survey gave the improvement team direct evidence from teachers as to whether the conversation protocol was working as intended.

Taken together, these four measures provided valuable real-time data as schools sought to integrate the feedback-support-observation process into their daily work. Much as the Asthma Control Team did in Cincinnati Children's Hospital, each school team used run charts to track how each component in the process was performing in their school. When a school team realized, for example, that coordination meetings were not routinely occurring, they designed and tested changes aimed at making sure they did.

At the same time, Baker and the districtwide improvement team were looking at the variation that was emerging among schools to see what they might learn from it. Figure 5.9 displays run charts on the frequency of feedback conversations for four schools. In schools B and N, teachers were getting feedback reliably every two weeks. In the other two schools, however, the length between feedback conversations had increased over time. While the year began well in schools G and O, by November the standard set for timely feedback was no longer being met.[11] Conversations with the teams in these two schools helped identify previously unseen problems. Meanwhile, schools B and N, where the process was working well,

Figure 5.9   A sample of school-level run charts on the number of days between feedback cycles (relative number of new teachers in parentheses)

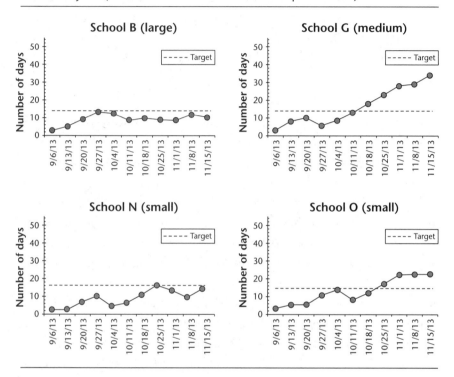

demonstrated some creative solutions that other schools might use. In short, good process data allowed schools to learn from observed variation.

AISD's initial goal was to improve reliability in its feedback processes—reliability across time, across teachers, and across school contexts. Interestingly, if the members of the AISD team had only looked at the average results among participating schools, they could easily have been misled. During the first semester of 2013, new teachers in these schools received feedback once every 13.5 days on average. This mean rate is consistent with the target set by the improvement team. However, in some schools, feedback occurred on average only once every 38 days; some new teachers went three months without having even a single conversation. Clearly, the process did not yet work reliably for all teachers in all schools. Achieving reliability required the improvement team to constantly examine the variability in performance. It demanded that they try to understand the causes of the variability, test new processes aimed at reducing it, and make wise use of what was learned along the way.

Watching for Unintended Consequences. As they worked to improve feedback for new teachers, the members of the AISD team began to worry about whether they might be adding too much to principals' already full plates. Would the new process create an impossible burden for these busy administrators? What would the principals stop doing to make room for this new work? In response to these concerns, the improvement team added a measure of the time that principals spent on the feedback-support-observation process.[12] Tracking this measure helped to focus attention to possible unintended disruptions in principals' work. It also served to build will with principals. Principals appreciated that the improvement team recognized the many demands of their job. Analyzing these data also provided some insights as to how principals might reasonably hope to schedule these conversations amidst their many other competing time demands.[13]

The time measure, developed by the AISD team, is an example of what is called a *balancing measure* in improvement science. It comes from recognizing that when a change is introduced into one part of a complex work system, it often produces unintended changes elsewhere. Gathering balancing measures helps improvers monitor other parts of the system that are not currently the target of improvement, but which may still be affected by the changes pursued.

Closing the Learning Loop

Zooming out a bit, Austin's work on the feedback-support-observation process was motivated by a larger aim: to improve the effectiveness and retention of new teachers. So while the district focused on changing a specific process, it also kept an eye on its overall theory of improvement. Basically, Austin had embraced a three-step causal cascade. Designing a feedback-support-observation process that could be implemented in diverse settings (Step 1) was seen as essential to improving the reliability of the feedback that new teachers received (Step 2), which in turn was viewed as essential to improving teacher effectiveness and retention (Step 3). The process measures described above guided the PDSA cycles on each of the five ramps illustrated in figure 5.7. To fully engage its working theory of improvement, however, AISD would also need data on both the primary driver it sought to effect—quality feedback to all new teachers—and on the ultimate aims for the overall project—improved teacher effectiveness and retention.

Measuring the Primary Driver: Quality of Feedback. Measuring the primary driver required AISD to operationalize "quality feedback." Without doing so, it could not assess whether process changes were resulting in improvement. In the end, the district settled on three key quality characteristics: new teachers should receive a manageable amount of actionable feedback that was consistent across the various people supporting their growth.[14] Developing a practical measure of this primary driver followed along the same lines as the process described in chapter 4 for operationalizing productive persistence. AISD subsequently introduced a short survey for new teachers to report every six weeks on these three aspects of the feedback received. Analyses of the data allowed the improvement team to check empirically whether the change developing at the process level linked to the primary driver they sought to effect.

Leading and Lagging Outcome Measures. Finally, to assess progress on its ultimate improvement goals, AISD needed measures of new teacher retention and effectiveness. The district already collected retention rates and effectiveness ratings for accountability purposes. By reorganizing these existing data to track individuals over time, the district would be able to monitor its progress with successive cohorts of new teachers.

However, retention rates and effectiveness scores are by nature *lagging outcome measures*; they are available only well after any intervention with new teachers is possible. So AISD also needed *leading outcome measures*. These measures should predict the ultimate outcomes of interest, but they should also be available on a more timely basis. Research pointed to two key factors as predictors of employee attrition and performance: teachers' sense of self-efficacy and their sense of being overwhelmed.[15] A carefully selected and varying subset of items was included in short surveys that new teachers took every six weeks.[16] (In keeping with the spirit of practical measurement, each survey took less than three minutes to complete.) Depending on how teachers responded over the course of the year, their probability of returning to the district the following year varied from 0.6 to over 0.9.[17] The school and district teams now had valuable data, every six weeks, to guide their efforts to improve the feedback-support-observation process. Increasingly, they were able to discern how, where, for whom, and under what conditions the process was resulting in better outcomes for new teachers.

Assembling a Full Measurement System. Figure 5.10 displays the overall set of measures that guided the improvement work in Austin. While the illustrative examples are particular to AISD's goals, the categories of measures apply more generally to efforts at improving complex systems. *Outcome measures (both leading and lagging)* help define and assess what is being accomplished. *Primary driver measures* inform about key intermediate outcomes that typically sit at critical junctures in the working theory of improvement (i.e., the link from process changes to key drivers to ultimate outcomes). *Process measures* feed back valuable information about how the specific changes, attempted in PDSA cycles, are performing under different conditions. *Balancing measures* keep an eye on the other parts of the system that might also be changing as a result. With such a system of measures in place, each of the hypothesized causal links in a team's working theory of practice improvement can be examined.

Figure 5.10   A practical measurement system to guide improvement

Type of measure	Description	Examples from Austin's measures
Outcome Measures	How is your system preforming? What is the result?	**Lagging:** Organizational measures of new teacher retention, instructional quality, and learning effectiveness (annually)
		Leading: Teacher reports of self-efficacy and being overwhelmed (every 6 weeks).
Primary Driver Measures	Testing working theory of improvement. Are process measures linked to intermediate outcomes and are they linked in turn to targeted aims?	Teacher reports of whether the overall feedback is actionable, consistent, and manageable (every 6 weeks)
Process Measures	The voice of the workings of the system. Are the specific processes performing as planned?	Quality of a specific feedback conversation (immediately after select feedback conversation) Number of days between feedback conversations (weekly) Time between logging the conversation and recording it on the online tool (as often as conversations occur) Frequency of coordination meetings
Balancing Measures	Looking at the other parts of the system. What unintended consequences accrue as we improve the outcome and process measures?	Time spent by the principal

CONCLUDING OBSERVATIONS

In sum, combining the PDSA methodology for inquiry with a system of practical measures provides networked improvement communities with a strong empirical infrastructure for learning their way into better outcomes. Beginning with a working theory of improvement and associated measures, improvement teams repeatedly test change ideas and gather evidence that continuously challenges what they think they know, what measures are actually telling them about how the system operates, and ultimately whether the processes being developed actually link to valued outcomes. Rigorously pursued over time, this process builds toward a robust base of professional knowledge about what works, for whom, and under what set of conditions.[18]

It is important to acknowledge that engaging a diverse community of practitioners, researchers, and institutional leaders in such efforts requires everyone to think and work in a new way. As Don Berwick has written: "[Quality improvement] is an applied field tethered to strong, formal science. Practitioners who lose touch with the science run aground; scientists who lose touch with application fly off into irrelevance."[19] Harnessing multiple forms of expertise, so that they join together as something considerably more than a sum of random parts, is essential for meaningful change. This is the challenge we take up next: how to engage a diverse community in productive, collective efforts to improve.

6

Accelerate Learning Through Networked Communities

[M]an's problem-solving capability represents possibly the most important resource possessed by a society. . . . Any possibility for evolving an art or science that can couple directly and significantly to the continued development of that resource should warrant doubly serious consideration.

—DOUGLAS ENGELBART[1]

It was December 9, 1968. Approximately 1,000 people, mostly computer scientists, had filled San Francisco's Brooks Hall for the biennial meeting of the Joint Computer Conference. They were there to witness the results of a research and development initiative titled the "Augmenting Human Intellect Project."[2] Douglas Engelbart sat alone center stage looking every bit the engineer of the day: short-sleeved white shirt, thin black tie, close-cropped hair, and visibly nervous about the public presentation that he was there to give. The goal of Engelbart's project was to explore the ways that a then-new technology, the digital computer, might enhance human functioning and performance. As he sat at his computer workstation, Engelbart had a keyboard directly in front of him, to the right sat a bulky device about half the size of a shoebox with three glowing buttons atop it.

A wire tailed from the box to the keyboard. This was the very first computer mouse, and Engelbart had invented it. This new tool was part of a grand vision that Engelbart proceeded to share with his audience about a truly interactive and personalized computing system with functionalities that the larger world would eventually come to know as windows, word processing, graphical user interface, and collaborative real-time editing.

Over the course of his career, Engelbart and colleagues articulated the basic concepts of what we now know as hypertext, groupware, shareware, social media, and cloud computing. Equally noteworthy, later in his career Engelbart drew attention to improving how groups organize for producing and using knowledge. For Engelbart, new technologies were tools for augmenting human intelligence, for helping people get better at what they innately do. Building on this idea of augmentation, Engelbart envisioned how systems of technologies might combine with human capabilities and organizational processes to enable more productive collective action. His understandings about the nature of social learning in organizations inspire our work. He also coined the name that we have adopted—*networked improvement communities.*

Figure 6.1 depicts the schema for individual and organizational learning developed by Engelbart.[3] In it, he describes three interrelated levels of learning. *Level-A learning* represents the knowledge acquired by front-line workers as they engage in their practice. For example, it is what teachers learn as they reflect individually on evidence from some new instructional practice they may have attempted or from their efforts to refine it. *Level-B learning* occurs across individuals within a workplace. It is the kind of knowledge generated, for example, in school-based learning communities where teachers gather around students' work or reports on school test scores to consider how they might improve them. Institutional research units in individual colleges and school districts may also generate this form of knowledge.

Learning can also occur across institutions, and Engelbart termed this *Level-C learning.* Recall the example in the introduction about how a group of labs across several countries, each operating independently but connected as a network, quickly identified the SARS virus and opened the

Figure 6.1   Schema for social learning (adapted from Engelbart)

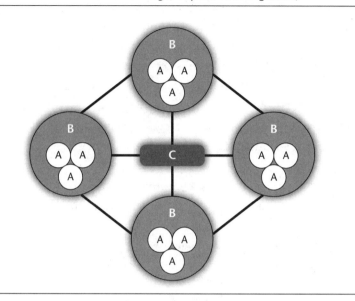

door for diagnostic testing and vaccine development. What might have taken months or years for any individual lab to solve occurred in just a matter of weeks. This is Level-C learning. It is an especially potent form of knowledge generated as ideas are elaborated, refined, and tested across many different contexts. The development of Level-C learning is not a simple, naturally occurring extension of Level-A and -B learning. Rather it requires deliberate organization. It is catalyzed and orchestrated by a network hub and relies on appropriate technologies for rapid communications about insights developing across distributed sites. Operating in this way enables a network to accelerate how it learns.

In essence, Level-B learning augments what individuals may learn on their own (Level-A). When individual insights are systematically pooled, collective capabilities grow. Moving this to Level-C learning radically speeds up this social learning process. When many more individuals, operating across diverse contexts, are drawn together in a shared learning enterprise, the capacity grows exponentially.

EXPLOITING THE POWER OF STRUCTURED NETWORKS

The networked improvement communities that are at the center of our work bring together Englebart's ideas about accelerating social learning with the methods of improvement science. Unlike more loosely formed or self-organizing networks, NICs are intentionally designed social organizations, and participants have distinct roles, responsibilities, and norms for membership. NICs maintain narratives that exemplify what they are about and why it is important to affiliate with them. Operationally, the key principles of improvement science detailed in the previous five chapters function as structuring agents, coordinating the efforts of many different individuals in addressing a focal problem. Getting these structuring agents right is key to unleashing individual creativity while advancing joint accountability for problem solving.

Formally, a NIC is marked by four essential characteristics. It is

- Focused on a well-specified common aim
- Guided by a deep understanding of the problem, the system that produces it, and a shared working theory to improve it
- Disciplined by the methods of improvement research to develop, test, and refine interventions
- Organized to accelerate the diffusion of these interventions out into the field and support their effective integration into varied educational contexts

Taken together, these features frame the NIC as a scientific learning community. Below, we sketch out some of the mechanisms that make NICs such a powerful system for accelerating improvement.

An Engine for Innovation

It is now well understood that large networks are powerful engines for innovation.[4] As an extremely large network, education has an extraordinary, and currently largely untapped, capacity to improve in this regard. Millions of educators are engaged every day in Level-A learning—confronting classroom problems, experimenting with new ways to respond, and learning as they go. Likewise, increasing numbers of educational institutions (schools, departments, and even whole districts and colleges) are engaged in Level-B learning. For almost any practical question we could ask, the chances are good that someone, somewhere, has been trying to answer it and developing some keen insights on which we might build.[5] However, lacking the common language infrastructure of a NIC, educators typically do not know who these individuals are or what specifically they have tried and learned. We live in separate silos. Much of value is being learned, but it lives and dies with those who learned it.

NICs, in contrast, are specifically structured to tap these latent resources. With ready access to data organized around a shared working theory of improvement, NICs are better able to identify "bright spots" or "positive deviants"—places where unusually positive outcomes are occurring—and to discern what it is that these places have actually done. Such cases provide inspiration about what is actually achievable; they also generate detailed practical knowledge about how the achievement was accomplished in a particular place. For example, by the third year of the Community College Pathways NIC, two colleges had successfully expanded Pathways instruction so that it could be offered to a majority of developmental mathematics students at their institutions. To accomplish this, they had to solve a wide array of very practical issues around scheduling, advising, expanding faculty capacity, and cross-program articulation. These two institutions have created a base of practical knowledge from which other colleges could now learn.

An Architecture for Broad Participation

A key feature of NICs, imported directly from networked science, is how a properly structured working theory of improvement enables broad participation.[6] By linking aims to key drivers and then detailing the many changes that might be tested, a NIC opens up numerous opportunities for individual members to engage with its problem-solving mission. More specifically, by parsing a very large problem into many discrete subtasks, it eases entry for individual participation. This strategy recognizes participants' busy lives and the limited time they may have to engage in improvement activity. An individual NIC member can work on just a single change idea embedded in the structure of a much larger improvement effort. The diversity of tasks also means that individuals will likely find a place to contribute that aligns with their particular interests and expertise. Consequently, enormous and previously largely untapped energy for change now gets released.

For example, community college faculty members, motivated by problems in their own classrooms, have been testing change ideas to improve students' attendance and homework corrections. Several of the PDSA cycles initiated by individual faculty have proved sufficiently promising that broader testing by other faculty is now proceeding. Importantly, these micro-change ideas, and the emerging evidence associated with them, connect directly back into the productive persistence driver for the CCP network. So the knowledge being generated through these individual faculty efforts is being recorded and can be easily accessed by others. (See further discussion on the knowledge management function of a network hub later in this chapter.)

Resourcing Social Capital

Over a half century of research has identified the importance of social connections as a key resource for innovation diffusion.[7] NICs recognize and build on these findings. When NIC participants come to know, respect, and trust one another, they are more likely to adopt the innovations of their colleagues and test and refine these innovations in their own contexts. A network hub, in turn, gathers and feeds back to the network key insights that emerge as innovations spread and are integrated into new contexts. This is another way in which Level-C learning occurs.

Central to making all of this work are deliberate efforts to nurture social capital across the network. In the context of the CCP initiative, these efforts include residential institutes that welcome new members into the community and periodic networkwide learning sessions (ideally face to face). In the interim, webinars, conference calls, and videoconferences sustain human contact and promote reciprocal accountability. As priorities emerge for networkwide design and development—for example, a new social learning platform to support students' out-of-class work and a professional development initiative tailored for adjunct faculty—they create additional opportunities for members to work together and strengthen their social ties while doing so.

Investigating Patterns and Identifying Improvement Targets from Network Data

The data that are shared networkwide provide further opportunities to accelerate improvement. By analyzing conditions and variations in performance across a network, a NIC taps into the law of large numbers. It allows participants to see things that may elude even the best individual educator.

For example, despite the high aspirations that community college faculty members have for their students, and their deep commitments to teaching, each year many students fail to achieve. A very basic aspect of our human nature kicks in at this point. We need an explanation. How do we reconcile perplexing outcomes that occur over and over that are seemingly beyond our control? If we have tried the best we can, and many of our students still fail, it is quite rational to look beyond the classroom for explanations. And so we craft a narrative. These students' lives are complicated. They have dependents to care for, and some are working too many hours to be able to study.

These accounts are truthful; the lives of many community college students *are* complicated, and sustaining the effort needed to achieve success can indeed be formidable. However, the NIC has learned through analyses conducted by the network hub that these factors are not the main sources of variation in outcomes that the NIC is observing.[8] As described in chapter 4, networkwide data have unearthed several different plausible explanations, one of which has to do with students' belonging uncertainty and associated stereotype threat. Confronting these social psychological threats and in attempt to protect themselves, students may withhold the effort needed to succeed. These data and explanation are important because they direct the NIC to consider possible changes in instruction and targeted interventions that might improve outcomes for these vulnerable students.

In short, network analytics have made it possible for CCP members to discern patterns across many different classrooms that few individual educators were likely able to see on their own. What is a recognizable phenomenon when we have data on large numbers of students may look highly particular in an individual classroom or to an individual faculty member. These networkwide findings (Level-C learning) can enhance both the efforts of individual colleges (Level-B) and also lead to subsequent Level-A learning.

Comparing Results and Learning from One Another

Along a related line, the common data collected by a network create opportunities for participants to examine comparative outcomes and to catalyze and inform continuous improvement at member sites. Within the safe collaborative environment of a NIC, two related processes become activated. First, comparing one's results to those of others can create a sense of moral urgency—if others can accomplish this, we can and should be able to do better too. This positive response stands in sharp contrast to the defensiveness that comparative data tend to generate in high-stakes accountability contexts. In the latter cases, the knee-jerk reaction is to discount the data, question their credibility, and explain away differences as others having better students or more support or better conditions, and so on. Second, when trusted colleagues are getting better outcomes in the same improvement system, participants are now more inclined to ask, "What exactly did you do to get those results?" Consequently, an explicit learning-to-improve opportunity is now created. So in these two ways participation in a NIC can enhance Level-B learning.

The account by Atul Gawande about the improvement efforts in the cystic fibrosis network, mentioned in chapter 2, offers a good example. Before the network was formed, no comparative information was available on health outcomes for cystic fibrosis patients across the major treatment centers in the United States. Each center believed that it was providing exemplary care until it actually saw data on what others were accomplishing. Clearly better performance could be achieved—and there was a member of their learning community who knew something about how to do it. So a new spirit is energized: "Let's go learn from them."

Supporting Translational Research

The applied researchers who participate in the NIC add still another distinctive resource for accelerating learning to improve. Their contributions occur in multiple ways. Researchers bring relevant academic knowledge to bear during the causal system analysis, helping to illumine the actual problems to be solved. Their discipline-based understandings are also invaluable in discussions aimed at developing a working theory of improvement. They may offer some very specific change ideas to be tested by the NIC. As especially vexing concerns arise, the academic researchers in the NIC also become conduits for possible translational research. They can assist a NIC in identifying promising findings in their respective disciplines and contributing to the design and development of workable interventions anchored around these ideas.

A good example was the rapid development of a growth mindset intervention under the productive persistence driver in the CCP networks.[9] The NIC structure made this possible. Common Institutional Review Board protocols and data-sharing agreements had been secured, and a common database existed. Trusting relationships among faculty, hub staff, and academic researchers had been nurtured. Resources were already available to invest quickly in this promising idea. So what might normally have taken two or more years under regular circumstances (e.g., recruiting participants, writing proposals and securing funding, developing IRB agreements, accessing extant data from different institutions, and converting it into a usable database), the NIC accomplished in five months. It began in March with a promising experimental intervention that needed to be translated into a practical experience for developmental math students in community colleges. Next, a very small test of change occurred in one classroom; then a larger test of change took place in a community college. This tailored version of a growth mindset intervention was introduced to the full network at the annual summer forum, and NIC-wide implementation began in August.[10] This is the NIC structure at work, accelerating learning to improve.[11]

STRUCTURING NIC PARTICIPATION

NICs afford extraordinary possibilities to advance improvement. Doing so, however, is not easy. As we elaborate next, a NIC makes demands on its participants to make a commitment to pursue specific measurable aims, set targets to guide continuous improvement, develop a common language, and adopt common measures of success. And it challenges participants to think differently about how they should do their work and relate to one another.

Aim Statements to Motivate and Direct Action

The commitment of participants to a specific, measurable aim is a distinguishing feature of NICs. In comparison, learning communities, communities of practice, and some forms of researcher–practitioner partnerships often describe their efforts as "learning together." Typically, these communities are convened around some common interest coupled with social affinity. Participants may engage in compelling discussions about a common problem and share reflections about things they have tried. However, they do not commit to achieving a specific improvement nor measure progress toward it.

As noted in chapter 3, an improvement aim articulates the specific problem to be solved and the measures of accomplishment to which the community will hold itself accountable. It imbues the community with its purpose. A good aim statement expresses lofty goals and specifies operational targets. It calls participants to action and offers explicit guidance as to what is to be accomplished by when and for whom. Consequently, aim statements can be framed in two different but closely related ways. Which of the two is most important to attend to depends on the context of use.[12]

Framed as a declaration of lofty purpose, a NIC aim statement should inspire individuals to see themselves as part of a larger narrative—as members of a community engaged in a highly valued pursuit. For this purpose, statements framed in language of "the lives we will touch" can be especially powerful. The Five Million Lives Campaign executed by IHI exemplifies this spirit.[13] The audacious aim of saving five million lives from needless harm in America's hospitals secured the active engagement of hundreds of health-care institutions across the United States. Well conceived and expressed, such a statement of aims captures the imagination, builds will, and encourages voluntary effort.

Following this lead, the CCP NIC set a significant goal in the summer of 2013 when participants at the National Community College Pathways Forum ratified an aim: "To reclaim 10,000 students' mathematical lives." These are students whose educational opportunities are blocked because they are unable to obtain the necessary college math credits to transfer to four-year institutions or qualify for select occupational training certificates. The CCP aim, framed in this fashion, engenders a sense of commitment among participants to a larger cause that no individual or single institution can advance alone. It creates both a reason and a need for collective action. Interestingly, the progress already made toward this goal by Pathways colleges is now inspiring a much more ambitious goal—to reclaim one hundred thousand students' mathematical lives.

Framed in a second fashion as a technical specification, a good aim statement details a precisely defined, measurable outcome and the statistics that will be used to chart progress. The initial aim specified for the CCP NIC was of this form: to increase from 5 percent to 50 percent the proportion of developmental math students successfully achieving college math credit within one year by enrolling in a Pathways course of study. This aim represented a tenfold increase over what is normally achieved.[14] An aim statement defined with this level of technical detail allows a NIC to identify a baseline comparison both overall and within each college so program impact can be charted over time college by college and classroom by classroom.[15]

We emphasize that these two different framings must meld smoothly together. They must align so that any declaration about "the number of student lives to be touched" is directly connected to the version being used to evaluate annual performance and inform NIC efforts to identify finer-grained improvement targets. Working in tandem, these two versions of an aim statement combine to motivate participation and direct specific improvement actions.

Targets to Guide Continuous Improvement

Digging a bit deeper into the actual operational dynamics of a NIC leads to the closely related topic of target setting. Targets are best understood in contrast to the aims that they serve. Whereas aims are intended to focus overall NIC efforts, targets are much more tailored. Targets may be specific to an institution or to particular subpopulations of students across the NIC. While aims are intended to sustain NICs over extended periods of time, targets guide the immediate work ahead. Key to this target setting is the availability of good comparative evidence.

For example, at the first institute to launch the CCP NIC, teams from each of the member colleges met to establish college-specific targets. They did so with relevant data from their own institution and comparative results networkwide. Each college followed a common inquiry protocol:

1. What has been the level of performance for developmental math students at our college historically? (*What's going on here?*)
2. What has been typical performance across member colleges more generally? (*What's going on in other similar places?*)
3. What does exemplary performance look like among NIC colleges currently? (*What has already been possible to achieve pre-innovation?*)
4. What is the aim for the NIC? (*Where are we trying collectively to get to?*)
5. What conditions unique to our college are likely to affect our performance?
6. What would be an appropriate reach target (challenging to stretch for but also potentially attainable) for the year ahead for us?

The first three questions provided an empirical basis for discerning what might actually be attainable by looking at data NIC-wide. Questions four through six challenged college teams to improve. Key here is that the process of establishing targets was both voluntary and transparent across the

NIC. In the latter regard, each college shared its deliberations with the others, and this prompted some to reach for more ambitious goals. At the same time, each college voluntarily adopted its own targets (as opposed to having them imposed from outside), which created motivational power. The governing spirit was now, "We set the targets; now let's go achieve them."

A similar process focusing on disparities in student success rates played out when first-year NIC results were shared at the second-year summer institute. While members celebrated achieving a 50 percent success rate networkwide, they also recognized that such success was not the case for all subgroups of students. In particular, students who scored low on a first-day assessment of basic mathematics conceptual knowledge (e.g., questions about number sense; the interconnections of fractions, decimals, and proportions; and algebraic thinking) were much less likely to succeed. Accordingly, an immediate NIC-wide priority was identified and a specific improvement target set: what will it take to move the success rate of these initially low-scoring students to at least 50 percent as well?

Stepping back a bit, while the role of aim statements in structuring network activity is quite general, the role of targets is more situation-specific. Learning to improve follows an evolutionary logic. Long-term goals can be articulated, and immediate next steps are often relatively clear; but the actual journey to the ultimate aims is created as we go. In this regard, target-setting processes structure conversations about the most productive next steps, both local and networkwide.

Common Language and Measures to Enable Social Learning

Educators often refer to the same phenomena by different names or, conversely, use the same names to refer to very different concepts or practices.[16] This gives rise to a version of the Tower of Babel problem. Many people work very hard attempting to accomplish some shared end, but absent a common language to organize the complex activities in which they are engaged, only frustration and failure ensue.

A common language, as represented in aim statements, driver diagrams, and system improvement maps, is essential for coordinating improvement in complex systems. By analogy, it would be impossible to orchestrate the construction of a skyscraper without architectural plans expressed in clear, precise, and unambiguous terms. To be sure, tweaks (and sometimes larger changes) are introduced on the job site as learning occurs through the act of building. But absent a shared understanding about the core elements of the plans, the construction would not be possible.

At base here is a straightforward idea. Teams working on complex problems need tools to organize their efforts.[17] The most basic of these tools is a common language for detailing the problem they are working on and how they will attempt to improve. This is why the framing of a driver diagram is especially important because, as a shared working theory of improvement, it can guide activity networkwide. Tests of change being carried out independently across diverse sites can now accumulate into a knowledge base. Likewise, the ability of others to access and use this knowledge depends on this shared framework and the clarity and consistency of the terms in which it is expressed. Put simply, this common language makes learning from each other possible.

Building on the common language framework is the adoption of common measures. We have argued that "we cannot improve at scale what we cannot measure," and we have detailed the forms of measurement necessary to support improvement work. Without common measures, the network cannot realize the benefits of Level-C learning because there would be no agreed-upon operational definitions as to what successful outcomes and improvements in primary drivers actually look like. Most important, these data, coupled with a shared working theory of improvement, provide the basis for conversations across the NIC about the causes and effects operating inside the problem the NIC is trying to solve. Such empirically grounded conversations strengthen the likelihood that a NIC's efforts will actually culminate in valued outcomes.

CHANGING ROLES AND RELATIONSHIPS AMONG PRACTITIONERS AND RESEARCHERS

NICs make demands on diverse forms of expertise. In most general terms, this expertise spans theoretical knowledge and empirical findings contributed by academic scholars, the know-how and professional judgments of practitioners, and a wide array of specialized skills, including materials and process design, improvement methods, large-data analytics, and online collaborative learning systems. A NIC values these forms of expertise, and to be effective, it must orchestrate well among them.

For practitioners, joining a NIC and embracing its improvement mission represent a commitment to a significant change in how they think about and carry out their work. In the CCP NIC, for example, all participating faculty members agree to use common materials and pedagogic practices. They also agree to collect and share the set of practical measures established by the NIC. We refer to these common materials, work practices, and measures as the *network's kernel resources*. Only those elements warranted by theory and empirical evidence and deemed essential to advancing the NIC's aim achieve kernel status. Other programmatic elements may be added or adapted locally in response to local needs.[18]

It is important to recognize that a delicate balance operates here. As previously discussed, local adaptations are often necessary for an intervention to be successfully implemented. Moreover, part of the power of large networks is what can be learned as individuals attempt to innovate in response to a perceived local need. Inevitably, some changes introduced locally will turn out to be genuine improvements of wider-scale significance. In a large network, these enhancements will almost surely occur with some regularity. Counterbalancing these opportunities for field-generated improvements, however, is a long history in education where local adaptations to promising interventions can easily turn into maladaptations. These failures will happen too; the key difference now is that a NIC is structured to learn from this too.

The disciplined inquiry embedded in the improvement model is key to negotiating this space successfully. As practitioners introduce a change to the kernel, they bear a professional responsibility to their network colleagues to address the three improvement questions: What is the problem we are trying to solve (i.e., why is some adaptation thought to be needed)? What change will be introduced and why (i.e., how is the proposed change consistent with the core concepts and design principles undergirding the network's working theory of improvement)? And what evidence will be considered to examine whether the change is actually an improvement? In essence, the call to innovate is accompanied by an obligation to document what was done, why it was done, and what was learned. Absent this documentation, the network cannot learn from other individuals' actions, and the commitment to collective problem solving is greatly weakened.

Participation in a NIC also has significant implications for academic researchers. In traditional research settings, academics largely control the action. Practitioners may serve as study advisors and occasionally contribute in modest ways to an intervention's design and development. More often than not, though, they are the subjects of field trials and program evaluations designed by others. A NIC creates a very different research-practice connection. Rather than simply looking for a receptive place to gather data and test their theories, researchers join a NIC so they can contribute their knowledge to making headway on a pressing practical concern. They work with practitioners in a negotiated space enlivened by a simple imperative: "How can we help each other best solve this problem?"[19] Within a NIC, research and practice truly fuse.

Organized by these norms of participation, a NIC activates multiple sources of innovation. Practitioners can be front-line innovators, developing ideas for small-scale testing in their own classrooms or institutions. They may also test change ideas from network colleagues. Academic researchers may originate initiatives in translational research and work with practitioners to design and develop them. Practitioners and researchers may also band into subnetworks to engage in iterative improvement cycles on high-priority needs. Any one or more of these organizational arrangements, and perhaps others not yet envisioned, may be most advantageous, depending on the problem and context. In this regard, the "who, what, and how" of learning fast to improve fast is a highly pragmatic enterprise. Regardless of the specific choices made, the work remains disciplined by theory and evidence and an overriding question, "How will this move us toward achieving our aims?"

ENABLING COLLECTIVE EFFORT: A NETWORK HUB

A NIC requires a set of supporting capacities, both to get started and to keep going. In principle, a variety of different structures can provide this support. Depending on their expertise and institutional resources, NIC members might share these functions. In other cases, a single organization might serve as a *network hub,* as the Carnegie Foundation has for the BTEN and CCP networks. Regardless of the structure chosen, the functions that must be supported remain largely the same. We describe each briefly next.

Improvement Science Capabilities

The methodology of improvement science is well understood and practiced in other fields, but few educational professionals are trained in these methods, and few have had opportunities to build their expertise through practice over time. Consequently, a NIC hub must assemble such expertise, serving as both trainer and coach. The hub at the Carnegie Foundation, for example, has made significant investments to support NICs through basic workshops, initiatives to train improvement coaches, residential fellowships, and the like. A gradually expanding group of individuals at the foundation, along with external consultants, now provides coaching in response to specific challenges that arise as NIC members undertake improvement projects.

Analytics

Because variation in performance is the core quality improvement problem to solve, analyzing such variation is a core hub function. The analytic team within the CCP hub helps to (1) pinpoint improvement priorities by regularly feeding back evidence about networkwide and college-specific outcomes; (2) examine variability in outcomes, contributing answers to the question, "What is working, for whom, and under what conditions?" (3) identify places where something may be working especially well and that may inspire others to adopt and test it further; and (4) provide a warrant that changes developed by the NIC are improvements deserving inclusion in the kernel and spread to other contexts. While serving these networkwide purposes (Level-C learning), the hub analytics team also seeks to enhance the capacities of member institutions to realize Level-B learning in their own sites.

Knowledge Management

We have discussed ways in which NICs can speed up the production of the practical knowledge needed to improve our educational institutions. We have also introduced strategies to improve how knowledge is built up and made accessible to others. These are twin engines for accelerating learning to improve. This directs us toward another key role that a hub plays. By formalizing the identification, capture, and organization of practical knowledge, a hub can accelerate the spread and use of the products of past improvement research. This enables the replication of successful processes and continued learning about them as others take them up. Simultaneously, an active knowledge management system also works to assure that new efforts at problem solving are informed by the best academic research in the field. It is an ongoing responsibility of the hub to work with NIC members to identify relevant research findings and make them easily accessible.[20]

Convenings, Communications, and Technological Support

As noted previously, an improvement network seeks to advance change ideas for which an empirical warrant has been established. A number of different mechanisms can be deployed for doing so. Face-to-face communication, especially when a NIC is being created and when new members are introduced, is essential. The CCP NIC, for example, arranges campus visits and holds an annual national forum and periodic regional meetings. Phone calls and emails augment face-to-face social ties and sustain them over time. It is a hub responsibility to facilitate these collaborative work processes and support the technologies needed to sustain them.

Lastly, we note that effective networks don't just happen automatically. They are the result of conscious effort to engage membership, focus collective effort, make it possible (even easy) to participate in the work, recognize and validate the contributions of members, and see to it that all share in the benefits of participation (emotional as well as intellectual). These servant leadership responsibilities also typically fall to members of the network hub. Consequently, the hub is part communications specialist, part traffic cop, part troubleshooter, and part evangelist. Although perhaps less visible than other hub functions mentioned previously, tending to the needs of the community is foundational for everything else.

STARTING AN IMPROVEMENT COMMUNITY

Increasingly, we are now asked, "How does one actually build a networked improvement community?" In responding to this question, we have come to recognize that network initiation is a distinct activity phase with its own unique demands.[21] Acknowledging that our practical experience continues to evolve rapidly in this domain, we share what we think we now know.

A Network Initiation Team

NICs require a core team to form the organization.[22] This *network initiation team* articulates the problem to be solved, analyzes the system that produces current undesirable outcomes, and develops the aim statement and an initial working theory of practice improvement. The initiation team also takes the lead in securing the necessary supports for the network (both political as well as material), recruiting initial members into the community, and engaging the academic and technical expertise relevant to the specific problem. These tasks demand a rich mix of skills: analytical thinking about the problem to be solved; systems thinking about the contexts in which solutions must be pursued; skills to facilitate conversations among diverse groups; and a good-sized dose of evangelizing leadership for showing why work on the problem is so important and why working on it in this way is the most promising approach.

The Carnegie Foundation assembled such teams in starting both the BTEN and CCP networks. While the composition of each team was problem- and context-specific, both teams engaged a diverse range of participants, from expert practitioners to select academic researchers to professional and policy leaders in the problem domain. We note that the composition of this team may evolve over time as the network moves from initial exploration and design into full operations. In the case of both the BTEN and CCP NICs, significant changes occurred in moving from the largely conceptual and strategic leadership required to form a NIC into the hub capabilities necessary to support its ongoing activities. While some of the initial leaders have continued throughout, others who played key roles during NIC initiation have moved on.[23]

Securing Membership

Having had opportunities to work with several outside organizations interested in forming NICs, we have identified a critical opening juncture—a classic chicken-or-egg question: Do we convene a small team to orchestrate the up-front work of refining the problem and framing a prototypical driver diagram and measures? Or do we first assemble the interested partners and have them identify a problem to pursue together? This strikes us as an important tactical decision. The second option appears more common, but we think there also are some good reasons to consider the first.

The strength of the "assemble-the-partners-first" strategy is that it brings a diverse group of potential improvement sites immediately to the table. Involving people from the outset, the thinking goes, enhances their commitment to the future effort. Further, identifying committed participants is often seen as essential for securing external funding.

The difficulty with this strategy is that a variant of solutionitis (chapter 1) can easily emerge. Participants tend to enter discussions with predefined solution ideas; they begin by saying something along the lines of "I'm really interested in trying . . ." or, in the case of academic researchers, "I am really interested in studying. . . ." While each individual perspective offers potential insights about the problem to be solved, each typically reflects only a partial understanding of the system that creates the problem. We note that this phenomenon plays out for both the researchers and practitioners. Researchers are accustomed to looking at problems of practice through a distinct theoretical lens that can deeply illumine some aspect of the problem to be solved, but they can remain blind to other important and related factors. Likewise, practitioners may gravitate toward a new idea, perhaps one touted recently in a professional publication, as "the solution." This instinct, too, reflects the same narrowness of insight.

Developing a good working theory of practice improvement can be very challenging in these situations. Recall from chapter 3 that the goal is to identify a small number of high-leverage drivers, and within each, the most promising changes that might be attempted.[24] This goal requires improvers to make critical choices that are disciplined both by extant research and professional expertise. Keeping all participants at the table, typically a concern under this scenario, amplifies the challenge in bringing forth a coherent and parsimonious improvement theory. The latter can take considerable time to achieve and may not ever really emerge.

The alternative scenario is that the initiation team develops the *charter* for the NIC, which includes the causal system analysis, aim statement, and initial working theory of improvement and related measures. Under this scenario, extensive work is carried out before participants formally join the network. This was the strategy the Carnegie Foundation used in launching the CCP initiative.

The advantage of this strategy is that NIC membership is informed participation. As community colleges joined the NIC, for example, members endorsed common measureable outcomes and a working theory for how to pursue them. Participating faculty agreed to common learning goals, instructional frameworks, pedagogical practices, student assessments, and a base set of common lessons. Applied researchers agreed to bring their analytical skills and relevant theoretical knowledge to bear in supporting faculty to achieve network aims.

The challenge with this arrangement is that it takes a significant commitment of resources up front to generate the initial charter and recruit members. And, there is no guarantee at the front end that "if we build it, they will come." So funders must be willing to accept a higher opening risk for any NIC developing along these lines.

A Distinctive Leadership Demand

A NIC is quite different from the traditional applied research center and many forms of research–practitioner partnerships. Typically, these other organizations consist of a collection of individual projects that are broadly related to one another through some fairly general conceptual rationale. They do not require the problem-solving discipline and theory of practice improvement that are central to a NIC. More to the point, the internal accountability logic is quite different. The critical test in these more traditional forms of collaboration is about whether "*my* project worked" rather than whether "*we* effected measureable improvements reliably across diverse contexts."

Regardless of how a NIC starts, its leaders must facilitate the complex process of forming a charter. Diverse views need to be sought out about the primary causes of the problem to be solved and the details of each. The initiating team for the CCP NIC, for example, convened several small meetings over the course of a year toward this end. The meetings involved community college faculty, institutional researchers, scholars knowledgeable about the problem area, leaders of professional organizations, and college presidents.[25] Facilitating these meetings demands challenging in-the-moment analysis. It requires the facilitator to honor the participants' many contributions while synthesizing them into a coherent framework (and on occasion respectfully discounting some individual comments as being without analytic or empirical merit).[26] To carry out this role well, the facilitator must hold broad academic knowledge relevant to the specific problem to be solved, have a good working understanding of the structure and functioning of organizations, and be sensitive to how local context considerations may come into play.

Critical judgment is especially important in the framing of the driver diagram. A good driver diagram is deeply rooted in the diverse concerns unearthed in the causal systems analysis. It must meld both clinical and research knowledge, including findings from relevant case studies, descriptive reports, and evaluations of promising interventions. It is a challenging task, in which good ideas must engage the practical, the logistical, and the political.

The Guiding Spirit: "Possibly Wrong and Definitely Incomplete"

Even with the extensive activity required to organize a NIC, it is important to recognize that the resultant working theory of improvement remains provisional. Network participants engage with it in the spirit of "possibly wrong and definitely incomplete." The working theory is constantly being tested against evidence generated in the crucible of improvement efforts. Errors and oversights are likely to surface. A driver may turn out to be less powerful than originally thought, and a new driver may emerge. For all these reasons, the working theory needs to be updated periodically. Meanwhile, it guides the work.

In this regard, the dynamic of learning to improve is more like the messiness of innovation development than the ideal of strategic planning. As we have noted, learning from failure is at the heart of improvement. A distinct set of intellectual dispositions sustains the activity. Participants must be able to tolerate ambiguity, to work with plausible competing conceptions that seemingly push in opposite directions, and to live with the uncertainty as to exactly how everything will come together. They must trust that the principles and processes of improvement will eventually guide them to a productive end.[27] NIC leaders need to remain open to recognize new issues as they emerge. An initially productive change in one primary driver may necessitate subsequent and different actions in other drivers for large-scale improvements to be realized and sustained. This dynamism is a natural consequence of the systems character of the educational phenomena we seek to improve.

FORMING MOTIVATION, IDENTITY, AND COMMITMENT

The tools and processes described throughout this book are largely technical and rational ones. But there is also a very human side to improvement work, one that is especially salient within NICs.

A NIC asks for a substantial voluntary commitment from its members. While participants sometimes receive modest remuneration if external resources are available, their primary incentives lie elsewhere. To attract and maintain the personal investments of its members, a NIC must nurture a culture that values both individual and collective improvement. For many individuals, engagement entails a significant change in professional identity. It is worth spending some time examining the confluence of factors that enable such transformation to occur.

A Case in Point: The National Writing Project

Although not formally a NIC, the National Writing Project (NWP) has much to teach us about the human side of networks.[28] Beginning in 1974, the NWP has grown to be one of the largest networks in the United States focused on the professional development of teachers. With nearly two hundred member sites serving all fifty states, it is composed of over seventy thousand members who care about the teaching of writing and the use of writing in students' learning. Building on a base of local resources, federal funds supported NWP for nineteen years. In 2011 federal funding came to a precipitous end—$25 million in network support one year, $0 the next. Given the rapid defunding, the program's demise seemed inevitable. But this did not happen. Of the 206 local sites in the network in 2011, 191 sites remain—a testament to extraordinary voluntary effort.[29]

When NWP funding was threatened, NWP members actively voiced their sentiments. They were teachers of writing, and they were writers, so they wrote. One teacher started a blog, and within forty-eight hours it had nearly five hundred lengthy postings. Thousands more followed. Embedded in these commentaries are rich insights about how a network secures and maintains member commitment.[30]

Extensive research on NWP has helped to illumine this social dynamic of participation.[31] Elyse Eidman-Aadahl, NWP's executive director, notes that teachers first come to the network for largely personal reasons. They want to be better teachers; they want to serve their students better. The NWP seeks to be responsive to these individual motives while also transforming them over time into collective responsibilities. Eidman-Aadahl says, "What you have to do early on is encourage new members to see themselves as part of the group. They have to recognize a larger narrative and be able to see themselves as having a place in that narrative. They have to be able to write themselves into the collective narrative."[32]

Since its inception, the NWP has been deliberate and skillful in craft-ing this narrative. The organization also has taken great care in how it welcomes new members. Four aspects stand out as central to the profes-sional identities that these new members come to embrace. First and fore-most is a widely shared belief that writing matters. Members affirm the importance that writing plays in representing and conveying knowledge and in helping to comprehend and improve the human condition. Echo-ing a widely held belief in NWP, Karen LaBonte, a longstanding NWP member, has written, "Writing is essential to communication, learning, and citizenship. It is the currency of the new workplace and global econ-omy. Writing helps us solve problems, convey ideas, and understand our changing world."[33]

The second key element in the NWP narrative is that all members are writers. To be a good teacher of writing, one must be a writer first of all. Jeremy Hyler, an NWP member, sums up the power of this idea. "I have always wanted to write, but when I finished with the Chippewa River Writing Project I found my voice, my confidence, and my niche in writ-ing. I now had the tools to create more powerful writing, and I learned to take those tools and enhance my students' learning of writing as well. The NWP propelled me to leadership and to a level of confidence I did not know existed in me as a writer."[34]

Third is the responsibility of members to improve their own perfor-mance as teachers. The calling to teach compels all to learn to do it well. As Kay McGriff says, "As a new teacher I struggled to find ways to connect my students to the power of words through reading and writing . . . [the NWP] transformed me as a teacher . . . I built connections to teachers as passionate about teaching and learning as I was. I now support others in their efforts, even as I continue to strive to improve my own teaching year after year."[35]

And fourth, NWP teachers are responsible not just for their own per-formance but for the advancement of their profession. The NWP's catch-phrase, "teachers teaching teachers," signals that NWP participants take on roles as providers of support and development to their colleagues and their school districts.

These four elements are demonstrated over and over at local sites and in larger regional and national meetings. The best example of this is the Invitational Summer Institute that each site sponsors every year. Participation in an institute is the core experience that binds all members of NWP together, no matter where in our fifty states they may do this. While each institute's program is locally defined, all share common elements. All participants read and discuss sets of writings, written for various purposes and audiences, in order to amplify their mission—that writing matters. It is also expected that all participants will share their own writing and respond to that of others. This activity reinforces a norm that to be a teacher of writing, one must write. During the course of local institutes, teachers also review new research on the teaching of writing as they continue to deepen their professional knowledge base. Lastly, to enculturate a sense of responsibility for improving both one's performance and that of the larger profession, participants offer demonstration lessons and engage with colleagues in the critique of each other's performance.

In short, common activities and a distinctive narrative reinforce one another. By engaging in NWP practices, one adopts an NWP way of professional living. What starts out as a personal motivation to improve is transformed through practice into a shared accountability for a much larger enterprise. Collective improvement becomes everyone's responsibility.

How This Plays Out in a Networked Improvement Community

The CCP NIC has sought to follow this same playbook by creating a structure in which participants engage in disciplined inquiry that supports both individual and collective improvement. All the while, the network reinforces a message about why improvement research is central to being a professional educator.

Individuals may join a NIC for many different reasons, such as personal improvement, professional recognition, the enjoyment of spending time with engaging colleagues and stimulating researchers. But membership in a NIC means accepting responsibility for something larger. The narrative of a NIC is that all participants are now improvement researchers.

Each is a generator of knowledge—knowledge that leads to solutions for shared problems and progress toward shared aims. In the CCP networks, small groups of faculty have engaged in a research protocol to create and improve particular lessons. A number of faculty are testing an online platform for student homework and assessments and advising the provider on how to improve the service. Still another group is piloting a network role in which accomplished faculty members mentor faculty members new to the Pathways community. Still others, as mentioned previously, are using PDSA cycles to improve attendance, homework completion, and student participation in class. Some of their network colleagues will begin testing the most promising of these ideas and reporting on outcomes in their classrooms. A subnetwork has begun to dig into the myriad organizational issues that must be resolved for Pathways enrollment to expand. And a few faculty are collaborating with educational researchers, cognitive scientists, and social psychologists to translate knowledge in their disciplines into practices that might help students.

Historically in education, there have been those who are seen as enacting the system (front-line educators) and those who are seen as defining and transforming it (system leaders, policy makers). There has been an equally sharp distinction between those who produce knowledge (researchers) and those who use it (practitioners). The vision of education R&D elaborated here blurs these boundaries and merges these roles. Everyone in a NIC is responsible for improving the system and producing and using the knowledge that can do so. All are improvers now. Hence, what may have begun as a seemingly marginal activity in an individual's life—another new project or teaching assignment—can transform his or her professional identity in a profound way.

Central to all of this is an essential normative understanding: NICs are *scientific communities*. Like scientific communities generally, work within a NIC is organized around a shared theory and shared measures for its central concepts. In the case of a NIC, it is a theory of practice improvement. The central concepts are the key drivers that comprise this theory and practical measures are associated with each. Again as is true of scientific communities, participants engage in discipline inquiries using established methods such as those illustrated in chapter 5. Likewise, this scientific practice has a public character within a NIC. Explicit predictions about improvement are offered; a rationale for each presented; and data are shared to warrant claims that some proposed change is indeed an improvement. Moreover, initially promising hypotheses are further tested, seeking to replicate findings and understand better the conditions under which positive outcomes are most likely to occur. Lastly, the network functions as its own social proof network, adjudicating claims as to what practice-based knowledge is worth entering the kernel. These are the forming elements of a scientific community. Hence, our claim that NICs are scientific communities, each organized to solve some specific high-leverage problem in educational practice.

A COMMUNAL IMPERATIVE TO IMPROVE

In closing, we return to an observation offered many pages ago. Silos of practice and silos of research characterize reform efforts in education. Currently, we fail to tap the extraordinary capacities embedded in large networks to innovate and improve. Imagine if we were better able to leverage the enormity of the education enterprise and the creativity and commitments of its professionals—constantly experimenting, trying something new, aiming to do better by our students. Networks organized around common conceptual frameworks, informed by common measures, and embracing the rudiments of disciplined inquiry open extraordinary possibilities for accelerating our learning to improve. The possibilities here dwarf even the most optimistic outcomes that we could imagine from our current research efforts.

Think of a future in which practical knowledge is growing in a disciplined fashion every day, in thousands of settings, as hundreds of thousands of educators and educational leaders continuously learn to improve. Rather than a small collection of disconnected research centers, we could have an immense networked learning community. To be sure, formal university-based scholarship remains the preeminent supplier of elemental ideas and technologies on which practical improvements can build. But we need to expand our vision—a more inclusive vision, but no less disciplined by scholarship and evidence. The call is urgent because our aim is so much grander than a published clinical trial or a peer-refereed academic paper. Our aim is nothing less than making progress against ignorance and the futures without hope that ignorance creates.[36]

7

Living Improvement

We can, whenever and wherever we choose, successfully teach all children whose schooling is of interest to us; we already know more than we need to do that.

—RON EDMONDS[1]

OUR AMBITION IN THIS volume has been to show readers how the rigorous application of the techniques of quality improvement, carried out through networked communities, can enhance how we educate students. We have sought to provide some useful tools and methods for those who have already started on this course, to offer examples that might encourage other educators to take up similar pursuits, and to provide grist for enlarging the conversation about a better way toward advancing a cherished national goal: a quality education for all.

As Ron Edmonds's quote suggests, the field knows a great deal more about what matters for educating children than teachers and administrators are able to effectively use day in and day out in our classrooms, schools, and districts. Edmonds highlights a phenomenon at the core of this book. To *know that* something is important is not the same thing as knowing how to make it happen regularly and well. Achieving reliability of this sort, we have argued, requires improving how systems operate.

Building greater *know-how* toward this end is the essential problem our field now needs to solve. And we believe it is within our reach to do so—to enliven the aspirations that Ron Edmonds set out over three decades ago.

Yet even as we embrace the promise of quality improvement, we remain realists. We know that improvement science is not without challenges. So we bring this volume to a close with a set of reflections based on our own direct experiences as well as what we have learned through the work of others. We highlight both the reasons for optimism as well as some of the formidable obstacles that still lie ahead. To set the context, we concisely recount the six improvement principles.

THE SIX IMPROVEMENT PRINCIPLES

1. *Make the work problem-specific and user-centered.* Quality improvement starts with a single question: "What specifically is the problem we are trying to solve?" It enlivens a codevelopment orientation. Engage key participants as problem definers and problem solvers from the earliest phases of development through large-scale implementation.

2. *Focus on variation in performance.* A networked improvement community aims to advance efficacy reliably at scale. Identifying and addressing the sources of variability in outcomes is essential. Rather than documenting simply "what works," as in estimating an on-average effect, aim to learn "what works, for whom, and under what set of conditions." Develop the know-how to make innovations succeed for different students across varied educational contexts.

3. *See the system that produces the current outcomes.* It is hard to improve a system if you do not fully understand how it currently operates to produce its results. Seek to understand better how local conditions shape work processes and resulting outcomes. Use this analysis to explicate a working theory of improvement that can be tested against evidence and further developed from what is learned as you go.

4. *We cannot improve at scale what we cannot measure.* Measure outcomes, key drivers, and change ideas so you can continuously test the working theory and learn whether specific changes actually represent an improvement. Constantly ask: "Are the intended changes actually occurring? Do they link to changes in related drivers and to desired system outcomes?" Anticipate and measure for unintended consequences too.

5. *Use disciplined inquiry to drive improvement.* Common inquiry protocols and evidentiary standards guide the diverse efforts of NICs. Engage in systematic tests of change to learn fast, fail fast, and improve fast. Remember that failure is not a problem; not learning from failure is. Accumulate the practical knowledge that grows out of failure, and build on it systematically over time.

6. *Accelerate learning through networked communities.* NICs aim to break down silos of practice and research. They enliven a belief that we can accomplish more together than even the best of us can accomplish alone. A shared working theory, common measures, and communication mechanisms anchor collective problem solving. Organize as a NIC to innovate, test, and spread effective practices sooner and faster.

A visitor to the Carnegie Foundation for the Advancement of Teaching will find these principles prominently displayed. They are deliberately posted together on one wall to reinforce the point that they operate as a system. While each element is important in its own right, attending to only one or two will not accomplish sustainable improvements in the complex enterprise that is education today. All six principles must be engaged to bring about improvement that is deep, widespread, and enduring.

As we work with groups interested in starting NICs, we have found that some of them find certain principles palatable but others harder to embrace. Teachers, for example, warm easily to the idea of being user-centered. But they may resist the directive to systematically test change ideas against process-level data. Data, after all, have historically been the purview of researchers and policy makers; the idea of educators using data to improve their work remains relatively new.[2] Likewise, practitioners may be partial to the power of collaborative networks, seeing them as the familiar communities of practice. They may not, however, immediately embrace the analytic and empirical rigor that characterizes NICs as scientific communities.

Accountability advocates will find a home in the principle that we cannot improve at scale what we cannot measure, but they may resist the idea of seeing the system. Policy makers prefer simple solutions, and the need to understand the seemingly mysterious behavior of complex systems runs deeply counter to that mentality. Similarly, serious empirical researchers will welcome the commitment to disciplined inquiry but may be troubled by the absence of a requirement for randomized control trials. The argument that the replicability of quality outcomes reliably at scale (rather than causal attribution) is the ultimate gold standard may feel disconcerting.

No matter who comprises the group, working in a structured improvement network challenges deeply established norms about individual and local autonomy. The latter pervades American education, from assertions about the needs of individual teachers, to claims about the uniqueness of each school and district, to the silos in professional training and research that characterize much of the education academy. But if we truly believe that we can accomplish more together than alone, we must embrace new forms of work, even if doing so represents a radical challenge to educators' identities.

EASY TO SAY BUT HARDER TO DO

Quality improvement, on its face, seems a simple notion. Yet putting improvement ideas into action can be challenging—something we now know from our own work and the experiences of others who have tried to launch NICs. Becoming an improver, and working in networks, calls us to very different methods, structures, and norms. Here we highlight a few places in which network initiation teams are likely to struggle.

Starting Well

Perhaps nothing is more fundamental than how the work of quality improvement begins. A key message throughout this volume is that quality improvement demands a clear and explicit problem to be solved. This problem needs to be deeply felt among participants, be concrete and actionable. One of our illustrative cases—the high failure rate among community college students in developmental mathematics—is an example of such a problem. When concerns like this one arise, various sources typically weigh in with a cacophony of ideas. Educational researchers may propose a solution anchored in a favorite theory about learning or socialization; microeconomists might suggest giving students monetary incentives; a policy analyst may argue to pay colleges to improve; designers might suggest prototyping an online tool or innovative classroom practice and so on. There is a deeply seductive quality to all of this. We all want to make a difference, and each new idea may seem compelling. However, absent a clear understanding of the nature and the causes of the specific problem to be solved, it is not always clear that each of these ideas addresses an actual, rather than an assumed, high-leverage problem. Moreover, even if all of this autonomous activity were properly aimed, no one is responsible for how all of it is supposed to combine together into productive large-scale change. Doing so is like trying to build a complex structure without an overall architecture, or even an explicit understanding of the essential elements needed to form such a design. This is another variant of solutionitis at work.

The discipline of improvement science directs us differently. To move forward, we must step back; we must try to understand how the system actually works to produce the problematic outcomes we currently see. Such critical analysis can provoke the kinds of difficult conversations that people tend to avoid. The desire to jump ahead to discuss new ideas and possible solutions is understandable. In fact, we have seen a number of groups' first attempts at articulating a problem statement phrased as the absence of some favored solution! These solution-centered conversations provide at best only a partial view of the system in operation, leaving critical features of the system unexamined.

The improvement science methods introduced in chapter 3 offer explicit processes and tools, such as fishbone diagrams and system improvement maps, to guide these analyses. They help improvement teams detail the problem, identify important interactions occurring within organizations, and clarify where to start work and why. They often direct attention to overlooked issues that function as critical contexts in designing for better outcomes. In short, they direct us toward gaining the actual know-how we need to be able to improve.

Next in the improvement process comes the seemingly simple problem of crafting a good aim statement. Over the last several years, we have had the opportunity to work with groups seeking to bring improvement thinking to a broad set of issues, ranging from the crisis in black male achievement to improving teacher education to smoothing the pipeline from K–12 classrooms to advanced STEM degrees. Many of these teams struggle with the aim statement; their initial attempts are typically immense in scope. They often involve the efforts of multiple institutions or organizational units. Handoffs between these units, as students move from one context to another, are frequently part of the problem. Many different work processes may be indicted that engage many different individuals and that stretch out over extended periods of time.

Specifically, the essence of crafting a workable aim, and all that flows from it in the form of a driver diagram, is managing scope. Drawing on the *Pareto principle* from improvement science that 80 percent of the variability in some outcome is often found to be associated with 20 percent of the possible causes, driver diagrams typically contain five or fewer judiciously selected primary drivers. Academics and practitioners alike may find it hard to embrace the idea that working theories of improvement are *incomplete by design*. Accepting that every conceptual nuance may not get represented is easier said than done.

Critical judgments, informed by research and professional experience, must be made about where to focus attention. An initial working theory of improvement must selectively put some stakes in the ground so that work can begin. Here the essential nature of the driver diagram—"definitely incomplete and possibly wrong"—helps moderate the uncertainty that can drive a network initiation team into "analysis paralysis." The driver diagram mantra reminds us all that we are embarking on a journey that may take unexpected turns. Critical gaps in initial thinking will become apparent, but often the only way to discover these gaps and begin to fill them is to get started on the learning journey.

Starting Smaller, Learning Fast, Aiming for Quality at Scale

We looked back on the education field's flawed efforts to create small high schools and saw how a powerful idea was sacrificed in the rush to scale too quickly. We saw similar problems with efforts to introduce instructional coaches—bringing on too many new coaches too fast. In both cases, districts pressed to scale a reform before they knew enough to make the complex changes actually work. And the phenomenon is not unique to education. Many organizations in diverse industries have fallen prey to the illusion that a great idea alone can guarantee success. History tells a different story. Deliberately learning our way to better outcomes is, in fact, how organizations improve quality and how interventions scale effectively.[3]

It is clear that given the conditions typical of educational reform, starting smaller is the key to learning faster, which in turn is the key to advancing quality outcomes reliably at scale. Why then does the education field keep pursuing reform after reform in the same dysfunctional way? There are surely many reasons, but among the most compelling is what Martin Luther King Jr. famously called the "fierce urgency of now"—the concern that time is passing, that problems are mounting, and immediate action is needed. And it's true: children's educational lives are being lost and something has to be done. But when leaders are pressed to act fast and wide, it diminishes their ability to learn fast with the result that districts spend enormous sums of time and money on the full-scale implementation of ill-thought-out initiatives. These efforts place enormous demands on classroom educators, and place school and system leaders at risk. These conditions often discourage critical internal analysis about what is actually happening or not. Failures stay private, and opportunities to learn from them go unrecognized.

Fortunately, there are good reasons to believe that using the discipline and structures described in this book can accelerate the processes of improvement. Much of educational R&D occurs within universities. Everything from the funding structure for educational research to human resource policies to the pacing of educational R&D is organized by larger forces that drive life in universities. These R&D settings are not especially agile, nor are they maximized for learning fast from problems of practice and for using these insights to propel improvement further forward. Likewise, as long as practitioners view change as largely an individual enterprise—as each practitioner having to figure things out on his or her own—we will fail to capitalize on Engelbart's insights about accelerating learning through improvement networks. In short, the mechanisms and structures we currently use to advance improvement are suboptimal and far from the limits of what is possible to accomplish.

The good news is that we can accelerate how we learn to improve. When individual organizations engage systematically in improvement research, they get better faster. When these same organizations join together in networks to solve shared problems, they learn faster still. This is the source of our optimism. We can move much more productively as we pursue the fierce urgency of now.

Failures Are a Treasure: Really?

We care deeply about the success of our educational systems. We believe fervently that every school and every teacher should be relentlessly focused on each student's success. We applaud leaders who insist that "failure is not an option." However, such beliefs also create the ground for what psychologists call "confirmation bias."[4] They lead us to look for, find, and favor information that matches what we believe or wish to happen.[5] As we have noted, advocates for past educational reforms have tended to see what they wanted to see until the evidence against their vision became so overwhelming that they discarded their favored ideas in favor of new ones.

In this instance, human nature does not serve us well. While we are wired to seek evidence of success, we actually learn more by studying our failures.[6] Cognitive scientists now tell us that when we struggle or experience a setback, the resulting dissonance often helps to deepen learning. This observation is at the heart of the iterative Plan-Do-Study-Act cycles used to test changes. When a predicted outcome fails to occur, it challenges us to ask why and to question deeply what we think we know. In the process, it catalyzes learning to improve.

In fact, failures are unavoidable when one is trying to change complex social systems. This is true whether we are talking about health care, education, or a social service agency seeking to ease its clients out of poverty. However, embracing failure as an opportunity to learn is much easier to talk about than to actually do. When things don't go well, we have a propensity to look for someone to blame. We fear that without personal accountability, people won't try their best to prevent failure the next time. And if they are held blameless, they will lapse into laissez-faire attitudes too comfortable with the status quo. So long as this way of thinking prevails, fostering improvement will remain very hard work—and quality improvement will be in short supply.

In contrast, an improvement culture puts learning to improve at its center and challenges everyone to put failure to work toward valued goals. This kind of culture encourages people to report when things don't go according to plan. It makes people feel safe because they know that failure means that their team is testing its theories and bettering the work of the organization. Part of the genius in the quality improvement logic of starting small and aiming to learn fast is that the costs of early failure are reduced and the dangers of confirmation bias—seeing only what we want to see—also lessened. In this regard starting small eases the path toward subsequent success.[7]

THE KNOW-HOW CHALLENGE

In our field, we have often not "closed the deal" with our efforts at reform. We regularly lack the know-how to transform good ideas into the tools, routines, human capabilities, and institutional arrangements necessary to make these ideas work effectively and reliably at scale. Consider the efforts now underway in many states to introduce the Common Core standards. Much attention is being focused on assuring that teachers know the new content to be covered and the conceptual understandings to developed in their students. But how to put these efforts into practice day in and day out, within time and resource constraints educators face, remains largely unknown. We hold onto a belief that if we show teachers a video of quality practice, send them to a workshop, or assign them take-home readings, the next step—how to use their newfound knowledge to effect quality outcomes in their classroom—will be straightforward. Tacitly, we act as if once educators know that something matters, they will figure out on their own how to make it work.[8]

This attitude also shapes the efforts of the educational research community. Attention to knowing that some things really matter has channeled the field to invest deeply in empirically grounded theory development, in studies that explore the association of student outcomes and malleable contributing factors, and in the development and tryout of new instructional approaches. Much of the latter focuses on the design of new tools, materials, or routines that embody theoretical insights drawn from the cognitive, learning, and social sciences. Typically, the goal of these inquiries is to demonstrate that various theoretical principles have applicability for education. How the artifacts that result from these studies can be used effectively beyond their initial design-development settings, however, receives much less attention.[9] Building rigorous know-how for improvement is not considered high-status work in the academy.

The policy community also exhibits certain myopia about these matters. Recent years have brought calls for greater use of *evidence-based practices* that are anchored in results from randomized field trials. But the collective set of resources of this sort currently available is miniscule in size and eclectic in content.[10] So from a purely pragmatic point of view, these arguments are more about an ideal vision for some long-term future rather than a near-term reality. Moreover, even if the volume of such randomized trials were orders of magnitude greater than we have now, evidence-based practices would still operate at best as building blocks for a larger enterprise aimed at improving student outcomes.

As noted in chapter 5, heterogeneity of effects is a common result in field trials. These varied outcomes provide ample evidence that implementation matters, even with the relatively well-defined interventions that have been subject to such study. How best to respond to this variability in performance—that is, how to achieve positive outcomes reliably for different students working with diverse teachers and in different organizational contexts—is just another manifestation of the know-how problem. The same issues still lurk, only behind a different banner, which insists that evidence-based practices be implemented with fidelity.

It is important to recognize that the interventions we seek for educational institutions are themselves often complex. Rarely a mechanical act, implementing an intervention often entails a complicated process of learning how to integrate new ideas, tools, and routines into practitioners' current understanding and work responsibilities. This learning process is at the heart of what we often hear about change—that each educator must make the intervention his or her own. Thus, given the nature of the changes we seek to make, variation in implementation is to be expected. This reality roots the second improvement principle—variation in performance is the quality improvement problem to solve. It is why it is so essential to develop modes of inquiry that accelerate learning from variation.

A Need for Practice-Based Evidence

As we have noted, knowing that better outcomes are possible is not the same thing as knowing how to generate these outcomes under different conditions. Learning how to make interventions work effectively in the hands of different individuals in varied contexts is the problem to solve. Developing this know-how—what might be called *practice-based evidence*—is the objective of improvement research carried out by networked communities.[11] It is an essential complement to the evidence-based practice movement that currently is gaining so much attention in education and other social policy circles.[12]

Building practice-based evidence directs attention to several important considerations. Improvement requires the development of *robust practice-based tools, materials, and routines.* As noted previously, much of design research in education today comes in the form of proving that a theoretical principle can be demonstrated in a tool, instructional resource, or teaching routine. These studies often result in prototypes, of sorts, whose continuous refinement is key to using them well at scale. Unfortunately, the field is much more likely to think that once a prototype has been shown to work under a limited set of conditions, it is now ready to be disseminated broadly.

Improvement research also recognizes that effective interventions often require the bundling of new work processes, tools, and routines along with changes in organizational structures and norms. As we described in chapter 3, these various components must *integrate well together as solution systems*. Returning to one of Atul Gawande's observations, cited at the beginning of chapter 3, the use of great components, even evidence-based components, does not assure that quality outcomes will result. Making all of the pieces fit together is a formidable and quite distinctive improvement task.

In addition, even after a solution system has undergone considerable testing and refinement, it will often need further honing as it moves into each new organizational setting. And this need for *adaptive integration into local contexts* remains even if the intervention appears modest. Recall that the Building a Teaching Effectiveness Network focused on improving just one high-leverage process—how principals provided feedback to teachers. Considerable adaptations were needed to get a new process to work reliably in different schools. In general, the principle of adaptive integration recognizes that each attempt to implement an intervention in a new setting is itself an act of design. Sometimes this may require significant changes in the intervention, and in the work settings into which it is being introduced, for the intervention to fit and achieve quality outcomes locally.

Then there is the human side of change. *Practicing educators must be core participants in generating practice-based evidence.* Unfortunately, in much of education today, the working out of tools, protocols, materials, and routines belongs to consultants, academics, and others who do not actually work in schools. The problems we seek to solve, however, exist on the job floor, so the refinement of tools, materials, and routines must happen there, too. In an improvement-centered world, practitioners are not just passive recipients of others' research, but active agents of change; they own problems, examine causes, and collaborate with researchers and others. For a genuine science of improvement to gain a foothold in education, practicing educators must become deeply engaged in the work, and an improvement culture must become the norm in schools.

Lastly, improvement science also calls for a *fusion of diverse sources of expertise.* Many different forms of expertise—academic, technical, and practical—must now meld together. And the significance of each must be explicitly acknowledged. Material designers, process developers, technologists, and academic researchers must join with practitioners in developing problem-solving knowledge bases. All must constantly ask the three improvement questions: What specifically is the problem to solve? What change might we introduce and why? And, how will we know if this change is actually an improvement?

In short, quality improvement is a shared commitment to a distinctive way of learning, leading, and working together. Living the principles would entail a genuine sea change for the field. It would place us on a path toward new ways in how we use evidence to improve, in whose role it is to initiate and carry out these changes, and how we embrace and build on each other's work.

An Essential Complementarity

Dichotomies are useful in bringing important issues into sharp relief. So it is with practice-based evidence as the complement to evidence-based practice. These two forms of inquiry, however, do not stand opposed to each other; rather, they exist in a symbiotic relationship. Together, they form a dynamic knowledge system for improving the social organizations that influence so many lives.

The natural question we should ask about any new reform idea is "Will it work?" This question is really an amalgam of two questions. First, is there any evidence that this intervention can succeed? The best form of this evidence comes from randomized field trials.

These studies are designed to empirically test whether some idealized set of tools, materials, or routines can produce desired outcomes. The genius of randomization is that the myriad of factors that contribute to the observed variation in outcomes are taken off the table. That is, in order to ascertain as clearly as possible one relationship (treatment → outcomes), the experimental design is willfully ignorant about all other causes of observed outcomes. It typically ignores how various aspects about students, teachers, and contexts may moderate the size of effects and even whether they actually occur.[13] But the strength of efficacy studies becomes a weakness when we shift to the second question: "Can the intervention produce positive outcomes reliably across the many different contexts where it is likely to be taken up and used?"

The second question directs us to find out if, when, and how an intervention can be made to be effective in various settings of practice. The work in this stream of inquiry necessarily happens across many contexts and involves iterative investigations aimed at refining interventions so that they are more likely to perform robustly. The impulse and insight for such improvement can start in different places. For example, in the Community College Pathways initiative, an intervention aiming to alter students' mindset about mathematics grew out of translational research anchored in decades of fundamental disciplinary inquiry. In contrast, our attention to belonging uncertainty derived from the NIC analytic team's effort to understand why some students failed to persist in Pathways classrooms. Interesting, while academic research documents that belonging uncertainty matters, extant academic research provides less guidance about how to moderate this social psychological mindset. This led individual community college faculty members in our NIC to carry out PDSA cycles that would help them test plausible changes. Likewise, the improvement efforts in BTEN are largely grounded in insights developed by school practitioners about key concerns affecting the work lives of new teachers.

In sum, reliable improvement at scale relies on both the knowledge of an intervention's promise and knowledge about how to realize that promise over and over again. In other words, quality improvement operates at the nexus of knowing *that* something matters (i.e., evidence-based practice) and knowing *how* to effect it reliably at scale (i.e., practice-based evidence). These different streams of evidence work in tandem with one another. We need to embrace and support both if we are to bridge the chasm that separates our rising aspirations for our educational systems and the quality of what is now delivered.

AN IMPROVEMENT PARADIGM

We have sought throughout this volume to introduce an integrated set of principles, tools, and inquiry processes, along with the structures and norms necessary for carrying out improvement research in networked communities. Together, they represent a coherent set of ideas about how this work should be considered and carried out. Formally speaking, this is the definition of a paradigm. Once embraced, the paradigm calls us to think and act in very different ways; it points our research, practice, and policy in new directions. Unlike paradigms in academic disciplines, the improvement paradigm has a very practical purpose—accelerating learning to improve. We hope that interest in and experience with this paradigm continues to grow. If it does, the ideas, tools, and methods described here will surely continue to evolve and improve.

At the risk of oversimplifying, we offer here a heuristic guide for this improvement paradigm (see figure 7.1).

Where the urgency for change has in the past caused educational reformers to implement fast and scale wide—ignoring the need for developing know-how—an improvement paradigm directs us to learn fast to subsequently implement well. A continued failure to follow this dictum will continue to relegate seemingly good reform ideas to the ever-growing waste heap of promises unfulfilled.

Where researchers and analysts have traditionally focused on the precise estimation of an effect size—the average difference in outcomes between a group receiving an intervention and a control group that did not—quality improvement directs us to scrutinize the myriad of factors that contribute to variation in outcomes and to use the insights gained

Figure 7.1 The improvement paradigm

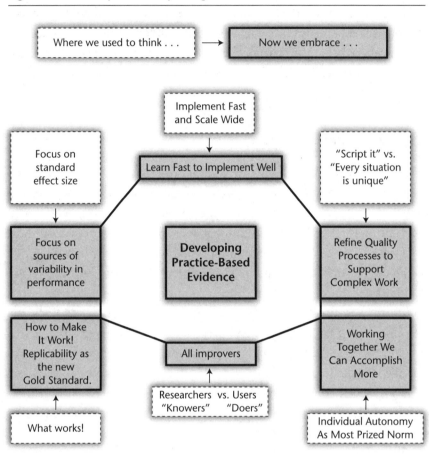

to fuel continuous improvement efforts. The capacity to replicate quality outcomes on a regular basis becomes the ultimate gold standard.

The improvement paradigm also represents a fresh way to resolve a long-standing dilemma for educational leadership, policy, and practice. As discussed in chapter 2, the field has swung back and forth between two polar opposites. On the one hand, the complexity of teaching and learning has led many educators to believe that every situation is unique and that, therefore, each educator, school, and district must invent practice on its own. While this view is grounded in a realistic understanding of the task and organizational complexity of schooling, those who subscribe to it are essentially accepting that wide variability in outcomes is inevitable.

On the other hand are those who, because they are frustrated with wide variability of student experiences and outcomes, advocate for scripting teachers so that every student might have the same opportunity to learn. But every student is not the same, nor is every context. The complexity of teaching and learning is real, and it cannot be side-stepped by standardizing all activity in an effort to "teacher-proof" instructional environments.

In contrast to both of these views, an improvement paradigm recognizes task and organizational complexity as a central concern. It also recognizes the high and sustained demands placed on educators for responding in the best way to each learner, the dynamics of each classroom, and the particular contexts of each school. Learning from other sectors and industries, the improvement paradigm understands how important it is for workers to know how to use well the kinds of tools and standard work process that enable quality work. Only in this manner can we free significant cognitive attention so that educators can focus on what is unique and distinctive in each particular setting. To be clear, standard work processes do not seek to automate teaching and learning. Rather, they seek to assure that the best practice-based evidence assists professionals to do best what only they can do. Developing such tools and standard work processes can help us bridge across the polarities described previously. This approach respects the complexity of the tasks of educating well, while also taking into account that important aspects of work can and indeed should follow standard protocols. We argue that this is the only way that our field can reach higher quality standards.

Operationalizing improvements also makes demands on what we measure and how we gather it. The field of education is now awash in data, mostly accountability data on students, teachers, schools, and districts. In addition specialized data are also collected for funded research projects, but these data, mainly used by researchers, typically have little or no practical utility for educators and students. In contrast, improvement research calls for data, not for purposes of ranking individuals or organizations, but for learning about how well specific processes actually work. These data offer the kind of evidence needed to discern whether changes in these processes are actually improvements. Introducing this kind of practical measurement poses a normative challenge for schools because educators have traditionally seen data as intended for someone else—for a distal actor seeking to hold them accountable or a researcher gathering information. Data have not been intended for educators to use to improve. Complicating matters further is the fact that time is the most restricted resource in education. The practical measurement challenge is to learn how to harvest just enough information in the most unobtrusive means possible to inform efforts to improve.

Relatedly, an improvement paradigm calls us to reconsider what has traditionally been the most prized educational norm: the autonomy of practice in classrooms and schools. In an earlier era, when we knew less, when teachers worked in simpler environments and (perhaps most significant) when our aspirations were more modest, it was reasonable to see the teacher as individual craftsman. Today, we have clearly reached the limits of what we can achieve by thinking of teachers in this way. Our problems now are too complex, the necessary knowledge and expertise too diverse. While some extraordinary individuals may well construct positive action on their own, when it is left to this device, quality will always be in short supply. Fortunately, education is a huge network. When properly structured, such networks have extraordinary capacities to innovate, test, and rapidly spread effective practices. The improvement paradigm calls us to activate these strengths. It calls us to embrace a new narrative: working together and learning together will make it possible to accomplish more for many more than ever before.

Improvement science also entails a different relational dynamic. The division between research and practice is legendary. We have tacitly accepted that there is a small class of "better knowers" and a much larger class of "doers," who should use the knowledge generated by the knowers. Quality improvement, in contrast, calls on both knowers and doers to work together. Respecting and valuing the varied expertise that is needed to solve educational problems, NICs embrace all involved as full members.

As has been the case in health care, the improvement paradigm in education promises to bring a valued but illusive goal—quality outcomes reliably at scale—within our reach. We return to the insight of Donald Berwick, the cofounder of the Institute for Healthcare Improvement, with whom we began chapter 1:

> [Achieving] quality is not just an intellectual endeavor; it is a pragmatic one. The point is not just to know what makes things better or worse; it is to make things actually better.[14]

IMPLICATIONS FOR POLICY, PRACTICE, AND THE ACADEMY

If the field of education is truly to embrace quality improvement, all of the major actors—those who make policy; those who teach; and those who train, research, and support educators—must change in fundamental ways. Next we outline what such changes might look like.

Educational Practice

Quality improvement calls educators toward a very different practice. It directs their attention to solving high-leverage problems using improvement methods and working through networked communities. It calls out for a new professional standard in which advancing quality improvement would become a central part of what it means to be a professional educator. In this new world, organizing improvement activity and being a leader in an improvement network would be recognized as high-status work. It would be at the core of what teacher leaders do.

For districts and other organizations that support schools, quality improvement means building the human capabilities and institutional capacities to support such efforts. Recognizing that improvement makes time demands on teachers, principals, and others, districts would adjust work assignments to facilitate deep engagement in this activity. They would recognize the important contributions that improvement leaders are making and remunerate accordingly.

Quality improvement would not be seen as a project but as an ongoing function in a high-performing organization. School districts, like health-care institutions, would operate quality improvement offices that provide technical staff and support capabilities to all educators in the district. Quality improvement also would anchor a new standard for leadership. Across many different sectors that take quality seriously, guiding improvement is what leaders at every level do. At a time when change is accelerating and has become part of the DNA of twenty-first century institutions, educational organizations would recognize that individuals who can lead improvement are among their most valued human resources. They help make the organization better at what it does every day.[15]

The Academy

The improvement paradigm calls on academic leaders, especially in schools of education, to rebalance their portfolios of applied research. Developing discipline-based theory and carrying out design-based experiments and rigorous evaluations will continue to generate, and ideally accelerate, the production of valuable knowledge about the fundaments of education. Complementing this would be an equally rigorous commitment to a science of improvement. Universities make natural hubs for problem-specific NICs, but to serve as such, they would need to become more hospitable to the kinds of expert teams necessary to support such activity. They would need to value great teams as much as great individual scholars. They would embrace a mission that directs intellectual resources both to advancing basic understanding about education problems and actively contributing to their solutions.

Professional education programs would embed improvement research methods in their training. The capstone experience for an advanced professional degree might be leading an improvement team in tackling a pressing problem. Teacher education programs would introduce quality improvement to the next generation of teachers and highlight it as part of teachers' career paths. New norms would come to characterize the practice of teaching. Rather than leaving it to new teachers to largely invent their own practice, teachers would build on what their predecessors have learned. Accumulating this know-how, and deeply understanding it, is the fertile ground from which genuine innovation springs. New teachers would take up membership in such a professional community and over time add to a collectively held body of practice-based evidence.

Policy

Quality improvement challenges policy actors toward more prudent aspirations. Wise leaders recognize the limits of what they actually know and are able to directly affect in a complex system. They understand that their efforts to intervene will almost surely beget unintended outcomes and that they can do harm as well as good. They understand why "the urgency of now" has compelled fast implementation, but they also recognize why this strategy will continue to frustrate all involved. Wise policy leaders embrace a new mantra; they promote *learning fast to implement well to achieve quality reliably at scale.*

Quality improvement also demands a more nuanced view of accountability. Evidence of student engagement and learning would continue to anchor improvement aims and help frame targets for change. Accountability systems, however, would also value educators paying serious attention to improvement. This means looking at more than just the outcomes themselves to also include process measures and evidence of progress on key drivers. It would hold educational institutions accountable for identifying high-leverage improvement problems and orchestrating and sustaining local action toward realizing improvement aims. These new accountability systems might inspect accounts of local failure, examine the evidence on subsequent changes attempted, and inquire as to what local educators are learning from these changes to further improve. They would recognize active participation in improvement networks and reward contributions to problem solving.

In addition, policy actors would aspire to create capabilities in every school and district where learning to improve becomes a lived force. It would make discretionary resources available so that districts could develop and sustain the ongoing institutional capacities necessary for continuous quality improvement to become "what we do here." In the not too distant future, it would change the narrative that any school visitor might hear. Rather than recounting the school's various new initiatives or its accountability category, a school leader would tell visitors: "Here is how we used to work and where we had been coming up short. Here is what we have tried so far. Here is what we have learned and where we are moving next."

Federal support for educational R&D would be directed toward NICs aiming to solve high-leverage problems of practice. Achieving measureable improvement targets would discipline the work of these NICs. The federal government would continue to support basic research programs aimed at the design and development of new tools and routines, as well as trials that provide evidence about what can work. Complementing this would be efforts to expand capacities to actually solve problems and to steadily increase the number of local educational leaders who are learning and improving, and who can mentor others how to do the same.

We have been living in an era of blame—calling out schools, districts, and, lately, individual teachers as failures. To be sure, chronic failures are a stain on public education, and they undermine the public's trust in the whole enterprise. These issues must be addressed. Yet we must also recognize that the larger problems we now seek to solve are the end result of the systems that our past policies have produced. We need a new and more ennobling vision that enables the best efforts from all involved and that begins with a belief that everyone wants to learn how to do better. In this new era, policy efforts would respect and enable our better selves to do the work of continuous improvement. They would redirect the holders of the policy reins toward servant leadership, demanding that they constantly ask: "What can we do better to support those upon whom we depend, and of whom we ask so much, to achieve what we highly value—a quality education for every child?"

EQUITY, PRACTICE, AND QUALITY IMPROVEMENT

We recognize that such new sensibilities are easy to talk about but very hard to embed in the fabric of public affairs. But we believe deeply that we must make the effort to do so. Quite simply, delivering on the promise of education depends on it. Every American president and every Congress for the last half-century has in one way or another recognized that a good education for all Americans is a key to the country's well-being and economic prosperity. The rhetoric has only intensified over the past two decades. While policy approaches have ranged from vouchers to accountability to new standards, the drumbeat has been a constant: education now matters more than ever before. Yet we clearly don't educate *all* Americans well, nor do we have a realistic strategy for doing so.

Quality improvement says every student matters, yet our current data and reporting systems only crudely acknowledge this belief. We divide students by gross social demographic characteristics and broad achievement levels. Even as we narrow gaps in performance between poor and not-poor and among black, Latino, and white, and even as we move students up a level from "basic" to "proficient," much remains hidden. Within these accountability categories are extraordinary possibilities for doing better—much better—for many more children. Reducing the minority gap, or the income gap, in third grade achievement would be a great accomplishment. But it would count as a far greater success if every child learned to read by the end of third grade, plus acquired the necessary cultural knowledge and dispositions to use reading skills to understand more complex subject matter in the years ahead. The education field knows enough to achieve this goal. We just don't know how to organize our systems to execute on this goal consistently in every school and with every child.

Achieving quality outcomes reliably at scale is a socially just aim around which we can all unite. It is important that our public institutions herald such just aspirations. But it is not enough simply to hold them as aspirations. Nor can those responsible for advancing equitable outcomes discharge that responsibility simply by telling educators to do better, extending rewards to those who somehow figure that out and imposing sanctions on those who don't. Leaders at all levels have a responsibility to create know-how on the job floor so that such valued accomplishments become regular occurrences rather than seemingly random events.

Quality improvement carried out in individual organizations, and through networked communities, is a new way of working that can move us from the aspirational realm toward a future where we actually achieve our goals. All across the nation, we are reaching for higher standards—whether we call this the Common Core, deeper learning, or some local definition of the same basic goal. The accountability paradigm created by the No Child Left Behind Act did much good in directing our attention to the learning of all children and in bringing data to the forefront. But, having guided us over the past decade, it is also revealing its limits. While test-based accountability has focused attention on better outcomes, by itself, it provides little guidance as to how actually to achieve them. It lacks what we have called in this volume a working theory of practice improvement. It also lacks the systematic methods for learning to improve, as well as the organizational arrangements necessary to accelerate efforts toward these ends. And most importantly, it fails to enable the educators—teachers, principals, and other school-based leaders—on whom we depend for improvement to actually be able to do so.

Improvement science and networked improvement communities offer us a shared language, access to diverse human capital, and rigorous methods to truly tackle the problem of providing an education of value. Building on the foundations of accountability, we view improvement research as the crucial next step in the long journey toward a quality education for all.

Glossary

THIS GLOSSARY ORGANIZES a selection of key terms used in this book that have formal meaning. In many cases our definitions align with those established in prior writing on improvement research and networked communities. In some cases they have been modified slightly for the education context. In a few cases they are original to this work. They have been grouped together topically in a way that, we hope, makes them a bit more meaningful while also still easily accessible.

ABOUT NETWORKED IMPROVEMENT COMMUNITIES

COLLEAGUESHIP OF EXPERTISE: A community of academic, technical, and clinical experts deliberately assembled to address a specific improvement problem. All involved are *improvers* seeking to generate strong evidence about how to achieve better outcomes more reliably.

NETWORKED IMPROVEMENT COMMUNITY: An intentionally designed social organization with a distinctive problem-solving focus; roles, responsibilities, and norms for membership; and the maintenance of narratives that detail what it is about and why affiliating with it is important. A NIC is marked by four essential characteristics. It is

- Focused on a well-specified common aim
- Guided by a deep understanding of the problem, the system that produces it, and a shared working theory to improve it
- Disciplined by the methods of improvement research to develop, test, and refine interventions
- Organized to accelerate their diffusion out into the field and effective integration into varied educational contexts

NETWORK HUB: A core group formed either as single organization or distributed across network members that carry out critical functions necessary for the support and effective operations of a networked improvement community. These functions include, but are not limited to, improvement science expertise, analytics, knowledge management, convenings, communications, and technological support.

NETWORK INITIATION TEAM: A team that accepts responsibility for the formation of a networked improvement community. It leads a set of processes that articulate the problem to be solved, analyzes the system that produces current undesirable outcomes, and develops the aim statement and an initial working theory of practice improvement. The initiation team also takes the lead in securing the necessary supports for the network (both political as well as material), recruiting initial members into the community, and engaging the academic and technical expertise relevant to the specific problem to be solved.

NIC AS A SCIENTIFIC COMMUNITY: An organization ordered around a shared theory and shared measures for its aim and primary drivers. Participants engage in discipline inquiries using established inquiry methods such as PDSA cycles. Promising results are subject to replication across the network to warrant claims that changes are improvements.

NIC CHARTER: A document that provides sustaining guidance to the distributed efforts of NIC members. It is typically composed of the network's aim, causal system analysis (often consisting of both fishbone diagrams and system improvement map), and the working theory of improvement (typically represented in a driver diagram).

ABOUT IMPROVEMENT SCIENCE AND QUALITY IMPROVEMENT

CONTINUOUS IMPROVEMENT: Improvement research that involves multiple iterative cycles of activity over extended time periods.

IMPROVEMENT RESEARCH: Particular acts of inquiry, or projects, that aim for quality improvement.

IMPROVEMENT SCIENCE: The methodology that disciplines inquiries to improve practice. Undergirding it is an epistemology of what we need to know to improve practice and how we may come to know it.

QUALITY IMPROVEMENT: An effort to increase the capacity of an organization to produce successful outcomes reliably for different subgroups of students, being educated by different teachers, and in varied organizational contexts.

SOLUTIONITIS: The tendency to jump quickly on a solution before fully understanding the actual problem to be solved. This behavior results in incomplete analysis of the problem to be addressed and fuller consideration of potential problem-solving alternatives. It is siloed reasoning—seeing complex matters through a narrow-angle lens—that can lure leaders into unproductive strategies.

ABOUT STANDARD WORK AND PROCESSES

HIGH-LEVERAGE PROCESS: A process that has the following properties: (1) it consumes substantial resources, especially teacher or student time; (2) its execution and outcomes vary considerably; and (3) there are reasons to believe that changes to it might improve resource efficiency and effectiveness.

MACRO PROCESS: A process for which the execution typically entails a sequence of more discrete micro processes.

MICRO PROCESS: An elemental activity or segment of work taken to achieve a particular end.

STANDARD WORK: Regularly occurring processes that are amenable to formulation as best practice routines within a networked improvement community. The purpose of these routines is to assist educators in carrying out their work by reducing the cognitive load associated with the performance of complex tasks. Such processes reduce undesirable variation in performance and free educators to better focus their attention, thereby advancing quality outcomes more reliably. High-leverage processes are attractive candidates for standard work.

ABOUT SYSTEMS

CAUSAL SYSTEM ANALYSIS: An analysis that directs attention to the question, "Why do we get the outcomes that we currently do?" In working through this analysis, participants develop a shared understanding of the specific problem(s) they are actually trying to solve. The process also provides a first test as to whether a team seeking to initiate a NIC can engage together productively as a focused improvement community.

FISHBONE DIAGRAM: A tool that visually represents a group's causal systems analysis (sometimes known as a cause-and-effect diagram or an Ishikawa diagram).

SYSTEM: An organization characterized by a set of interactions among the people who work there, the tools and materials they have at their disposal, and the processes through which these people and resources join together to accomplish its goals.

SYSTEM IMPROVEMENT MAP: An analytic tool that represents what we learn through the causal system analysis about the different organizational levels (e.g., classrooms, schools, and districts) and key organizational subsystems (e.g., human resources, finance, instruction) relevant to solving the identified problem.

ABOUT DRIVER DIAGRAMS AND WORKING THEORIES OF PRACTICE IMPROVEMENT

CHANGE IDEA: An alteration to a system or process that is to be tested through a PDSA cycle to examine its efficacy in improving some driver(s) in working theory of improvement.

CONCEPT FRAMEWORK: [also may be referred to as *design principles*] An account that provides conceptual detail and relevant research findings that form design principles for key drivers and change ideas. It also provides a conceptual basis for the development of practical measures.

DRIVER DIAGRAM: A tool that visually represents a group's working theory of practice improvement. The driver diagram creates a common language and coordinates the effort among the many different individuals joined together in solving a shared problem.

IMPROVEMENT AIM: A goal for an improvement effort that answers the question, "What are we trying to accomplish?" Improvement aims should clearly specify how much, for whom, and by when. They sit at the far left end of a driver diagram.

PARETO PRINCIPLE: A principle anchored in a long history of organizational studies that 80 percent of the variability in organizational performance is often associated with only 20 percent of the possible causes. It aids in the selection of primary, and when needed, secondary drivers.

PRIMARY DRIVER: Representation of a community's hypothesis about the main areas of influence necessary to advance the improvement aim.

SECONDARY DRIVER: A system component that is hypothesized to activate each primary driver. The "how" of change.

WORKING THEORY OF PRACTICE IMPROVEMENT: A small interrelated set of hypotheses about key drivers necessary for achieving an improvement aim and specific changes associated with each driver. It requires a creative blending of observations arising from the causal system analysis with relevant research that bears on this problem together with wise judgments from expert educators.

ABOUT DOING IMPROVEMENT RESEARCH

ADAPTIVE INTEGRATION: Learning how to integrate a change package into different settings. This may require significant changes in the intervention, and in the work settings into which it is being introduced, for the intervention to fit and achieve quality outcomes locally.

PDSA (PLAN-DO-STUDY-ACT): A pragmatic scientific method for iterative testing of changes in complex systems. Each cycle is essentially a mini-experiment in which observed outcomes are compared to predictions and discrepancies between the two become a major source of learning.

PROCESS MAP: A tool for visualizing the steps in a process that can assist an improvement team in identifying gaps, strengths, and opportunities for improvement.

RUN CHART: A graphical display of some measured characteristic over time. Data from PDSAs are often displayed in run charts.

SOLUTION SYSTEM: An intervention that consists of multiple interrelated components that must mesh well together. Formally, such interventions have a systems character. For positive effects to occur reliably, coordinated improvements need to occur across all of the drivers that comprise the solution system. A material weakness in any one driver can undermine the efficacy of the overall solution.

ABOUT MEASUREMENT

BALANCING MEASURE: A measure that helps improvers keep an eye on the other parts of the system that are not currently the target of improvement but nevertheless may be affected by the changes being pursued.

LAGGING OUTCOME MEASURE: A measure that is available only well after an intervention has been initiated.

LEADING OUTCOME MEASURE: A measure that predicts the ultimate outcome of interest but is available on a more immediate basis.

MEASUREMENT FOR ACCOUNTABILITY: A broad, general measure that aims to sort individual or organizational units into performance categories. This use introduces increased formality into the measurement process and places primacy on the reliability of individual scores. Often used as a measure for improvement aims.

MEASUREMENT FOR IMPROVEMENT: A measure that directly links to the specific drivers and work processes that are the object of change. It provides evidence for testing changes and examining hypothesized causal connections in the working theory of improvement.

MEASUREMENT FOR RESEARCH: A detailed measure developed by researchers to represent particular theoretical constructs. It is used in academic research to test relational propositions among key constructs that form a theory. It is often useful as a basis for developing practical measures.

OUTCOME MEASURE: A measure that operationalizes the aim statement in the driver diagram. These data provide a way of assessing whether progress is being made on the specific problem to be solved. Accountability measures are often used here.

PRACTICAL MEASUREMENT: Data to inform improvement that is embedded in regular work. Since the intent is to inform continuous improvement, practical measures are collected frequently to assess whether positive changes are in fact occurring. Since the focus is on specific populations and contexts, the measures are framed in a language that is natural and comprehensible to those asked to respond to them.

PRIMARY DRIVER MEASURE: A measure associated with primary drivers. Since these drivers are intermediate outcomes in the working theory of improvement (i.e., intermediaries between process changes and leading and lagging outcomes), they play a key role in the testing of a working theory of improvement.

PROCESS MEASURE: A measure that feeds back valuable information about how specific processes being tested are performing under different conditions.

ABOUT EVIDENCE FOR IMPROVEMENT

LEVEL-A, -B, -C LEARNING: Three interrelated levels of learning, developed by Douglas Engelbart, that together form a schema for individual and organizational learning. Level-A learning represents the knowledge acquired by front-line workers as they engage in their practice. Level-B learning occurs across individuals within an organization. Level-C learning is orchestrated by a network hub and coupled with appropriate technologies to support rapid communications across distributed sites. This confluence is what enables the network to accelerate how it learns to improve.

EVIDENCE-BASED PRACTICE: Tools, materials, or sets of routines, typically grounded in theoretical principles, that have been subject to rigorous empirical study. Their use is warranted by results from a rigorous field trial that demonstrated that the intervention can work because it has somewhere.

KNOW-HOW: The detailed practical knowledge necessary to get good ideas actually to work in classrooms, schools, and districts.

PRACTICE-BASED EVIDENCE: Evidence that grows from practice and can be used to improve it. This evidence, emerging from improvement research, demonstrates that some process, tool, or modified staff roles and relationships works effectively under a variety of conditions and that quality outcomes will reliably ensue. It is the evidence of know-how.

Appendix

Responses to Some Frequently Asked Questions

IMPROVEMENT SCIENCE AND networked improvement communities represent a different paradigm for inquiry and action in education. Increasingly, we are fielding questions about this methodology as interest grows in these ideas. Some are raised by groups directly interested in advancing practical improvements in educational institutions. Others are asked by researchers who engage in rigorous program evaluations, and still others by policy leaders seeking to promote use of more effective practices in schools. While the improvement paradigm represents a compelling and internally consistent framework for inquiry and action, it is also quite different from how most individuals have been trained and what they have come to think of as best professional practice. Consequently, they struggle in different ways to integrate the ideas presented in this book into their working understandings. Here are some of the questions we are frequently asked and our responses to them.

STARTING SMALL TO LEARN FAST, REALLY?

One might reasonably ask: How could we possibly start with just a few teachers or just a handful of principals or just a few schools given pervasive problems affecting hundreds of thousands of students? The key here is to recognize that modest beginnings are not antithetical to widespread improvements. Rather, starting small increases the likelihood that when we get to scale, the changes introduced will actually produce the outcomes sought. Put succinctly, it is about learning fast in order to implement well.[1]

The trajectory of learning to improve resembles a classic organic growth curve. Progress is slow at first but accelerates over time as future changes build on a gradually enlarging base capacity. (See the black curve in figure A.1.) Early PDSA cycles create a base of knowledge and expertise that speeds subsequent efforts and makes widespread improvement the more likely result.[2] The alternative, illustrated as the gray curve in figure A.1, depicts how change typically occurs in education. With great promise, reforms move quickly into practice. Some immediate effects may occur, but the dysfunction embedded in this strategy eventually takes hold. Rates of improvement diminish or flatten entirely, and accomplishments fall far short of expectations.

Figure A.1   Comparative learning to improve trajectories

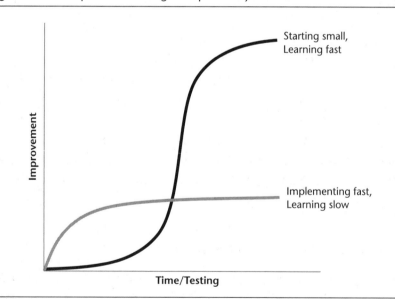

ISN'T THIS JUST A PILOT PROGRAM?

The notion of starting small is not entirely new to education. Many prior reform efforts have used pilots as a first step toward full-scale implementation. A district might, for example, introduce a new teacher-mentoring initiative into twenty-five schools one year before moving it district-wide the next. In the best cases, the pilot produces some learning that improves the model before it goes to scale. Typically, most of the design decisions made in developing the pilot are considered fixed and in place, leaving little more than the possibility of modest tweaks thereafter.

To be clear, the main point in starting small is to organize a process so that improvers can systematically learn by doing. The essential feature is carrying out *iterative cycles of change*. Yet many teams often miss the significance of iteration. We have seen enthusiastic improvement groups go through a reasonably rigorous causal system analysis and develop a workable driver diagram only to proceed directly to test a full-blown solution. Typically, there is little or no engagement of individuals on the job floor, and the idea of multiple quick tests of change is nowhere to be found.

Along a related line, a pilot program is now viewed in the education science community as a first step toward a large-scale field trial.[3] The goal of the pilot is to demonstrate sufficient efficacy to warrant the larger study. This sequence characterizes the evidence-based paradigm that emerged in medicine and is now being mimicked in education. While there is good rationale for staging activities in this fashion, it too is not principally a strategy for learning to improve. Rather, it assumes a set of favorable conditions that often do not exist in education. Program designers, for example, typically do not know ahead of time precisely how to execute their change ideas in different settings. The pilot test, however, requires that the design of the intervention be held constant across sites and over the duration of the study so that an effect size can be estimated. This requirement prevents investigators from changing the intervention based on what they are learning as the trial goes forward. Efforts to improve must be deferred to some future time. In contrast, improvement research uses iterative PDSA cycles to turn promising ideas into workable processes, useful tools, and more productive work environments. If this is the learning goal, then the pilot test strategy tends to be too slow, cumbersome, and costly, as well as suboptimal from practitioners' perspectives.

WHAT IS EVIDENCE FOR RELIABLE IMPROVEMENT?

Each PDSA cycle follows the basic logic of disciplined inquiry. Improvers pose a hypothesis about a potentially productive change, make a prediction about what will happen, and gather evidence to determine whether the change is actually an improvement. As they analyze the evidence, two different things can happen.

Especially during the early stages of an improvement effort, it is likely that the predicted outcomes will not occur. The improvement team asks, "Why? What did we not take into account?" Their analytic probing helps them form the next PDSA cycle on the iterative journey toward reliable change.

Alternatively, it is possible that the predicted outcomes do occur. This does not mean that the team has proven anything yet. Rather, they simply have one bit of evidence that the change idea, as currently formulated, might work. A positive result suggests that the improvement team should test the idea further, perhaps with different individuals working in different organizational contexts. If initial hunches turn out to be wrong and the process deficient, the idea will eventually break down, and the predicted outcomes will not repeat. Such failures are valuable grist for improvement efforts. Reflecting on these failures causes improvers to question critically, "What did we miss? Does the change protocol need to be refined further? Do we need to make adaptations to make it work in this new context?"

In sum, the multiple iterative trials of improvement research aim to accumulate robust evidence over time and across different contexts. This warrant develops when improvers systematically test and refine a set of changes under an increasingly diverse set of conditions. It is only as the change repeatedly demonstrates improved outcomes over diverse conditions that its worth becomes established.

BUT DON'T YOU STILL NEED A RANDOMIZED CONTROL TRIAL?

The methods introduced here for assessing change may seem foreign to those formally trained in research design and program evaluation. On numerous occasions we have been asked, "How can you really know that a change actually produced the improvement? Don't you need a randomized control trial?"

This question is important, and we need to detour briefly to explain why quality improvement directs us toward alternative methods. First, we need to be clear about what a randomized control trial (RCT), as typically implemented in education, tells us and what it does not. The RCT is a powerful method for addressing a very specific type of question. Can some change "a" cause some set of desirable outcomes to happen? A significant result from an RCT means that on average the outcomes were somewhat higher under condition "a" than under some control situation. This result implies that somewhere in the study sample better results occurred. This is what the expression *evidence-based practice* means: we have evidence that a practice can work because it did somewhere for somebody.[4]

However, evidence-based practice does not mean that better results occurred everywhere or even in most places or with most of the teachers and students. In fact, in education the opposite is often the case. Over the last fifty years, studies have found that many interventions can be made to work in some places but that virtually none work everywhere. In fact, this finding has become so common with education-related RCTs that it has taken on its own technical name: *effects heterogeneity.*[5]

To the point, the on-average difference documented in an RCT tells us nothing about the conditions necessary for better outcomes to occur. Likewise, it tells us nothing about how an intervention can be effectively adapted so that good outcomes can emerge in different settings. This perspective brings different light to common understandings about "what works." At their best, the rigorous field trials summarized in the What Works Clearinghouse tell us *what can work* because empirical evidence exists that an intervention did work somewhere.[6] However, these studies provide little or no information about *how to make it work* effectively in the hands of diverse individuals working under varied organizational conditions.[7] Yet this is precisely what practitioners need to know as they seek to implement an intervention in their local schools, colleges, and districts.

Improvement research has different aims. Rather than just knowing that better outcomes are possible, the gold standard in quality improvement is the capacity to replicate positive outcomes. Developing "know-how" to accomplish this goal is what we have referred to as *practice-based evidence.*

To be clear, this is not an argument about the supremacy of one method over another, but rather the pragmatic matching of methods to questions. The inferential logic of improvement research is tied to the nature of the problem we are trying to solve—how to get quality outcomes to occur more reliably at scale. The design of iterative inquiries toward this end is highly pragmatic. It directs us to learn fast across increasingly variable conditions so that eventually we can implement well at scale. In some instances, that might involve an RCT. For example, an early PDSA in the Community College Pathways NIC involved a small randomized trial in one classroom as a first test of an intervention to shift students' mindsets about learning mathematics. In this case, the trial was a quick way to learn whether an experimental protocol with strong laboratory evidence could be adapted to work in a community college classroom.[8] In contrast, the challenge of integrating a growth mindset into diverse developmental math classrooms, and assuring that instruction builds on it, is a very different problem. It demands an organized learning process about what works, for whom, and under what conditions.

WHAT ABOUT IMPLEMENTATION FIDELITY?

How we think about implementation is also part of the problem. If the work of schooling were straightforward, its organizations simple, and the proposed changes discrete, the mechanical implementation of fixed changes would be quite sensible.[9] Practitioners would just need to follow the directions, and the desired outcomes should ensue. But, as discussed in chapter 3, this is not the reality of contemporary schooling. The tasks we seek to improve, as well as the organizations in which they are embedded, are quite complex. Often this is true as well for the solutions that are being introduced. Absent an appreciation of this complexity, many efforts to change schools just add to their dysfunction.

We now know from quality improvement efforts in other sectors that the introduction of interventions into different contexts often creates new problems, problems that are as important to solve as the initial design and development of the intervention itself. This perspective points the issue of implementation away from a simple conception of fidelity; it means we also have to study how to *adaptively integrate* interventions into different contexts if we are to attain improved outcomes reliably.

Quality improvement efforts in health care help illustrate this point. In *The Checklist Manifesto,* Atul Gawande explains that he began his improvement efforts with several quick attempts to see if he could first make a checklist work in his own surgeries.[10] After Gawande accumulated evidence subsequently about the checklist's efficacy across his medical center, a different question arose: What would it take to make the surgical checklist work in other places, such as health-care centers in Third World countries, other First World hospitals, and in context with non-Western cultures and social values? Recognizing that adaptations were inevitable, Gawande's improvement team zeroed in on how to assure efficacy as the checklist was taken up in these varied contexts. Rather than treating issues of context as externalities—for example, other surgeons failed to implement the checklist as designed—they treated these concerns as the next critical problems to solve. A life-saving checklist is of little value if it cannot be effectively integrated into the vastly different work environments of health care in America and across the world. Engineering robust adaptations to local contexts proved essential to saving lives.

Notes

Preface

1. Anthony S. Bryk and Louis Gomez, "Ruminations on Reinventing an R&D Capacity for Educational Improvement," prepared for the American Enterprise Institute Conference, Side of School Reform and the Future of Educational Entrepreneurship, October 25, 2007. Revised and subsequently published as Anthony S. Bryk and Louis Gomez, "Reinventing a Research and Development Capacity," in *The Future of Educational Entrepreneurship: Possibilities for School Reform,* ed. Frederick M. Hess (Cambridge, MA: Harvard Education Press, 2008): 181–206.

2. On a personal note, Louis and I (Tony) came to the work of urban school reform from very different disciplinary perspectives. Louis was trained as a cognitive psychologist and had worked for a period of time at Bell Laboratories. My initial training had been in educational statistics; gradually over time I also became an organizational sociologist. So our professional lives started in very different places. Our collaboration began with a series of conversations going back and forth between Northwestern, where Louis was on the faculty, and my academic home at that time, the University of Chicago. One day as we sat in my office, Louis commented that he had read virtually nothing among the books on the shelves behind my desk. I confessed that I had had a similar experience sitting in his NWU office. We were most unusual colleagues, neither joined by discipline, institution of employment, nor research specialization. We did, however, share a common concern—how rigorous, practical inquiry could contribute to fundamental improvements in student learning in the Chicago Public Schools.

3. This paper focuses on problem-solving R&D in education. Key institutions supporting this activity are professional schools of education. While our remarks here can be interpreted as an implied criticism of these institutions, the concerns raised here can be, and have been, raised more generally about professional schools. Warren G. Bennis and James O'Toole, "How Business Schools Lost Their Way," *Harvard Business Review,* May 1, 2005, 96–104, for example, offers a similar critique of graduate schools of business.

4. James Hiebert, Ronald Gallimore, and James W. Stigler, "A Knowledge Base for the Teaching Profession: What Would It Look Like and How Can We Get One?" *Educational Researcher* 31, no. 5 (2002): 3–15; Anne K. Morris and James Hiebert, "Creating Shared

Instructional Products: An Alternative Approach to Improving Teaching," *Educational Researcher* 40 (2011): 5–14.

5. In our 2008 paper we called this Design-Educational Engineering-Development, or *DEED* for short.

6. Charles Kenney, *The Best Practice: How the New Quality Improvement Movement Is Transforming Medicine* (New York, NY: Public Affairs, 2008).

7. W. Edwards Deming's theory of profound knowledge is seminal in this field: W. Edwards Deming, *The New Economics for Industry, Government, Education* (Cambridge, MA: Massachusetts Institute of Technology, Center for Advanced Engineering Study, 1993). Its best known application is the Toyota Quality Management System, which stands as a model worldwide for quality manufacturing. See, for example, Mike Rother, *Toyota Kata: Managing People for Improvement, Adaptiveness, and Superior Results* (New York, NY: McGraw Hill, 2009).

   For a general introduction to its practical uses, see Gerald J. Langley et al., *The Improvement Guide: A Practical Approach to Enhancing Organizational Performance* (Indianapolis, IN: Jossey-Bass & Management Series, 2009).

8. See IHI's Web site (www.ihi.org) for information about its 100,000 Lives Campaign and 5 Million Lives Campaign. Numerous other examples are documented in *Best Care at Lower Cost: The Path to Continuously Learning Health Care in America* (Washington, DC: Institute of Medicine, 2012), http://www.iom.edu/Reports/2012/Best-Care-at-Lower-Cost-The-Path-to-Continuously-Learning-Health-Care-in-America.aspx.

9. Kenney, *The Best Practice*.

10. The IHI Web site is replete with numerous useful materials including an open introductory course on quality improvement, called Open School. See Institute for Healthcare Improvement (www.ihi.org).

11. Each of these points is extensively documented in the Institute of Medicine report, *Best Care at Lower Cost*, http://www.iom.edu/Reports/2012/Best-Care-at-Lower-Cost-The-Path-to-Continuously-Learning-Health-Care-in-America.aspx. For more, see: Atul Gawande, "How Do We Heal Medicine?" Ted Talk, April 2012, http://www.ted.com/talks/atul_gawande_how_do_we_heal_medicine.html.

12. For research on communities of practice, see Etienne Wenger, *Communities of Practice: Learning, Meaning, and Identity* (New York, NY: Cambridge University Press, 1998).

   For a treatment on action research, see Cathy Caro-Bruce et al., *Creating Equitable Classrooms Through Action Research* (Thousand Oaks, CA: Corwin Press, 2007).

   For research on lesson study, see James W. Sigler and James Hiebert, *The Teaching Gap* (New York, NY: Free, 1999); Catherine C. Lewis, *Lesson Study: A Handbook of Teaching-Led Instructional Change* (Philadelphia, PA: Research for Better Schools, 2002).

   For discussions on the scholarship of teaching and learning, see Ernest L. Boyer, *Scholarship Reconsidered: Priorities of the Professoriate* (Princeton, NJ: Carnegie Foundation for the Advancement of Teaching, 1990); Lee S. Shulman, "Taking Learning Seriously," *Change: The Magazine of Higher Learning* 31, no. 4 (1999): 10–17; Pat Hutchings and Lee S. Shulman, "The Scholarship of Teaching: New Elaborations, New Developments," *Change: The Magazine of Higher Learning* 31, no. 5 (1999): 10–15; Mary Huber and Pat Hutchings, "Building the Teaching Commons," *Change: The Magazine of Higher Learning* 38, no. 3 (2006): 24–31.

13. Donald J. Peurach, Joshua L. Glazer, and Sarah W. Lenhoff, "The Developmental Evaluation of School Improvement Networks." *Educational Policy* (In press). Michael Quinn Patton, *Developmental Evaluation: Applying Complexity Concepts to Enhance Innovation and Use* (New York, NY: Guilford Press, 2010). See also: Jon R. Dolle et al., "More Than a Network: Building Communities for Educational Improvement," in *Design-Based Implementation Research: Theories, Methods, and Exemplars,* eds. Barry J. Fishman and William R. Penuel, vol. 112 of National Society for the Study of Education Yearbook (New York, NY: Teachers College Record, 2014), 443–463.

14. For a good overview of this work, see Fishman and Penuel, *Design-Based Implementation Research.*

Introduction

1. James Hiebert, Ronald Gallimore, and James W. Stigler, "A Knowledge Base for the Teaching Profession: What Would It Look Like and How Can We Get One?" *Educational Researcher* 31, no. 5 (2002): 3–15.

2. "Tom Vander Ark—Testimony for the House Appropriations Committee," published online via the Bill & Melinda Gates Foundation, Press Room, May 22, 2001, http://www .gatesfoundation.org/media-center/speeches/2001/05/tom-vander-ark-2001-house -appropriations-committee.

3. There were actually many practice-based roots to the small schools movement. One of the leading resources here was Michelle Fine and colleagues in the Philadelphia Schools Collaborative that developed small schools-within-schools (later called small learning communities) in the early 1990s. For case studies of effective urban small high schools, see Thomas Toch, *High Schools on a Human Scale* (Boston, MA: Beacon, 2003).

4. For examples, see Valerie E. Lee and Anthony S. Bryk, "A Multilevel Model of the Social Distribution of High School Achievement," *Sociology of Education* 62, no. 3 (1989): 172; Valerie E. Lee and Julia B. Smith, "High School Size: Which Works Best and for Whom?" *Educational Evaluation and Policy Analysis* 19, no. 3 (1997): 205. Small size was also a factor identified by Anthony S. Bryk, Peter B. Holland, and Valerie E. Lee, *Catholic Schools and the Common Good* (Cambridge, MA: Harvard University Press, 1993).

5. A question has been raised as to exactly how much the Bill & Melinda Gates Foundation spent on this initiative. Bill Gates mentioned the frequently cited figure of $2 billion in an annual letter in 2009. More recently, Gates Foundation spokesman Chris Williams claimed the actual amount was $650 million. See Valerie Strauss, "How Much Bill Gates's Disappointing Small-Schools Effort Really Cost," *Washington Post,* June 9, 2014, http:// www.washingtonpost.com/blogs/answer-sheet/wp/2014/06/09/how-much-bill-gatess -disappointing-small-schools-effort-really-cost/.

6. Penny Bender Sebring et al., *Charting Reform: Chicago Teachers Take Stock* (Chicago, IL: Consortium on Chicago School Research, 1995); Anthony S. Bryk and Barbara Schneider, *Social Trust: A Moral Resource for School Improvement* (Chicago, IL: Consortium on Chicago School Research, 1996). See also Anthony S. Bryk and Barbara L. Schneider, *Trust in Schools: A Core Resource for Improvement* (New York, NY: Russell Sage Foundation, 2002).

7. Becky Smerdon and Barbara Means, *Evaluation of the Bill & Melinda Gates Foundation's High School Grants Initiative: 2001–2005* (Washington, DC: American Institutes for Research/SRI International, August 2006).

8. Karen S. Louis and Sharon D. Kruse, *Professionalism and Community: Perspectives on Reforming Urban Schools* (Thousand Oaks, CA: Corwin Press, 1995).

9. For a further discussion of this design-development orientation, see Anthony S. Bryk and Louis Gomez, "Reinventing a Research and Development Capacity," in *The Future of Educational Entrepreneurship: Possibilities for School Reform,* ed. Frederick M. Hess (Cambridge, MA: Harvard Education Press, 2008), 181–206. In the original paper we referred to such activity as Design-Educational Engineering-Development (DEED). In the interests of simplicity, this book uses the shortened term, *design-development.* The latter also provides a more ready connection to closely related, emerging literature on design-based implementation. See, for example, Jon R. Dolle et al., "More Than a Network: Building Communities for Educational Improvement," in *Design-Based Implementation Research: Theories, Methods, and Exemplars,* eds. Barry J. Fishman and William R. Penuel, vol. 112 of National Society for the Study of Education Yearbook (New York, NY: Teachers College Record, 2014), 443–463.

10. For an evocative general account of this problem in other organizational fields, see the discussion of "clusterfug": Huggy Rao and Robert I. Sutton, *Scaling Up Excellence* (New York, NY: Crown Business Books, 2014). They describe a set of circumstances in which three factors join: Illusion that it is possible to spread a reform faster than the facts warrant, Impatience in rolling out reform because of emotional commitments to an urgency for change, and Incompetence where decision makers truly lack the requisite knowledge and skill to effect the desired reforms. High school redesign was a "clusterfug."

11. This failure is the nature of innovation where we may have a great idea but really don't yet know exactly how to make it work. Learning from failure is the core analytic disposition in design-development activities, continuous quality improvement, and entrepreneurial start-ups. For sample conversations about this in contexts outside education, see Martin Dewhurst, Bryan Hancock, and Diana Ellsworth, "Redesigning Knowledge Work," *Harvard Business Review,* January–February 2013. Also see Ronald A. Heifetz and Donald L. Laurie, "The Work of Leadership," *Harvard Business Review,* December 2001. See also Gerald J. Langley et al., *The Improvement Guide: A Practical Approach to Enhancing Organizational Performance* (Indianapolis, IN: Jossey-Bass & Management Series, 2009). Within the education context, see Dolle et al., "More Than a Network."

12. The final evaluation report commissioned by the Bill & Melinda Gates Foundation (Smerdon and Means, *Evaluation of the Bill and Melinda Gates Foundation's High School Grants Initiative,* August 2006) concluded that "although there have been some isolated examples of apparently successful small schools emerging from the restructuring of a large high school, these have been the exception rather than the rule." In a harsh appraisal, the Huffington Post concluded that the movement was an abject failure; Leonie Haimson, "The Most Dangerous Man in America," *Huffington Post,* July 10, 2010, http://www.huffingtonpost.com/leonie-haimson/the-most-dangerous-man-in_b_641832.html.

Subsequent research has selectively modified this opinion. A report released by MDRC, Howard S. Bloom, and Rebecca Unterman, *Sustained Positive Effects on Graduation Rates Produced by New York City's Small Public High Schools of Choice* (New York City: MDRC Policy Brief, 2012) documents the success in New York City for many of the New Century High Schools initiated by Michele Cahill at the Carnegie Corporation of New York and Robert Hughes at New Visions for Public Schools.

Unlike the implement fast and wide strategy characteristic of most of the small schools initiatives, this effort was anchored in deep understanding of both the problems to solve and how to convert good ideas into constructive action, had access to considerable expertise necessary to undertake the work, and was a green field initiative (i.e., start small and grow over time, based on what one learns along the way). It also benefited from the considerable design-development expertise at New Visions, which acted as a learning hub supporting the launch of these schools. So in significant ways, New Century High Schools developed largely along the lines of a networked improvement community.

13. Daniel, Golden, "Bill Gates' School Crusade," *Bloomberg Businessweek,* July 17, 2010.

14. See, for example, Steven Brill, "The Rubber Room," *New Yorker,* August 31, 2009. http:// www.newyorker.com/magazine/2009/08/31/the-rubber-room.

15. Value-added analyses had emerged as a powerful source of evidence in policy analyses and evaluation of various human resource development strategies. Many new technical and logistical issues arose in moving to use these procedures to evaluate the performance of individual teachers.

    Extensive research continues on the technical properties of value-added statistics, particularly their reliability and validity when used to make judgments about individual teachers. Significant summaries can be found at Carnegie Knowledge Network (www .carnegieknowledgenetwork.org), a series of papers published by The Brookings Institution (www.brookings.edu/research/topics/education), and the MET Project (http:// metproject.org).

16. Examples abound here. To name just a few: (1) most districts do not operate data systems that reliably document the linkage between teachers and the students they actually instruct; in many instances, the organization of instruction does not permit a simple one-to-one mapping of teachers and students (e.g., team teaching arrangement with push-in supplemental services for lower-performing students); (2) the necessary assessment data to compute value-added scores exist only for between 25 and 30 percent of teachers; (3) annual learning gains, the basis for value-added estimates, also include summer effects for which classroom teachers are not responsible; and (4) little consideration has been given to possible unintended consequences that might ensue.

17. Ronald F. Elmore and Deanna Burney, *Investing in Teacher Learning: Staff Development and Instructional Improvement in Community School District #2, New York City* (Washington, DC: National Commission on Teaching and America's Future, 1997); Ronald F. Elmore and Deanna Burney, *Continuous Improvement in Community District # 2, New York City* (Pittsburgh, PA: High Performance Learning Communities Project, Learning Research and Development Center, University of Pittsburgh, 1998).

18. Elaine Fink and Lauren B. Resnick, "Developing Principals as Instructional Leaders," *Phi Delta Kappan,* 82, no. 8 (April 2001): 598–606.

19. For example, the incidence of test-score cheating accelerated, and select students were ignored as accountability schemes directed attention toward some students but not others. On test-score cheating, see, for example, Brian A. Jacob and Steven D. Levitt, "Rotten Apples: An Investigation of the Prevalence and Predictors of Teacher Cheating," *Quarterly Journal of Economics,* 118, no. 3 (2003): 843–877. Public scandals about test cheating subsequently emerged in a number of cities. Among the most extensively investigated are the Atlanta public schools: "Deal Releases Findings of Atlanta School Probe," released July 5,

2011, http://gov.georgia.gov/press-releases/2011-07-05/deal-releases-findings-atlanta-school-probe.

For research on the emergence of "bubble kids," see Jennifer Booher-Jennings, "Below the Bubble: 'Educational Triage' and the Texas Accountability System," *American Educational Research Journal* 42, no. 2 (2005): 231–268.

20. G. Alfred Hess, *Restructuring Urban Schools: A Chicago Perspective* (New York, NY: Teachers College, Columbia University, 1995); Anthony S. Bryk et al., *Charting Chicago School Reform: Democratic Localism as a Lever for Change* (Boulder, CO: Westview, 1998).

21. The idea of "disruptive change" is an educational buzzword that has taken on great salience in the past few years since the publication of Clayton M. Christensen, Michael B. Horn, and Curtis W. Johnson, *Disrupting Class: How Disruptive Innovation Will Change the Way the World Learns* (New York, NY: McGraw-Hill, 2008).

22. See the Huffington Post postmortem on high school redesign in note 12. Another prominent example is the effects of Chicago's retention-in-grade policy on neighborhood high schools. The policy dramatically increased the number of special education students assigned to these schools, making these already stressed school environments even harder to improve. See Melissa Roderick et al., *Ending Social Promotion: Results from the First Two Years* (Chicago, IL: University of Chicago Consortium on Chicago School Research, December 1999); Melissa Roderick et al., *Update: Ending Social Promotion: Passing, Retention, and Achievement Trends Among Promoted and Retained Students, 1995–1999* (Chicago, IL: University of Chicago Consortium on Chicago School Research, September 2000); Jenny Nagaoka and Melissa Roderick, *Ending Social Promotion: The Effects of Retention* (Chicago, IL: University of Chicago Consortium on Chicago School Research, March 2004); and Elaine Allensworth, *Ending Social Promotion: Dropout Rates in Chicago After Implementation of the Eighth-Grade Promotion Gate* (Chicago, IL: University of Chicago Consortium on Chicago School Research, March 2004).

For a further elaboration on this theme, see chapter 1 of Huggy Rao and Robert I. Sutton, *Scaling Up Excellence* (New York, NY: Crown Business Books, 2014), 3–32. Although working independently, both we and Rao and Sutton drew on similar bodies of scholarship and practice to come to the same conclusion about the importance of going slow to scale better and faster later.

23. We introduce and use throughout this book a number of key terms and concepts from improvement science and networked communities. These terms appear in italics when introduced for the first time. A brief description for each also appears in the glossary at the back of the book. In striving for clarity in this regard, we minimize other uses of italics throughout the text.

24. Bryk and Gomez, "Reinventing"; Dolle et al., "More Than a Network."

25. For documentation of this phenomenon in educational reform, see Paul Hill and Mary Beth Celio, *Fixing Urban Schools* (Washington, DC: Brookings Institution Press, 1998); Paul Hill, Christine Campbell, and James Harvey, *It Takes a City: Getting Serious About Urban School Reform* (Washington, DC: Brookings Institution Press, 1999).

26. This theme about learning in practice has a long tradition reaching back to contributions from both John Dewey and Kurt Lewin. See, for example, John Dewey, *Democracy and Education: An Introduction to the Philosophy of Education* (New York, NY: Macmillan, 1916); and Kurt Lewin, *A Dynamic Theory of Personality: Selected Papers* (New York & London: McGraw-Hill Books, 1935).

27. There is a long-standing and well-documented research-practice divide in education. See, for example, *Recommendations Regarding Research Priorities: An Advisory Report to the National Education Research Policy and Priorities Board* (Washington, DC: National Academy of Education, 1999); M. Suzanne Donovan and James W. Pellegrino, eds., "Learning and Instruction: A SERP Research Agenda" (research for the National Research Council, The National Academies Press, Washington, DC, 2003); John D. Bransford et al., eds., *The Role of Research in Educational Improvement* (Cambridge, MA: Harvard Education Press, 2009); and Cynthia E. Coburn and Mary Kay Stein, *Research and Practice in Education: Building Alliances, Bridging the Divide* (Lanham, MD: Rowman & Littlefield, 2010).

28. For a discussion along these lines, see Rocco J. Perla, Lloyd P. Provost, and Gareth J. Parry, "The Seven Propositions of the Science of Improvement," *Quality Management in Health Care* 22, no. 3 (2013): 170–186.

29. See Gerald J. Langley et al., *The Improvement Guide*, 217.

30. Donald Berwick, "The Science of Improvement," *JAMA* 299, no. 10 (2008): 1182–1184. He argues that quality improvement in health-care organizations, which are large complex human-social-technical systems, requires a different kind of methodology than is associated with, for example, assessing the efficacy of a specific drug. He makes a compelling argument that the methodology of quality improvement is a form of disciplined inquiry that is properly seen as a scientific endeavor.

31. For an inspiring account along these lines, see Ken Robinson, "Bring On the Learning Revolution!" http://www.ted.com/talks/sir_ken_robinson_bring_on_the_revolution.html.

32. This story is recounted by James Surowiecki, *The Wisdom of Crowds* (New York: Anchor, 2005). The original account can be found in the following report on the World Health Organization, "A Multicentre Collaboration to Investigate the Cause of Severe Acute Respiratory Syndrome," *The Lancet* 361 (2003): 1730–1733.

33. These examples and more are detailed in Michael Nielsen, *Reinventing Discovery: The New Era of Networked Science* (Princeton, NJ: Princeton University Press, 2012).

34. The development of Wikipedia and the Linux operating system are exemplars of the latter. For a detailed discussion of the Linux network, see Steven Weber, *The Success of Open Source* (Cambridge, MA: Harvard University Press, 2004); Anthony S. Bryk, Louis M. Gomez, and Alicia Grunow, "Getting Ideas into Action: Building Networked Improvement Communities in Education," in *Frontiers in Sociology of Education*, ed. Maureen T. Hallinan (New York, NY: Springer, 2011), 156–159.

35. This theme is developed by both Surowiecki, *The Wisdom of Crowds*, and Nielsen, *Reinventing Discovery*.

36. As discussed later, key here is the role of the network hub or, more specifically, how a specific set of network functions is exercised within collaborative improvement inquiries. We are indebted to Goldsmith and Eggers for articulating the critical role that hubs play in learning to improve networks. See Stephen Goldsmith and William D. Eggers, *Governing by Network: The New Shape of the Public Sector* (Washington, DC: Brookings Institution Press, 2004).

   Many of these same functions are characteristic of one of the roles played by comprehensive school reform organizations such as America's Choice and Success for All. See Donald J. Peurach and Joshua L. Glazer, "Reconsidering Replication: New Perspectives on Large-Scale School Improvement," *Journal of Educational Change* 13, no. 2 (2012):

155–190. See also David K. Cohen et al., *Improvement by Design* (Chicago, IL: University of Chicago Press, 2014).

37. For work on professional learning communities, see Richard DuFour, Rebecca Burnette DuFour, and Robert E. Eaker, *Revisiting Professional Learning Communities at Work: New Insights for Improving Schools* (Bloomington, IN: Solution Tree Press, 2008).

   For work on communities of practice, see Etienne Wenger, *Communities of Practice: Learning, Meaning, and Identity* (New York, NY: Cambridge University Press, 1998).

   For work on faculty inquiry groups, see Mary T. Huber, *The Promise of Faculty Inquiry for Teaching and Learning Basic Skills,* report for Strengthening Pre-collegiate Education in Community Colleges (SPECC) (Stanford, CA: The Carnegie Foundation for the Advancement of Teaching, 2008).

38. See Bryk et al., "Getting Ideas."

39. Larry Cuban, "Reforming Again, Again, and Again," *Educational Researcher* 19, no. 1 (1990): 3.

40. See indicators 25 and 28 of Grace Kena et al., "The Condition of Education 2014" (NCES 2014-083, Washington, DC: U.S. Department of Education, National Center for Education Statistics, 2014).

41. The 2011 MetLife survey of teachers shows morale at the lowest level in twenty years; the number of teachers who are very or fairly likely to leave the profession is 29 percent, up from 17 percent in 2009; those who are very satisfied are at 44 percent, down from 59 percent in 2009. "The MetLife Survey of The American Teacher," March 2012, https://www.metlife.com/assets/cao/contributions/foundation/american-teacher/MetLife-Teacher-Survey-2011.pdf.

42. The Triple Aims of Improvement is a signature initiative of the Institute for Healthcare Improvement. Its formulation of the Triple Aims consists in improving the quality of the patient experience, improving the overall health of a population, and reducing per capita costs. Our formulation is a slight adaptation for education that draws directly on the IHI's framework.

Chapter 1

1. Donald M. Berwick, foreword to *The Improvement Guide: A Practical Approach to Enhancing Organizational Performance* by Gerald J. Langley et al. (Indianapolis, IN: Jossey-Bass & Management Series, 2009).

2. Jonah Lehrer, "Imagine That: Fostering Creativity in the Workplace," NPR, added March 21, 2012, http://www.npr.org/2012/03/21/148607182/fostering-creativity-and-imagination-in-the-workplace.

3. Jonah Lehrer, *Imagine: How Creativity Works* (Boston, MA: Houghton Mifflin, 2012).

4. This idea is supported in neo-institutional theory. See Paul J. DiMaggio and Walter W. Powell, "The Iron Cage Revisited: Institutional Isomorphism and Collective Rationality in Organizational Fields," *American Sociological Review* 48 (1983): 147–160. In the absence of a broadly recognized professional status, institutions affirm their legitimacy in symbolic ways—by being on the cutting edge of reform. The new idea has currency precisely because it is new, regardless of what the problem actually is and the presence or absence of any evidence warranting the claims made.

5. The authors wish to acknowledge Chris Thorn's contribution in developing the TIF case. Chris provided technical assistance to TIF grantees throughout this time period and

had access to a variety of published and unpublished communications as this initiative proceeded forward.

6. See, for example, Thomas S. Dee and Benjamin J. Keys, "Does Merit Pay Reward Good Teachers? Evidence from a Randomized Experiment," *Journal of Policy Analysis and Management*, 23, no. 3 (2004): 471; Matthew G. Springer et al., *Teacher Pay for Performance: Experimental Evidence from the Project on Incentives in Teaching* (Nashville, TN: National Center on Performance Incentives at Vanderbilt University, Society for Research on Educational Effectiveness, 2011); Julia A. Marsh et al., *A Big Apple for Educators. New York City's Experiment with Schoolwide Performance Bonuses: Final Evaluation Report* (Washington, DC: Fund for Public Schools, 2011, http://www.rand.org/content/dam/rand/pubs/monographs/2011/RAND_MG1114.pdf); U.S. Department of Education, "Legislation, Regulations, and Guidance—Race to the Top Fund," http://www2.ed.gov/programs/racetothetop/legislation.html; U.S. Department of Education, "September 23, 2011: Letter to Chief State School Officers Regarding NCLB Flexibility," http://www2.ed.gov/policy/gen/guid/secletter/110923.html; U.S. Department of Education, "Funding Status—Teacher Incentive Fund," http://www2.ed.gov/programs/teacherincentive/funding.html; Bill & Melinda Gates Foundation, "Foundation Commits $335 Million to Promote Effective Teaching and Raise Student Achievement," http://www.gatesfoundation.org/Media-Center/Press-Releases/2009/11/Foundation-Commits-$335-Million-to-Promote-Effective-Teaching-and-Raise-Student-Achievement; Steven Glazerman and Allison Seifullah, *An Evaluation of the Teacher Advancement Program (TAP) in Chicago: Year Two Impact Report* (Chicago, IL: Joyce Foundation, 2010), http://www.mathematica-mpr.com/publications/pdfs/education/tap_yr2_rpt.pdf; U.S. Department of Education, "Funding Status—Race to the Top Early Learning Challenge Program," http://www2.ed.gov/programs/racetothetop-earlylearningchallenge/funding.html.

7. A major national evaluation conducted by SRI in 2012 underscored the complexity of implementing compensation reform, including significant technical challenges still remaining in implementing such reforms. The evaluation offered a strong cautionary tale for policy makers eager to quickly introduce fundamental change to educator compensation. Daniel C. Humphrey et al., *Teacher Incentive Fund: First Implementation Report, 2006 and 2007 Grantees* (Washington, DC: U.S. Department of Education & SRI International, 2012), http://www2.ed.gov/rschstat/eval/teaching/tif/report.pdf.

8. Dan C. Lortie, *Schoolteacher: A Sociological Study* (Chicago: University of Chicago, 1975), offered a seminal contribution on the sociology of teaching. This effort has been updated and further refined in the work of numerous scholars, including Susan Moore Johnson, *Teachers at Work: Achieving Success in Our Schools* (New York: Basic, 1990); Milbrey W. McLaughlin, Joan E. Talbert, and Nina Bascia, *The Contexts of Teaching in Secondary Schools: Teachers' Realities* (New York, NY: Columbia University Press, 1990); and David Cohen, *Teaching and Its Predicaments* (Cambridge, MA: Harvard University Press, 2011).

9. Melissa A. Clark et al., *The Effectiveness of Secondary Math Teachers from Teach For America and the Teaching Fellows Programs (NCEE 2013-4015)* (Washington, DC: National Center for Education Evaluation and Regional Assistance, Institute of Education Sciences, U.S. Department of Education, 2013). See also Steven M. Glazerman, Daniel Mayer, and Paul Decker, "Alternative Routes to Teaching: The Impacts of Teach For America on Student Achievement and Other Outcomes," *Journal of Policy Analysis and Management*, 25, no. 1 (2006), 75–96.

10. Thomas J. Kane, Jonah E. Rockroff, and Douglas O. Staiger, "What Does Certification Tell Us About Teacher Effectiveness? Evidence from New York City," *Economics of Education Review* 27, no. 6 (2008): 615–631.

11. See a review by Richard Ingersoll and Jeffrey M. Kralik, "The Impact of Mentoring on Teacher Retention: What the Research Says," *Research Review: Teaching Quality* (Denver, CO: Education Commission of the States, February, 2004). And also see Kavita Kapadia, Vanessa Coca, and John Q. Easton, "Keeping New Teachers: A First Look at the Influences of Induction in the Chicago Public Schools," (Consortium on Chicago School Research at the University of Chicago, January 2007).

12. According to one survey in 2012, teachers work on average ten hours and forty minutes out of every school day. Scholastic, "Primary Sources: 2012, America's Teachers on the Teaching Profession" (project completed by Scholastic and the Bill & Melinda Gates Foundation, 2012): 13.

13. According to Pfeffer [Jeffrey Pfeffer, "Changing Mental Models: HR's Most Important Task," *Human Resource Management* 44, no. 2 (2005): 123–128.]: "There is a lot of evidence . . . that the growing emphasis on individual accountability—something, by the way, that is completely inconsistent with the lessons of the quality movement—hinders learning and even discovering mistakes" (126).

14. Jarrod Bolte, personal communication, 2014.

15. (Later renamed *The Design of Everyday Things*): Donald A. Norman, *The Design of Everyday Things* (London: MIT, 1998).

16. It's noteworthy that Elliot Soloway and colleagues took up Norman's message with a movement in scholarship called learner-centered design. Elliot Soloway, Mark Guzdia, and Kenneth E. Hay, "Learner-Centered Design: The Challenge for HCI in the 21st Century," *Interactions* 1, no. 2 (1994): 36–48. This work, while important, has not gained traction in the construction of large-scale interventions like those described here.

17. This is true, for example, among national board-certified teachers. Dan Goldhaber, "National Board Teachers Are More Effective, But Are They in the Classrooms Where They're Needed the Most?" *Education Finance and Policy* 1, no. 3 (2006): 371–381.

18. See, for example, Suzanne Wilson, ed. "Teacher Quality" (White paper, National Academy of Education, Washington, DC, 2009).

19. Jeffrey Pfeffer and Robert I. Sutton, *The Knowing–Doing Gap: How Smart Companies Turn Knowledge into Action* (Cambridge, MA: Harvard Business Press, 2000).

20. Bringing the voice of users into design can be accomplished in many ways. Sometimes the most appropriate approach is to observe and study people in their work contexts—in essence, using explicit techniques to see and understand the nature of work on the job floor. At other times it is more appropriate to engage users on design. These approaches are called codesign. Here users are actors in the design process. Both of these approaches are among a family of techniques that allow designs to be more user-centered.

21. Jal Mehta, *The Allure of Order: High Hopes, Dashed Expectations, and the Troubled Quest to Remake American Schooling* (Oxford: Oxford University Press, 2013).

22. Mike Rother, *Toyota Kata: Managing People for Improvement, Adaptiveness, and Superior Results* (New York, NY: McGraw-Hill, 2009), describes why Toyota was so willing to share with competitors various process solutions that it had developed. The key to quality and to Toyota's premier status in the field was the culture of improvement that imbued throughout the organization. All who work there are potential improvers, and all who

manage there are coaches for such improvement. These are the "two Kata" defined at Toyota: an improvement Kata and the coaching Kata.

23. Andrew Delano Abbott, *The System of Professions: An Essay on the Division of Expert Labor* (Chicago, IL: University of Chicago, 1988).

Chapter 2

1. Stephen Jay Gould, "The Median Isn't the Message," *Discover* 6 (1985): 40–42.
2. Andrew F. Beck et al., "Improved Documentation and Care Planning with an Asthma-Specific History and Physical," *Hospital Pediatrics*, 2 (2012): 194–201.
3. Chaya Merrill and Pamela L. Owens, "Reasons for Being Admitted to the Hospital Through the Emergency Department for Children and Adolescents, 2004" (statistical brief #33, June 2007, http://www.hcup-us.ahrq.gov/reports/statbriefs/sb33.pdf).
4. *President's Task Force on Environmental Health Risks and Safety Risks to Children: Coordinated Federal Action Plan to Reduce Racial and Ethnic Asthma Disparities* (Washington, DC: Environmental Protection Agency, May 2012, http://www.epa.gov/childrenstaskforce/).
5. Jeffrey Simmons, personal communication, 2014.
6. The efforts of Tony Alvarado, Elaine Fink, and District 2 colleagues were detailed by the High Performing Learning Communities Project. It remains, even today, an extraordinary exemplar of ambitious teaching and learning carried out with reliability at a relatively large scale. See Richard Elmore and Deanne Burney, "School Variation and Systemic Instructional Improvement in Community School District #2, New York City," http://files.eric.ed.gov/fulltext/ED429264.pdf.
7. Michael S. Garet et al., *The Impact of Two Professional Development Interventions on Early Reading Instruction and Achievement* (no. 20084034, Washington, DC: Institute of Education Sciences, 2008).
8. Irene Fountas and Gay Su Pinnell, *The Continuum of Literacy Learning, Grades PreK-8*, 2nd ed. (Portsmouth, NH: Heinemann, 2010).
9. For more information, see www.literacycollaborative.org.
10. Gina Biancarosa, Anthony S. Bryk, and Emily R. Dexter, "Assessing the Value-Added Effects of Literacy Collaborative Professional Development on Student Learning," *Elementary School Journal* 111, no. 1 (2010): 7–34.
11. On the significance of relational trust, principal leadership, and school-based professional community on changes in student learning over time, see Anthony S. Bryk et al., *Organizing Schools for Improvement: Lessons from Chicago* (Chicago, IL: University of Chicago Press, 2010).
12. For the results on the variability in coaching exposure, see Allison Atteberry and Anthony S. Bryk, "Analyzing Teacher Participation in Literacy Coaching Activities," *Elementary School Journal*, 112, no. 2 (2011): 356–382. For results documenting the variability in the quality of comprehensive literacy instruction in classrooms, how this changed over time, and how this linked to differences in classroom-level value-added learning, see Heather J. Hough et al., "Assessing Teacher Practice and Development: The Case of Comprehensive Literacy Instruction," *School Effectiveness and School Improvement* 24, no. 4 (2013): 452–485.
13. On balance, the causal warrant for the IES field trial is in principle stronger in that the study was designed as a randomized field trial. In contrast, the accelerated longitudinal

cohort design used in the Literacy Collaborative study is subject to one major source of confounding: other factors being introduced into study schools occurring coterminus with the intervention. Biancarosa, Bryk, and Dexter, "Assessing the Value-Added Effects," examine and discount the plausibility of this alternative explanation, but it cannot be completely eliminated.

It is well known that there is an inherent tension between concerns about internal validity (i.e., did A truly cause B in this particular instance?) and concerns about external validity (i.e., what is the evidence that results generalize to other contexts?). The traditional RCT places almost exclusive premium on the first. Improvement research, while attending to internal validity issues, places premium on the second. That is, how do we achieve "B results" over and over again, regardless of conditions? For a seminal discussion on this topic, see Donald T. Campbell and Julian C. Stanley, "Experimental and Quasi-Experimental Designs for Research on Teaching," in *Handbook of Research and Teaching*, ed. N. L. Gage (Washington, DC: American Educational Research Association, 1963), 171–246.

14. A seminal contribution on this point can be found in Herbert A. Simon, *The Sciences of the Artificial* (Cambridge, MA: MIT, 1996). Simon demonstrated that combinations and interactions even among a small number of primary factors can result in enormous complexity in what we observe. The key point is that while observed activity may look highly variable—unique—sitting beneath the observed may well be regularities that can be identified and become a resource for improvement.

15. Atul Gawande, *Better: A Surgeon's Notes on Performance* (New York, NY: Metropolitan, 2007).

16. We acknowledge that concerns have been raised about the overuse of C-sections in childbirth situations. Our point is not to argue about the appropriateness in choice of the procedure. Rather it is about how a process can be carefully detailed so as to produce quality outcomes reliably over and over—in this case, in the hands of different doctors working under varied health-care conditions.

17. Sian Beilock, *Choke* (New York, NY: Free Press, 2011). Also Daniel Kahneman, *Thinking, Fast and Slow* (New York, NY: Farrar, Straus and Giroux, 2011).

18. Edwin Hutchins, "How a Cockpit Remembers Its Speeds," *Cognitive Science* 19, no. 3 (1995): 265–288.

19. Psychologists refer to this as automaticity. Such automaticity plays a key role in expertise development. It is a key feature distinguishing between novices and experts, and its development marks a key juncture in moving toward expertise. See K. Andres Ericsson, Ralf Th. Krampe, and Clemens Tesch-Romer, "The Role of Deliberate Practice in the Acquisition of Expert Performance," *Psychological Review* 100 (1993): 393–394. See also Bent Flyvbjerg, *Making Social Science Matter: Why Social Inquiry Fails and How It Can Succeed Again* (Oxford, UK: Cambridge University Press, 2001).

20. V. Agora et al., "Communication Failures in Patient Sign-Out and Suggestions for Improvement: A Critical Incident Analysis," *Quality and Safety in Health Care* 14, no. 6 (2005): 401–407.

21. Charles Kenney, *The Best Practice: How the New Quality Movement Is Transforming Medicine* (New York, NY: Public Affairs, 2008), 171. See also David Leonhardt, "Making Healthcare Better," *New York Times Magazine*, November 3, 2009, http://www.nytimes .com/2009/11/08/magazine/08Healthcare-t.html?pagewanted=all&_r=0, for an account

of the extraordinary improvement efforts led by Brent James at Intermountain Healthcare system.

22. Patricia Graham wrote about this long-standing progressive dilemma almost three decades ago; see Patricia A. Graham, "Schools: The Raw, the Cooked, and the Half Baked," *Massachusetts Association of School Committees Journal* 18, no. 3 (1985): 12–17. She offers a contrasting metaphor of a baked apple versus a pork chop. A baked apple can be under- or overcooked, and it remains edible. A pork chop when well done is succulent, the basis of a delicious meal. When undercooked, however, it can kill you. In this account, the crafts view of teaching is analogous to the pork chop.

23. For a further discussion of these polar opposites, see Anthony S. Bryk, Louis M. Gomez, and Alicia Grunow, "Getting Ideas into Action: Building Networked Improvement Communities in Education," in *Frontiers in Sociology of Education*, ed. Maureen T. Hallinan (New York, NY: Springer: 2011), 181–206.

24. The choice of words *practice-based evidence* is deliberate. We aim to signal a key difference in the relationship between inquiry and improvement under a quality improvement framework versus that typically assumed in the more commonly used expression *evidence-based practice*. Implicit in the latter is that evidence of efficacy exists somewhere outside local practice and practitioners should simply implement these evidence-based practices. Improvement work, in contrast, is an ongoing activity that is continuously anchored in evidence, emerging from local practice, as to what might be done next to further improve it.

We are indebted to Lawrence Green for introducing us to the concept of practice-based evidence and how it relates and contrasts with formulations about evidence-based practice. See Lawrence W. Green, "Making Research Relevant: If It Is an Evidence-Based Practice, Where's the Practice-Based Evidence?" *Family Practice* 25, Supplement 1 (2008): I20–I24. See also Michael Barkham and John Mellor-Clark, "Bridging Evidence-Based Practice and Practice-Based Evidence: Developing a Rigorous and Relevant Knowledge for the Psychological Therapies," *Clinical Psychology & Psychotherapy* 10, no. 6 (2003): 319–327.

25. For further details about each of these, see Isabel L. Beck and Margaret G. McKeown, "Text Talk: Capturing the Benefits of Read-Aloud Experiences for Young Children," *Reading Teacher* 55, no. 1 (September 2001): 10–20; Irene C. Fountas and Gay Su Pinnell, *Guided Reading: Good First Teaching for All Children* (Portsmouth, NH: Heinemann, 1996); Irene C. Fountas and Gay Su Pinnell, *Guiding Readers and Writers: Teaching Comprehension, Genre, and Content Literacy* (Portsmouth, NH: Heinemann, 2000); Irene C. Fountas and Gay Su Pinnell, *Teaching for Comprehension and Fluency: Thinking, Talking, and Writing About Reading, K–8* (Portsmouth, NH: Heinemann, 2006); Andrea McCarrier, Irene C. Fountas, and Gay Su Pinnell, *Interactive Writing: How Language and Literacy Come Together, K–2* (Portsmouth, NH: Heinemann, 2000); and Irene C. Fountas and Gay Su Pinnell, *Word Matters: Teaching Phonics and Spelling in the Reading-Writing Classroom* (Portsmouth, NH: Heinemann, 1998).

26. In general, a process may have many levels to it. Simply distinguishing macro from micro suffices for the purposes of the discussion in this book.

27. See http://uchicagoimpact.org/step for more information on this issue. Also see Irene C. Fountas and Gay Su Pinnell, *Fountas and Pinnell Benchmark Assessment System 1 Grades K–2, Levels A–N* (Portsmouth, NH: Heinemann Press, 2008).

28. For further details on this research on practice improvement see Hough et al., "Assessing Teacher Practice and Development."

29. In an earlier essay I referred to this an instructional system operating with a professional community; see Anthony S. Bryk, "Support a Science of Performance Improvement," *Phi Delta Kappan* 90, no. 8 (2009): 597–600. This aligns closely with David Cohen's detail of the essential infrastructure for teaching; see David K. Cohen, *Teaching and Its Predicaments* (Cambridge, MA: Harvard University Press, 2011). For application of these ideas in analysis of the functioning of a charter management organization, Achievement First, see Seneca Rosenberg, "Organizing for Quality in Education: Individual and Systemic Approaches to Teacher Quality," (dissertation, University of Michigan, 2012).

30. Atul Gawande, "The Difference Between Coaching and Teaching," *Askwith Forum*, Harvard Graduate School of Education, Cambridge, MA, November 2, 2012, https:// www.youtube.com/watch?v=VabtGPVVihA.

31. Richard T. Pascale, Jerry Sternin, and Monique Sternin, *The Power of Positive Deviance: How Unlikely Innovators Solve the World's Toughest Problems* (Boston, MA: Harvard Business, 2010).

32. See Gawande, *Better*.

Chapter 3

1. Atul Gawande, "How Do We Heal Medicine?" (TED Talk, March 2012, https://www.ted .com/talks/atul_gawande_how_do_we_heal_medicine).

2. The lack of full predictability about the consequences of a change is a basic property of complex adaptive systems. For further elaboration of this property, see Robert M. Axelrod and Michael D. Cohen, *Harnessing Complexity: Organizational Implications of a Scientific Frontier* (New York, NY: Free, 1999); John H. Miller and Scott E. Page, *Complex Adaptive Systems: An Introduction to Computational Models of Social Life* (Princeton, NJ: Princeton University Press, 2007).

3. *Best Care at Lower Cost: The Path to Continuously Learning Health Care in America,* (Washington, DC: Institute of Medicine, 2012, http://www.iom.edu/Reports/2012/Best -Care-at-Lower-Cost-The-Path-to-Continuously-Learning-Health-Care-in-America.aspx).

4. Institute of Medicine, *Crossing the Quality Chasm: A New Health System for the 21st Century* (Washington, DC: The National Academies Press, 2001).

5. Gawande, "How Do We Heal Medicine?"

6. Task complexity manifests in work activities that involve multiple nonrepetitive micro processes, in which a number of different tools may be used to carry them out and contingent action may be demanded (i.e., if this happens, then do the following; alternatively, if something different happens, then pursue this path).

    For example, in an earlier era round-robin reading was a common instructional practice. Each child in the class, one after another, read a few sentences aloud from a basal reader with the teacher correcting occasional errors. This instructional activity has a relatively simple, repetitive character. In contrast, the process of guided reading described in chapter 2 is intellectually much more demanding on teachers, as it requires a high degree of contingent action within each micro process.

7. This is now a well-known property of complex adaptive systems. For examples of this in health care, see Atul Gawande, "The Difference Between Coaching and Teaching," *Askwith Forum* Harvard Graduate School of Education (Cambridge, MA, November, 2012),

https://www.youtube.com/watch?v=VabtGPVVihA; see also Atul Gawande, "The Bell Curve," *New Yorker,* December 6, 2004: 82–91.

8. See, for example, research on one-to-one computing: Mark Warschauer, *Laptops and Literacy: Learning in the Wireless Classroom* (New York, NY: Teachers College Press, 2006). Also see Brian M. Stecher et al., "Class-Size Reduction in California: A Story of Hope, Promise, and Unintended Consequences," *Phi Delta Kappan,* 82, no. 9 (2003): 670–674.

9. Consider, for example, the fifty thousand–plus students who now apply each year to Teach For America. Those selected from this pool by TFA take on some of the most challenging teaching assignments across our nation. And there are thousands of other students just like them, graduating every year from our postsecondary institutions. At the Carnegie Foundation for the Advancement of Teaching, for example, we now have a dozen recent college graduates in a juniors fellows program. The fellows come from diverse colleges and universities all across the country. What these young people can do is impressive, well beyond what earlier generations could do at that age.

10. See *The Nation's Report Card: A First Look: 2013 Mathematics and Reading (NCES 2014-451)* (Washington, DC: Institute of Education Sciences, U.S. Department of Education, 2014).

11. Charles Kenney, *The Best Practice: How the New Quality Movement Is Transforming Medicine* (New York: Public Affairs, 2008), 19.

12. Anthony S. Bryk was an advisor to the Aspen Urban Superintendents program for fifteen years. The program brings together a small group of superintendents from leading districts all across the United States. In the privacy of their meetings, he has observed this conversation play out on several occasions.

13. See, for example, Steven Brill, "The Rubber Room," *New Yorker,* August 31, 2009, http://www.newyorker.com/magazine/2009/08/31/the-rubber-room. Interestingly, this same line of thinking characterized medicine in the pre-quality improvement era. See Kenney, *The Best Practice,* 19.

14. Comments offered by Tom Nolan at the Assessing-Teaching Improving-Learning September 2012 Forum, "Revisiting Teacher Evaluation." The "six percent" idea derives from application of the Pareto principle. In brief, this key principle in improvement science directs us toward identifying the major sources, typically five or six in number at most, contributing to undesirable outcomes and then focusing change efforts on these sources. Interestingly, as new teacher evaluation systems have rolled out, contrary to reformers' expectations, the percentage of teachers designated unsatisfactory remains small. The vast majority of teachers are in a broad middle group for whom improving teaching is the primary problem to solve.

15. Gerald J. Langley et al., *The Improvement Guide: A Practical Approach to Enhancing Organizational Performance* (Indianapolis, IN: Jossey-Bass & Management Series, 2009), 84.

16. As a point of clarification, when we use the term *predictable failures,* we mean this as a systems property. Predictably, the system will fail on some number or percent of occasions. We typically don't know exactly when or where or precisely for whom this will happen. Consequently, we have to address the system that generates the predictable failures.

17. See Donald M. Berwick, "Continuous Improvement as an Ideal in Health Care," *New England Journal of Medicine* 320, no. 1 (1989): 53–56. For a general treatment on this topic, see Langley et al., *The Improvement Guide.* For a discussion of this in the context

of leadership for human resource management, see Jeffrey Pfeffer, "Changing Mental Models: HR's Most Important Task," *Human Resource Management* 44, no. 2 (2005): 123–128. Also see Steven J. Spear, *The High-Velocity Edge: How Market Leaders Leverage Operational Excellence to Beat the Competition* (New York: McGraw-Hill, 2009).

18. Seneca Rosenberg, "Organizing for Quality in Education: Individual and Systemic Approaches to Teacher Quality" (dissertation, University of Michigan, 2012), uses this concept in analyzing how the charter management organization, Achievement First, is organizing itself to advance quality reliably as it scales.

19. See Berwick, "Continuous Improvement."

20. See, for example, William and Flora Hewlett Foundation, "Education Program: Strategic Plan," www.hewlett.org/uploads/documents/Education_Strategic_Plan_2010.pdf.

21. See David K. Cohen, *Teaching and Its Predicaments* (Cambridge, MA: Harvard University Press, 2011).

22. See the account of the Hancock School in Anthony S. Bryk et al., *Organizing Schools for Improvement: Lessons from Chicago* (Chicago, IL: University of Chicago Press, 2010). This school made substantial improvements in student outcomes over a six-year period. Because of the school's success, the principal was subsequently promoted to the central office and brought her lead staff developer with her. Their replacements at Hancock encountered difficulties in keeping the school moving forward. A few of the school's best teachers left. Support arrangements with community organizations atrophied, and collective faculty work on instructional improvement diminished. A few years later, the school had returned to the watchlist of underperforming schools in the Chicago Public School system.

23. For a detailed theoretical account and empirical analysis of systems organization and effects at the school site level, see Bryk et al., *Organizing Schools for Improvement*.

24. The phenomenon of new problem emergence is another property of complex adaptive systems (see Axelrod and Cohen, *Harnessing Complexity*, and Miller and Page, *Complex Adaptive Systems*). As a classic case of how changing conditions wrought disaster, see the account of fire jumpers in Norman Maclean, *Young Men & Fire* (Chicago, IL: University of Chicago Press, 1992). Donald M. Berwick, *Escape Fire: Designs for the Future of Health Care* (San Francisco: Jossey-Bass, 2004), uses the well-known account to describe the emerging health-care crisis in the United States. Similar analyses of the functioning of complex systems have been offered for the space shuttle disasters and nuclear plant meltdowns. These disasters are described in Spear, *The High-Velocity Edge*.

25. This description is a generic account of a phenomenon that operates in large school districts. The specific details, as experienced by an individual teacher, will of course vary among both schools and districts.

26. Many districts now deploy these interim tests, which are closely aligned to the end-of-year high-stakes accountability tests. While they are often described as formative assessments to improve instruction, some critics refer to these systems as "teaching to the test."

27. We need to distinguish between the ideas about system improvement developed here and early work on the concept of "systemic reform"; see Marshall S. Smith and Jennifer O'Day, *Teaching Policy and Research on Teaching* (Stanford, CA: CERAS, School of Education, Stanford University, 1988). They share common ground in that both deploy basic ideas about systems, for example, concerns about coordination, alignment, and reduction of redundancies and conflicting guidance. Systemic reform was principally a policy initiative

operating at a macro level. It was concerned with how federal and state governments could drive more coherent local action through aligning learning goals, curriculum, assessments and professional development. In contrast, the improvement of organizational operations, the principal focus of this book, starts on the job floor and makes the day-to-day work of principals, teachers, and others its focal activity. It sees these professionals as active improvers rather than primarily passive receivers of policies passed down from above. The initiative for change is situated in structured networks among educational professionals rather than in policy analysts and governmental leaders.

28. A compendium of these tools that emerged from over five decades of activity across diverse industries can be found in Langley et al., *The Improvement Guide*.

29. See Thomas Bailey, Dong Wook Jeong, and Sunny-Woo Cho, "Referral, Enrollment, and Completion in Developmental Education Sequences in Community Colleges," *Economics of Education Review* 29, no. 2 (2010): 255–270; Jenna Cullinane and Uri Treisman, "Improving Developmental Mathematics Education in Community Colleges: A Prospectus and Early Status Report on the Statway Initiative" (paper prepared for the NCPR Developmental Education Conference: What Policies and Practices Work for Students? Teachers College, Columbia University, NY, September 23–24, 2010); Anthony S. Bryk and Uri Treisman, "Make Math a Gateway, Not a Gatekeeper," *Chronicle of Higher Education,* April 18, 2010, B19–B20.

30. In the improvement literature, this diagram is also referred to as an Ishikawa diagram after organizational theorist Kaoru Ishikawa.

31. In addition to the fishbone diagram, several other tools may also assist in the problem analysis phase, depending on the nature of the particular problem under consideration. (See Langley et al., *The Improvement Guide*, 410, for a discussion of these options.) One that can be especially useful is process mapping. Some educational problems are in essence "pipeline problems." An example of this is the small numbers of minority students going into teaching careers in math and science. The unsatisfactory outcomes that we see here are the end result (akin to standing at the end of pipeline) of many preceding processes. At each step along the way, some students are lost. For problems of this sort, the root cause analysis focuses on mapping out these cascading processes as a precursor to identifying critical change points.

32. We note that this brief subsystem description focuses only on the programmatic aspects of educational organizations most germane to the identified improvement problem.

33. We developed this simplified version of the Community College Pathways system improvement map for inclusion in this book. We present only short summary headers for each box in figure 3.2. In the full map, each box contains multiple layers of descriptive detail. The first level typically consists of two sentences. One describes the organizational element; the second details how the organizational element links to student outcomes. The next level of description connects the organizational element, represented in the box, to the key factors identified in the causal system analysis. How does this aspect of the formal organization contribute to the undesirable student outcomes we continue to observe? Any known interventions that have been attempted on this "micro problem" would be tracked here as well. Systemic interconnections among boxes are also noted.

34. The target condition for the Community College Pathways NIC also includes a precise definition of student population for the initiative. This population definition creates a local, college-by-college, comparison group of students for charting progress. The full

NIC improvement target actually includes two goals. In addition to advancing student persistence toward successful completion within one academic year, the second goal focuses on evidence from common end-of-course and end-of-pathways assessments. These make manifest the ambitious learning goals set out for Pathways students.

35. See, for example, Douglas O. Staiger, Robert Gordon, and Thomas J. Kane, "Identifying Effective Teachers Using Performance on the Job" (Hamilton Project discussion paper, Brookings Institution, Washington, DC, 2006); Steven G. Rivkin, Eric A. Hanushek, and John F. Kain, "Teachers, Schools, and Academic Achievement," *Econometrica* 73, no. 2 (2005): 417–458; and Eric Hanushek and Steven G. Rivkin, "Using Value-Added Measures of Teacher Quality," *National Center for Analysis of Longitudinal Data in Educational Research,* Brief 9, http://www.caldercenter.org/publications/upload/1001371 -teacher-quality.pdf.

36. For general cognitive research, see K. Anders Ericcson, "Deliberate Practice and Acquisition of Expert Performance: A General Overview," *Academic Emergency Medicine* 15 (2008): 988–994. K. Anders Ericsson, Ralf Th. Krampe, and Clemens Tesch-Romer, "The Role of Deliberate Practice in the Acquisition of Expert Performance," *Psychological Review* 100 (1993): 363–406. Harold Pashler et al., "Enhancing Learning and Retarding Forgetting: Choices and Consequences," *Psychonomic Bulletin and Review* 14 (2007): 187–193.

    For research in the specific context of mathematics instruction, see James Hiebert and Douglas A. Grouws, "The Effects of Classroom Mathematics Teaching on Students' Learning," in *Second Handbook of Research on Mathematics Teaching and Learning*, ed. Frank K. Lester (Greenwich, CT: Information Age, 2007), 371–404; Richard A. Schmidt and Robert A. Bjork, "New Conceptualizations of Practice: Common Principles in Three Paradigms Suggest New Concepts for Training," *Psychological Science* 3, no. 4 (1992): 207–217; Jo Boaler, "Open and Closed Mathematics: Student Experiences and Understandings," *Journal for Research in Mathematics Education* 29 (1998): 41–62.

    The pilot study on community colleges is by James W. Stigler, Karen B. Givvin, and Belinda J. Thompson, "What Community College Developmental Mathematics Students Understand About Mathematics," *MathAMATYC Educator* 10 (2010): 4–16.

37. One key productive persistence activity was a direct-to-student growth mindset intervention delivered either in class as a worksheet or via the Internet during the first week of the course. The growth mindset intervention is a precise, brief (thirty minutes) theory-based persuasive reading and writing exercise that is designed to shift students' beliefs away from the view that being a "math person" or not is something that is fixed and toward the view that math ability can be grown and developed. For more on growth mindset activities, see Carol S. Dweck, *Mindset* (New York: Random House Publisher, 2006). Also see David S. Yeager and Carol S. Dweck, "Mindsets That Promote Resilience: When Students Believe That Personal Characteristics Can Be Developed," *Educational Psychologist* 47 (2012): 1–13.

38. See, for example, Kim Gomez et al., "Increasing Access to Mathematics Through a Literacy Language Lens" (paper presented at the American Mathematical Association of Two-Year Colleges [AMATYC], Jacksonville, FL, 2012). Also see Alan H. Schoenfeld, "When Good Teaching Leads to Bad Results: The Disasters of 'Well Taught' Mathematics Courses," *Educational Psychologist*, 23, no. 2 (1988): 145–166.

39. These change ideas are sometimes referred to as tertiary drivers. Additional levels beyond three can be added. In the interest of moderating the complexity of this example,

we have limited our exposition to three. In most general terms, the driver diagram is a nested set of conceptual structures that can have any number of levels to it. Any element in the diagram might in turn interact with other elements within the same or different primary drivers.

40. *Benchmarking and Benchmarks: Effective Practice with Entering Students* (Austin, TX: Center for Community College Student Engagement, 2010).

41. This is a general property of a solution system. For a further discussion of the concept of essentiality and its relationship to organizational systems, see Bryk et al., *Organizing Schools for Improvement*.

42. See, for example, the What Works Clearinghouse at http://ies.ed.gov/ncee/wwc/aboutus.aspx.

43. For an interesting example of the significance of context in health-care quality improvement, see chapter 7 of Atul Gawande, *The Checklist Manifesto* (New York: Metropolitan Books, 2009), 136–157, on testing the surgical checklist. On the surface, a checklist is a simple solution—a single piece of paper detailing a two-minute process. Regardless, to test the checklist fully, Gawande's team took the protocol out to eight different hospitals varying in economic resources and cultural conditions all around the word. That the checklist could work was already known. In contrast, what it would take to make it work in these different contexts was largely unknown.

44. Noelle V. Rivera, Kimberley Burly, and James S. Sass, *Evaluation of School-Based Professional Development* (Los Angeles, CA: Los Angeles Unified School District Program Evaluation and Research Branch; Planning, Assessment and Research Division Publication No. 187, 2002–2003).

45. Such zones of wishful thinking are common occurrences. See Paul Hill and Mary Beth Celio, *Fixing Urban Schools* (Washington, DC: Brookings Institution Press, 1998); Paul Hill, Christine Campbell, and James Harvey, *It Takes a City: Getting Serious About Urban School Reform* (Washington, DC: Brookings Institution Press, 1999).

46. See Anthony S. Bryk, Heather Harding, and Sharon Greenberg, "Contextual Influences on Inquiries into Effective Teaching and Their Implications for Improving Student Learning," *Harvard Educational Review*, 82, no. 1 (2012): 27–50, where this issue about generic versus instructional system–specific educational practice is further discussed.

47. For a very readable account on this point and research-based advice about how to respond, see Chip Heath and Dan Heath, *Switch: How to Change Things When Change Is Hard* (New York, NY: Broadway Books, 2010).

48. For a discussion on the role of relational trust in school improvement, see Anthony S. Bryk and Barbara L. Schneider, *Trust in Schools: A Core Resource for Improvement* (New York, NY: Russell Sage Foundation, 2002), and also Bryk et al., *Organizing Schools for Improvement*.

Chapter 4

1. William Shakespeare, *Measure for Measure*, ed. Davis P. Harding (New Haven, CT: Yale University Press, 1954).

2. Donna Foote, *Relentless Pursuit: A Year in the Trenches with Teach for America* (New York: Alfred A. Knopf, 2008).

3. Ted Quinn (Senior Vice President of Strategy and Research, Teach For America), in discussion with the authors, July 7, 2014.

4. For a discussion of how the absence of key human resources can undermine effective organizational expansion, see Larry Bossidy, Ram Charan, and Charles Burck, *Execution: The Discipline of Getting Things Done* (New York, NY: Crown Business, 2002). For a case study description of this tension, see Mike Rother, *Toyota Kata: Managing People for Improvement, Adaptiveness, and Superior Results* (New York, NY: McGraw-Hill, 2010).

5. Research documents these school-based organizational attributes as critical components in the retention and success of new teachers. See Richard M. Ingersoll, "Teacher Turnover and Teacher Shortages: An Organizational Analysis," *American Educational Research Journal* 37, no. 3 (2001): 499–534. See also Kavita Kapadia, Vanessa Coca, and John Q. Easton, *Keeping New Teachers: A First Look at the Influences of Induction in the Chicago Public Schools* (Chicago, IL: Consortium on Chicago School Research, January 2007). For a more general treatment on this matter, see Susan Moore Johnson, *Teachers at Work: Achieving Success in Our Schools* (New York, NY: Basic, 1990).

6. In the context of a driver diagram for TFA, improving the selection of corps members would be one of the primary drivers. TFA also invested in and pursued improvement on additional drivers including the quality of its teacher preparation, ongoing support, and alumni leadership cultivation.

7. Malcolm Gladwell, "Most Likely to Succeed," *New Yorker*, December 15, 2008, http://www.newyorker.com/magazine/2008/12/15/most-likely-to-succeed-2.

8. Douglas O. Staiger and Jonah E. Rockoff, "Searching for Effective Teachers with Imperfect Information," *Journal of Economic Perspectives* 24, no. 3 (2010): 97–118.

9. The initial list of twelve consisted of persistence, commitment, integrity, flexibility, oral communication skills, enthusiasm, sensitivity, independence, assertiveness, self-evaluative skills, ability to work within an organization and operate without student approval, and conceptual ability/intellect (achievement, perseverance, critical thinking, organizational ability, influencing others, respect, fit with TFA).

10. Steven Farr, personal communication, April 7, 2013.

11. From transcript of Harvard Educational Review Roundtable, Spring 2012. For a summary of the fuller discussion, see Anthony S. Bryk, Heather Harding, and Sharon Greenberg, "Contextual Influences on Inquiries into Effective Teaching and Their Implications for Improving Student Learning," *Harvard Educational Review* 82, no. 1 (Spring 2012): 83–106.

12. For a further discussion of this issue, see Richard J. Shavelson and Lisa Towne, *Scientific Research in Education* (Washington, DC: National Academy, 2002), for the core elements that form the disciplined inquiry characteristic of a science.

13. Ted Quinn, personal communication, October 16, 2012.

14. See Samuel Messick, "The Interplay of Evidence and Consequences in the Validation of Performance Assessments," *Educational Researcher* 23, no. 2 (1994): 13.

15. For closely related ideas in the context of health-care accountability, research, and improvement, see Lief Solberg, Gordon Mosser, and Sharon McDonald, "Three Faces of Performance Measurement," *Journal on Quality Improvement* 23, no. 3 (March 1997): 135–147. Also see Donald M. Berwick, Brent James, and Molly Joel Coye, "Connections Between Quality Measurement and Improvement," *Medical Care* 41, no. 1 (2003): I30–I38.

16. See Heather J. Hough et al., "Assessing Teacher Practice and Development: The Case of Comprehensive Literacy Instruction," *School Effectiveness and School Improvement* 24, no. 4 (2013): 452–485. We note the unusual composition of the team: clinical experts in

literacy practice and teacher and coach development; technical expertise in instrument design and deep data analytic capacity. The combination of expertise is often needed to build practical measures.

17. This perspective on expertise development closely follows more general findings about the development of expertise across diverse practices. Bent Flyvbjerg, *Making Social Science Matter: Why Social Inquiry Fails and How It Can Succeed Again* (Oxford, UK: Cambridge University Press, 2001), for example, elaborates five developmental levels in the learning process from novice to expert. The first three levels reflect rule-based thinking and logically based action, or procedural knowledge. At this stage of expertise development, the focus is on following rules and using trial-and-error experimentation, but there is not yet skill in addressing more novel problems or contexts. In contrast, learners at the higher levels of expertise have both developed procedural expertise and can more readily recognize patterns as they are dynamically occurring.

    For a very readable account of these differences in cognition, see Sian Beilock, *Choke: What the Secrets of the Brain Reveal About Getting It Right When You Have To* (New York, NY: Free, 2010).

18. Perverse responses are also not hard to imagine. Picture a teacher who is rated low on a rubric element measuring the frequency of discussion and questioning techniques. In an effort to improve, the teacher starts using more discussions throughout the day, even at points where a discussion is not the most effective instructional technique. The point here is that the lack of explicit connection between the rubric and the instructional model limits its informative value for guiding improvement.

19. Interestingly, the Danielson rubric was first published in 1996, with aspirations to help support teacher development. The use of the rubric exploded rapidly in the past few years when it became the instrument of choice for many states and districts for teacher evaluation. The evolution of the instrument has reflected this accountability use. Rubric descriptors now provide less detail but are easier to score objectively. "As the stakes in the teacher evaluation become higher, this increased accuracy is absolutely essential" [Charlotte Danielson, "The Framework for Teaching Evaluation Instrument" (framework by the Danielson Group, Princeton, NJ, 2013): 5]. Compare this to treatment in 1996: "Reliability is essential in a high-stakes environment. If an individual's teacher licensure depends on the results of several classroom observations, the assessors' judgments must be reliable. But if a framework for teaching is used within a school or district primarily for mentoring and coaching, with support and professional dialogue as the principal purpose, then inter-rater agreement is less critical" [Charlotte Danielson, *Enhancing Professional Practice: A Framework for Teaching*, (Alexandria, VA: Association for Supervision and Curriculum Development, 1996), 12].

20. To learn more about the Literacy Collaborative, go to www.literacycollaborative.org/index.php.

21. The ideas presented in this section summarize arguments that can be found in David S. Yeager et al., "Practical Measurement" (working paper, Carnegie Foundation for the Advancement of Teaching, Stanford, CA, 2014), which details how these distinctions evolved in the course of building the theory and measurement for productive persistence in the Community College Pathways NIC.

22. The latter is much more a design and engineering task than is commonly the concern of academic researchers. See the work of the International Society for Design and

Development in Education (www.isdde.org). See also Bent Flyvbjerg, *Making Social Science Matter*; and Donald A. Schön, *The Reflective Practitioner: How Professionals Think in Action* (New York, NY: Basic, 1983).

23. As an example, drawing on research from Deepa Marat, "Assessing Self-Efficacy of Diverse Students from Secondary Schools in Auckland: Implications for Academic Achievement," *Issues in Educational Research* 15, no. 1 (2005): 37–68. What is a practitioner supposed to do, for example, if self-efficacy for *cognitive strategies* is low but self-efficacy for *self-regulated learning* is high?

24. See *Best Care at Lower Cost: The Path to Continuously Learning Health Care in America* (Washington, DC: Institute of Medicine, 2012, http://www.iom.edu/Reports/2012/Best-Care-at-Lower-Cost-The-Path-to-Continuously-Learning-Health-Care-in-America.aspx), where an electronic patient-centered record system was a core recommendation in accelerating learning in health care.

25. See Jeffrey Pfeffer, "Changing Mental Models: HR's Most Important Task," *Human Resource Management* 44, no. 2 (2005): 123–128; Donald P. Moynihan, Sanjay K. Pandey, and Bradley E. Wright. "Setting the Table: How Transformational Leadership Fosters Performance Information Use," *Journal of Public Administration Research and Theory* 22, no. 1 (2011): 143–164.

26. An advantage of this outcome measure is that it is universally available across all community college institutions for all developmental math courses. Thus, it is a highly practical choice as an overall measureable target for the network and for providing comparable data on students pursuing a more traditional course of study. The measure, however, does not operationally define exactly what it is students are to know and be able to do as they complete a statistics or quantitative reasoning pathway. For this reason the NIC added common end-of-course exams. While faculty remain free as to how they use exam results in grading their students, these data are especially important in analyses of variation in performance—what works where and for whom? Formally, the common end-of-course exams are a measure associated with the instructional system primary driver. They can also be viewed as a balance measure. If grading standards, for example, became more lax, allowing more students to "pass the Pathways," this would manifest itself in declining achievement over time on the common exams.

27. For reviews, see Camille A. Farrington et al., *Teaching Adolescents to Become Learners. The Role of Noncognitive Factors in Shaping School Performance: A Critical Literature Review* (Chicago, IL: University of Chicago Consortium on Chicago School Research, June 2012). See also Carol S. Dweck, Gregory M. Walton, and Geoffrey L. Cohen, "Academic Tenacity" (white paper, prepared for the Bill & Melinda Gates Foundation, Seattle, WA, 2011).

28. We note that such operational definition is a key feature of improvement research. See Rocco J. Perla, Lloyd P. Provost, and Gareth J. Parry, "Seven Propositions of the Science of Improvement," *Quality Management in Health Care* 22, no. 3 (2013): 170–186.

29. For more information on this innovation development process, see Sandra Park and Sola Takahashi, *90-Day Cycle Handbook* (Stanford, CA: Carnegie Foundation for the Advancement of Teaching, August 2013). The Institute for Healthcare Improvement was the source of this development strategy. For more information on the IHI's use of it, see www.ihi.org/about/pages/innovationscontributions.aspx.

30. See David S. Yeager et al., *Measures of Developmental Math Student Motivation and Engagement* (Stanford, CA: Carnegie Foundation for the Advancement of Teaching,

December 2010). Also see Elena Silva and Taylor White, *Pathways to Improvement: Using Psychological Strategies to Help Community College Students Master Developmental Math* (Stanford, CA: Carnegie Foundation for the Advancement of Teaching, 2013, http://www.carnegiefoundation.org/sites/default/files/pathways_to_improvement.pdf).

31. See Yeager et al., "Practical Measurement."

32. See, for example, Jon A. Krosnick, "Survey Research," *Annual Review of Psychology* 50 (1999): 537–567. Also see Howard Schuman and Stanley Presser, *Questions and Answers in Attitude Surveys: Experiments on Question Form, Wording, and Context* (New York, NY: Academic Press, 1981).

33. For instructions, see, for example, Stanley Presser et al., *Methods for Testing and Evaluating Survey Questionnaires* (New York, NY: John Wiley Press, 2004).

34. To elaborate a bit further, items that are correlated with each other add less predictive value to the overall set. At base here is a simple idea from regression analysis. The maximum percentage of variance explained in an outcome occurs when the predictor variables are unrelated to each other. In such situations each variable (in our case each item or small cluster of items) is adding new information.

35. For further details about the measure and its statistical properties see Yeager et al., "Practical Measurement."

36. See Jonathan E. Cook et al., "Chronic Threat and Contingent Belonging: Protective Benefits of Values Affirmation on Identity Development," *Journal of Personality and Social Psychology* 102 (2012): 479–496.

37. See David S. Yeager, Dave Paunesku, Gregory M. Walton, and Carol S. Dweck, "How Can We Instill Productive Mindsets at Scale? A Review of the Evidence and an Initial R&D Agenda" (white paper prepared for the White House meeting on "Excellence in Education: The Importance of Academic Mindsets," Washington, DC, May 2013); and David S. Yeager and Carol S. Dweck, "Mindsets That Promote Resilience: When Students Believe That Personal Characteristics Can Be Developed," *Educational Psychologist* 47 (2012): 1–13.

38. The at-riskness indicator tapped the three subdomains of productive persistence that focus directly on the student: (1) skills and habits for succeeding in college, (2) fixed mindset about math ability, and (3) mindsets about social belonging. For further details, see Yeager et al, "Practical Measurement."

39. This result persists even after controlling for background math knowledge and demographic–personal characteristics such as race/ethnicity, income, number of dependents in the home, and number of hours worked.

40. See Gregory M. Walton and Geoffrey L. Cohen, "A Brief Social Belonging Intervention Improves Academic and Health Outcomes Among Minority Students," *Science* 331 (2011): 1447–1451; Gregory M. Walton and Geoffrey L. Cohen, "A Question of Belonging: Race, Social Fit, and Achievement," *Journal of Personality and Social Psychology* 92 (2007): 82–96.

Chapter 5

1. Attributed to Kurt Lewin, in Charles W. Tolman et al. (eds.), *Problems of Theoretical Psychology* (North York, Ontario: Captus Press, 1996), 31.

2. Gerald J. Langley et al., *The Improvement Guide: A Practical Approach to Enhancing Organizational Performance* (San Francisco, CA: Jossey-Bass, 2009).

3. For further details about run charts and the statistical methods used for drawing inferences based on such data, see Rocco J. Perla, Lloyd P. Provost, and Sandra K. Murray, "The Run Chart: A Simple Analytical Tool for Learning from Variation in Healthcare Processes," *BMJ Quality & Safety* 20, no. 1 (2011): 46–51. Also see Lloyd P. Provost and Sandra K. Murray, *The Health Care Data Guide: Learning from Data for Improvement* (San Francisco, CA: Jossey-Bass, 2011).

4. See Larry Bossidy, Ram Charan, and Charles Burck, *Execution: The Discipline of Getting Things Done* (New York, NY: Crown Business, 2002).

5. For a history of the PDSA cycle, see Ronald D. Moen, "Circling Back," *Quality Progress* 43, no. 11 (2010): 22–28. For a more in-depth discussion for how to use the PDSA cycles in different stages of an improvement effort, see Langley, *The Improvement Guide*.

6. Adapted from Langley et al., *The Improvement Guide*.

7. One of the most robust findings in the teacher effectiveness research is that teachers in their first three years of teaching are less effective than their more experienced counterparts. See, for example, Dan Goldhaber, "Everyone's Doing It, but What Does Teacher Testing Tell Us About Teacher Effectiveness?" *Journal of Human Resources* 42 (2006): 765–794; and Donald Boyd et al., "How Changes in Entry Requirements Alter the Teacher Workforce and Affect Students' Achievement," *Education, Finance, Policy* 1, no. 2 (2006): 176–216.

8. A Carnegie Foundation team provided improvement research training and support throughout this three-year effort. This was the Austin district's first attempt at using improvement research methods to address a problem of practice.

9. Note that this preliminary aim statement lacks the detail and specificity found in the Cincinnati Children's example. Early versions of aim statements are often of this form and need to be honed over time into more refined targets.

10. Even though BTEN officially closed with the end of the 2013–2014 academic year, a large new group of Austin educators came to Carnegie the following summer to learn how they too could take up and use these methods on other local problems.

11. The first hypothesis that AISD considered was that perhaps the design was unrealistic for schools with many new teachers. This turned out not to be the case. The team found examples of schools with both small and large numbers of new teachers that show process degradation. They also had one school with a very large number of new teachers that maintained the feedback standard. So the team had to dig deeper and investigate other hypotheses about what was going on.

12. Note that if the team had a strong notion about specific work that would suffer as a result of the feedback work (i.e., principals' attendance at meetings, district paperwork, etc.), they may have included a specific balancing measure attached to that work. In this case, collecting principals' time was more practical and was sufficient for remaining mindful of pulling principals away from other important activities.

13. More generally, how much time our educational solutions require of educators is an important, yet often ignored, aspect of reforms. We add, without accompanying subtractions, as if principals and teachers had an extra supply of time that was not already allocated. Getting quality with reliability at scale will require attention to how the existing changes fit in with the other work that is already occurring in schools.

14. These decisions made by AISD were informed by a ninety-day cycle performed by the Carnegie Foundation for the Advancement of Teaching on relevant research findings

regarding factors affecting new teacher development and persistence in practice. See Sandra Park, Sola Takahashi, and Taylor White, *Developing an Effective Teacher Feedback System,* (Stanford, CA: Carnegie Foundation for the Advancement of Teaching, 2014), http://www.carnegiefoundation.org/sites/default/files/CF_Feedback_90DC_2014.pdf.

15. The identification and development of the specific measures began with a scan, conducted by the Carnegie Foundation, of the constructs and associated measures thought to predict employee retention and development both inside and outside education. With the help of the American Federation of Teachers (one of the BTEN partners), the larger set of potential measures was tested on a pilot population of new teachers. Cognitive interviews with new teachers asked about how they interpreted each item. This aided revisions to the wording of select items to improve their clarity for these particular work settings. Psychometric analyses guided the selection of a small set of items that could effectively measure each construct. After the first year of use, the measures were validated in terms of how well they predicted new teacher retention and efficacy.

16. In general, each six-week survey was designed to take three minutes or less to complete. The surveys were administered on six different occasions over the course of an academic year. The overall design was based on a matrix sampling of survey items. The item pool was organized by separate construct, and a rating scale measure was developed for each construct. The latter allowed us to sample different items within constructs to compose different survey forms for each administration. No single question was asked more than twice in one year. For assessing efficacy and burnout, clusters of four items were included in three of the six-week surveys spaced out over the course of the year. For further details, see Sola Takahashi and Hannah Hausman, "The New Teacher On-Track Survey: A Tool for Tracking the Consequential Experiences of Early Career Teachers," (working paper, Carnegie Foundation for the Advancement of Teaching, Stanford, CA, 2014).

17. These results are from the administration of these same surveys in the Baltimore school district as part of their participation in the Building a Teaching Effectiveness Network. The AISD collected items only on teachers' sense of being overwhelmed, as self-efficacy items were already being asked as part of an annual districtwide survey of teachers.

18. See James Hiebert and Anne K. Morris, "Building a Knowledge Base for Teacher Education: An Experience in K–8 Mathematics Teacher Preparation," *The Elementary School Journal* 109, no. 5 (2009): 475–490; also see James Hiebert, Ronald Gallimore, and James W. Stigler, "A Knowledge Base for the Teaching Profession: What Would It Look Like and How Can We Get One?" *Educational Researcher* 31, no. 5 (2002): 3–15.

19. Langley et al., *The Improvement Guide,* xii.

Chapter 6

1. Douglas C. Engelbart, *Augmenting Human Intellect: A Conceptual Framework* (Menlo Park, CA: Stanford Research Institute, 1962).

2. For those with a taste for such things, the entirety of the presentation is available for viewing on YouTube. The talk is now known as "Mother of All Demos" in computer science circles. (YouTube, "The Mother of All Demons, presented by Douglas Engelbart," https://www.youtube.com/watch?v=yJDv-zdhzMY).

3. See Douglas C. Engelbart, "Toward High-Performance Organizations: A Strategic Role for Groupware," *Proceedings of the GroupWare* 92 (1992): 3–5.

4. See Clay Shirky, *Here Comes Everybody: The Power of Organizing Without Organization* (New York, NY: Penguin Books, 2008).

5. This idea was popularized by James Surowiecki in his widely read book, *The Wisdom of Crowds*. James Surowiecki, *The Wisdom of Crowds* (New York, NY: Anchor, 2005).

6. For a further elaboration on this point, see Michael A. Nielsen, *Reinventing Discovery: The New Era of Networked Science* (Princeton, NJ: Princeton University Press, 2012), 25–36. Nielsen argues that complex problems actually require the solution of many particular component problems. He posits that no one individual can possess all the relevant knowledge to solve this problem array. He terms this knowledge that applies to some part of a complex problem as "micro-expertise." The building of the atomic bomb, for example, necessitated the solution of problems that required carpenters, metal workers and electricians, alongside theoretical and applied physicists and mathematicians.

7. For the seminal work on this topic, see Everett M. Rogers, *Diffusion of Innovations* (New York, NY: Free Press, 1983).

8. In networkwide data analyses, the numbers of hours that students worked and responsibility for dependents are very weak predictors of persistence to completion and learning outcomes.

9. This work was led by Carnegie Fellow, David Yeager, Department of Psychology at the University of Texas–Austin, in collaboration with Jane Muhich, a Seattle Community College faculty member in-residence at Carnegie, in close consultation with Carol Dweck, Greg Walton, and colleagues.

10. Drawing on this research, David Yeager, Carnegie's Fellow for Productive Persistence, and Roberta Brown, a Pathways faculty member from Valencia Community College and a psychological researcher, adapted the initial mindset intervention to align with community college constraints. They shortened the intervention to thirty minutes, changed the reading level of the article to match that of the community college level, and made the article content more relevant for an adult student population. Brown tested the modified intervention in her spring Algebra I course at Valencia in a small, randomized control trial. Running in parallel was a somewhat larger randomized trial at Santa Monica Community College. Brown and Yeager presented their findings to the rest of the Pathways network at their summer national forum in July. Three weeks later, this intervention had become a part of the first day of instruction in a hundred different classrooms across twenty-two different colleges. As a result, this intervention has been embedded within the Pathways instructional system ever since. For more on this, also see David S. Yeager et al., "Practical Measurement" (working paper, Carnegie Foundation for the Advancement of Teaching, Stanford, CA, 2013).

11. This NIC strand of activity we refer to as an alpha lab. For further discussion of this and activities under way here, see www.carnegiealphalabs.org/.

12. Formally, this dualism in the statement of aims responds to the "Rider and Elephant" analogy for change developed by Heath and Heath in *Switch* [Chip Heath and Dan Heath, *Switch: How to Change Things When Change Is Hard* (New York, NY: Broadway Books, 2010)]. They maintain that all change processes—individual, organizational, and institutional—share this Janus-faced quality. The appeal to the rider is rational and technical—hence, the focus on explicating clear measurable outcomes and attainment targets. The appeal to the elephant is more emotional. It is to inspire, foment will, and

compel action toward change. Such aim statements focus on the human side—the faces we can actually see, the lives we actually touch.

13. See IHI's Web site (www.ihi.org) for information about its Five Million Lives Campaign.

14. Working with institutional researchers at NIC colleges, the network hub had established that the typical success rate of developmental math students (i.e., achieving college math credits within one year of enrollment) was 5 percent. This number functioned as the measured baseline for improvement.

15. See Scott Strother, James Van Campen, and Alicia Grunow, *Community College Pathways: 2011–2012 Descriptive Report* (Stanford, CA: Carnegie Foundation for the Advancement of Teaching, 2012), http://www.carnegiefoundation.org/sites/default/files/CCP_Descriptive _Report_Year_1.pdf; James Van Campen, Scott Strother, and Nicole Sowers, *Community College Pathways: 2012–2013 Descriptive Report* (Stanford, CA: Carnegie Foundation for the Advancement of Teaching, 2013), http://www.carnegiefoundation.org/sites/default/files/pathways/CCP_Descriptive_Report_Year_2.pdf; and Hiroyuki Yamada and Scott Strother, "How Successful Are We Unlocking the Mathematical Gate?: Assessing the Year 1 Success of the Community College Pathways Program" (paper presented at the Society for Research on Educational Effectiveness Spring Conference, Washington, DC, March 6, 2014), for further validation of these results based on a propensity score matching strategy in which each Pathways student was matched on forty-four different indicators to from three to five comparable students in the same college who pursued the traditional program of study instead.

16. See, for an illustration of this issue, Melinda M. Karp and Georgia W. Stacey, *What We Know About Nonacademic Student Supports* (New York, NY: Community College Research Center, Teachers College, Columbia University, 2013).

17. See chapter 3 in the *Checklist Manifesto* for further elaboration on this analogy. Atul Gawande, *The Checklist Manifesto* (New York, NY: Metropolitan Press, 2010), 48–71.

18. In the case of the Community College Pathways NIC, these kernel resources broadly speaking consist of the Pathways structure and learning outcomes; a base of common lessons organized around evidence-based instructional principles; an online platform for student homework, core assessments, and other student-level measures; a set of interventions and classroom practices designed to support students' productive persistence through the Pathways; and participation by faculty new to the Pathways in a year-long professional program that introduces them to these Pathways resources, supports them as they learn to use these resources well, and welcomes them into active membership in the improvement community. For more information, see www.carnegiefoundation.org/developmental-math.

We also note that, at any given point in time, numerous other change ideas may be under exploration by individual participants or subgroups of participants. Some of these may eventually also warrant kernel-level status. Consequently, the kernel is not static, but rather continues to evolve over time through NIC efforts at learning to improve.

19. This same spirit is also reflected in the line of work described as design-based implementation research. For a further discussion of this, see Barry J. Fishman and William R. Penuel, eds., *Design Based Implementation Research* (New York, NY: National Society for the Study of Education Yearbook, 2013).

20. Carnegie sometimes accomplishes this through an expert convening that is sharply focused on a specific issue raised within a NIC. On other occasions, borrowing on another process developed at IHI, the hub might undertake a ninety-day cycle process to quickly identify promising practices. For more information on ninety-day cycles, see Sandra Park and Sola Takahashi, *90-Day Cycle Handbook* (Stanford, CA: Carnegie Foundation for the Advancement of Teaching, 2013).

21. On this point, we are now forming a separate team at the Carnegie Foundation focusing specifically on issues concerning network initiation and growth and how we might best support the efforts of others in this regard. A practical framework for NIC initiation called "A Framework for Network Improvement Community Initiation" is now under development at the foundation, and we have initiated pilot efforts around its use.

22. See the discussion on the important role of evangelizing leadership in Anthony S. Bryk, Louis M. Gomez, and Alicia Grunow, "Getting Ideas into Action: Building Networked Improvement Communities in Education," in *Frontiers in Sociology of Education*, ed. Maureen T. Hallinan (New York, NY: Springer: 2011), 181–206.

23. Joining Anthony Bryk on the initial thought leadership team were Bernadine Chuck Fong, Louis Gomez, Sharon Greenberg, Magdalene Lampert, Nicole Pinkard, Myra Snell, Jim Stigler, and Uri Treisman. Bernadine Chuck Fong eventually took on the role as senior partner at the Carnegie Foundation for the Community College Programs. Both Louis Gomez and Jim Stigler remain senior fellows at the foundation engaged with the CCP NIC and other NIC-related activities.

24. This approach is based on the *Pareto principle* established in improvement science. Typically, this means working on five or six big things that must be integrated into a coherent solution system. A practical working theory of improvement is intentionally incomplete in this regard; it does not seek to work on everything, just the five or six at most high-leverage practices for transformation.

25. We learned a key process lesson along the way. In the first few meetings, we presented a very rudimentary version of the causal system analysis based on our internal conversations and asked others to react to it. These discussions did not prove as productive as we had hoped. We then changed the process. With each new group we joined in a fresh task of identifying causes. We facilitated the group to push this as far as they thought useful. In a second activity later in the day, we then shared with the group the current working version of the diagram synthesized from earlier convenings. It was presented in the spirit of being possibly wrong and definitely incomplete. We asked participants to tell us what was missing, what was unclear, and where the working diagram failed to represent adequately their earlier discussion. Key observations invariably arose in the course of this process that led to further refinement of the diagram, which then would be tested at the next convening. Through multiple iterations of this sort, this process eventually converged on version 1.0 of a working theory of improvement.

26. These may be expressions, for example, of frustrations encountered with a particular institutional leader that focus on aspects of personality rather than system causes.

27. For an engaging case study account, see Mike Rother, *Toyota Kata: Managing People for Improvement, Adaptiveness, and Superior Results* (New York, NY: McGraw-Hill, 2010).

28. James Gray, *Teachers at the Center: A Memoir of the Early Years of the National Writing Project* (Berkeley, CA: National Writing Project, 2005). See also Ann Lieberman and

Diane Wood, *Inside the National Writing Project: Connecting Network Learning and Classroom Teaching* (New York, NY: Teachers College Press, 2002).

29. Elyse Eidman-Asdahl, personal communication, National Writing Project Annual Report, January 20, 2014, and June 11, 2014.

30. See *Cooperative Catalyst*, http://coopcatalyst.wordpress.com/tag/blog4nwp/.

31. See Sherry Seale Swain, *I Can Write What's on My Mind: Teresa Finds Her Voice* (New York, NY: Heinemann, 1998); Ann Lieberman and Lynne Miller, eds., *Teachers in Professional Communities: Improving Teaching and Learning* (New York, NY: Teachers College, Columbia University, 2007); and Ann Lieberman and Linda D. Friedrich, *How Teachers Become Leaders: Learning from Practice and Research* (New York, NY: Teachers College, Columbia University, 2010).

32. Elyse Eidman-Asdahl, personal communication, June 11, 2014.

33. Karen LaBonte, "It's the Writing, Stupid," blog post, *All Hands on Deck: Reflections on Teaching and Learning in a Time of Change,* April 6, 2011, http://klabonte.edublogs.org/2011/04/06/its-the-writing-stupid/.

34. Jeremy Hyler, "NWP—I Am a Writer!" blog post, *Jeremyhyler40*, March 20, 2011, http://jeremyhyler40.wordpress.com/2011/03/20/nwp/.

35. Kay J. McGriff, "Teachers Write the Way," blog post, *Kay Jernigan McGriff,* March 20, 2011, http://kaymcgriff.edublogs.org/2011/03/20/teachers-write-the-way/.

36. We wish to acknowledge a commentary from Don Berwick quoted in Charles Kenney, *The Best Practice: How the New Quality Improvement Movement Is Transforming Medicine* (New York, NY: Public Affairs, 2008), 284. The spirit of this closing section takes its root there.

Chapter 7

1. Ronald Edmonds, "Effective Schools for the Urban Poor," *Educational Leadership* 37, no. 1 (1979): 23.

2. See Kathryn P. Boudett, Elizabeth A. City, and Richard J. Murnane, *Data Wise: A Step-by-Step Guide to Using Assessment Results to Improve Teaching and Learning* (Cambridge, MA: Harvard Educational Press, 2005), as opening up this space by engaging teachers around evidence of student learning. Improvement research expands the realm of inquiries to focus explicit attention on the actual work processes that contribute to observed student outcomes.

3. See Huggy Rao and Robert I. Sutton, *Scaling Up Excellence* (New York, NY: Crown Business Books, 2014).

4. We note that this thinking is not peculiar to education. It has been widely noted as a problem in medical decision making. See Jerome E. Groopman, *How Doctors Think* (Boston, MA: Houghton Mifflin, 2007). For a treatment on this topic in the context of human cognition more generally, see Daniel Kahnerman, *Thinking, Fast and Slow* (New York, NY: Farrar, Straus and Giroux, 2011). Also, see Eva Jonas et al., "Confirmation Bias in Sequential Information Search After Preliminary Decisions: An Expansion of Dissonance Theoretical Research on Selective Exposure to Information," *Journal of Personality and Social Psychology,* 80, no. 4 (2001): 557–571.

5. Peter C. Wason and Philip N. Johnson-Laird, *The Psychology of Reasoning: Structure and Content* (Cambridge, MA: Harvard University Press, 1972).

6. Kate Kornell et al., "Unsuccessful Retrieval Attempts Enhance Subsequent Learning," *Journal of Experimental Psychology: Learning, Memory and Cognition* 35, no. 4 (2009): 989–998.

7. Chip and Dan Heath single out this idea of "easing the path" as a critical element in promoting individual, organizational, and institutional change. Chip Heath and Dan Heath, *Switch: How to Change Things When Change Is Hard* (New York, NY: Broadway Books, 2010).

8. For a further discussion of this theme and a critical analysis of what genuine support for teaching improvement entails, see David K. Cohen, *Teaching and Its Predicaments* (Cambridge, MA: Harvard University Press, 2011).

9. The paradigm sketched out here represents the basic goals framework that guides the research efforts of the Department of Education's Institute of Education Science. The vast majority of proposals to IES focus on exploration and design-development studies. Far fewer proposals for efficacy and large-scale field-trial evaluations are received. The latter are predominately for commercial products and services already on the market.

10. A search of the What Works Clearinghouse database turned up 473 studies approved without reservations and another 305 approved with reservations (see http://ies.ed.gov/ncee/wwc/ReviewedStudies.aspx). This is a cumulative knowledge base spanning back almost twenty-five years. Many of these studies are about very specific practices at select grade levels and student subpopulations. A small number are large-scale evaluations of commercial products. While the number of entries is now increasing, this knowledge base is still miniscule and unable to provide coherent practical guidance. To put the efforts of the WWC in perspective, over twenty-seven thousand randomized trials were conducted on clinical medical practice in just 2010 alone (see *Best Care at Lower Cost: The Path to Continuously Learning Health Care in America,* Washington, DC: Institute of Medicine, 2012), http://www.iom.edu/Reports/2012/Best-Care-at-Lower-Cost-The-Path-to-Continuously-Learning-Health-Care-in-America.aspx).

11. Michael Barkham and John Mellor-Clark, "Bridging Evidence-Based Practice and Practice-Based Evidence: Developing a Rigorous and Relevant Knowledge for the Psychological Therapies," *Clinical Psychology & Psychotherapy* 10, no. 6 (2003): 319–327. Barkham and Mellor-Clark offer taxonomy of the landscape of research and development. They divide the landscape into (1) efficacy research, (2) effectiveness research, (3) practice research, and (4) service systems research.

12. See Lisbeth B. Schorr, "Broader Evidence for Bigger Impact," *Stanford Social Innovation Review* (Fall 2012): 50–55. Also see Lisbeth B. Schorr and Frank Farrow, *Expanding the Evidence Universe* (New York, NY: Center for the Study of Social Policy, December 2011).

13. The concept of willful ignorance is central to historical development of probability theory. For a full elaboration of these ideas and its application in experimental design, see Herbert I. Weisberg, *Willful Ignorance: The Mismeasure of Uncertainty* (Hoboken, NJ: John Wiley & Sons, 2014).

14. Gerald J. Langley et al., *The Improvement Guide: A Practical Approach to Enhancing Organizational Performance* (San Francisco, CA: Jossey-Bass, 2009), xii.

15. Developing human resources for improvement is a central feature, for example, in the Toyota Quality Management system. It also appears as a common feature in quality leaders in health care such as Cincinnati Children's Hospital, Virginia Mason Medical Center, Kaiser Permanente, and Intermountain Health Services.

Appendix

1. There is ample evidence now across many different fields of work that going slower initially is key to scaling faster and better later. For elaborations on this point, see Robert I. Sutton and Hayagreeva Rao, *Scaling Up Excellence: Getting to More Without Settling for Less* (New York, NY: Crown Business, 2014).

2. Building a Teaching Effectiveness Network was the Carnegie Foundation's first attempt to support an improvement process in large public school district contexts. The rate of progress was slowed by limited on-the-ground capacities to guide this work and by the novelty of the processes that the foundation was asking district and school-based leaders to engage in. Much time was spent on making the case for starting small, for developing a shared working theory of practice improvement, for gathering evidence about process changes being attempted, and the need to introduce a practical measurement system that linked process changes to ultimate aims. Were educators accustomed to the logic and protocols of improvement research, the rate of moving through these various stages could have occurred more quickly and wider-spread change resulted faster. In essence as we started BTEN, the Carnegie Foundation was operating toward the lower end of its own learning to improve growth trajectory.

3. Pilots are conceptualized this way, for example, in the goal structure for funding programs at the Institute of Education Sciences.

4. To pursue this a bit further, most educational RCTs are done on a small convenience sample, that is, with whoever is willing to participate in the study. Technically, this means that inferences from these results are limited to only those contexts. Now even if large, truly random samples were drawn for educational evaluation studies, the issue described here would still not disappear. In all likelihood we would continue to see effects of heterogeneity and have little guidance as to how to achieve quality outcomes reliably at scale.

5. See, for example, a recent SREE meeting in Spring 2014, "Improving Education Science and Practice: The Role of Replication," where this was the central theme for the conference.

6. These results put aside a more basic problem that many of the WWC entries report null findings, which technically tell us nothing. While it is common to interpret such reports as evidence that an intervention does not work, we learn in basic statistics that one can never prove a null hypothesis. Consequently, interpreting null findings as a general inference that an intervention cannot work is logically flawed.

7. For a further discussion of this point, see Robert G. Granger, Vivian Tseng, and Brian L. Wilcox, "Connecting Research and Practice," in *Societal Contexts of Child Development Pathways of Influence and Implications for Practice and Policy,* eds. Elizabeth T. Gershoff, Rashmita S. Mistry, and Danielle A. Crosby (New York, NY: Oxford University Press, 2013): 205–219.

8. See Carol S. Dweck, *Mindset: The New Psychology of Success* (New York, NY: Random House, 2006); also David S. Yeager and Carol S. Dweck, "Mindsets That Promote Resilience: When Students Believe That Personal Characteristics Can Be Developed," *Educational Psychologist* 47 (2012): 1–13.

9. This topic has a long intellectual history, actually much longer than most contemporary discussions of the topic acknowledge. See, for example, seminal papers by Paul Berman and Milbrey Wallin McLaughlin, "Implementation of Educational Innovation," *The*

Educational Forum 40, no. 3 (1976): 345–370; Richard F. Elmore, "Backward Mapping: Implementation Research and Policy Decisions," *Political Science Quarterly* 94, no. 4 (1979): 601; Eleanor Farrar, John E. Desanctis, and David K. Cohen, "Views from Below: Implementation Research in Education," *Teachers College Record* 82, no. 1 (1980): 77–100; and also Milbrey Wallin McLaughlin, "Learning from Experience: Lessons from Policy Implementation," *Educational Evaluation and Policy Analysis* 9, no. 2 (1987): 171–178.

10. When differences associated with a new practice are large and consistent, as apparently was the case here, one does not need powerful experiment designs to detect them. Such interoccular effects literally hit us between the eyes. Consequently, the surgical checklist was not subject to an RCT. It was, however, subject to rigorous external validity tests and analyses. See chapters 5 and 7 in Atul Gawande, *The Checklist Manifesto: How to Get Things Right* (New York, NY: Metropolitan Press, 2010), 86–113, 136–157.

Acknowledgments

Learning to Improve: How America's Schools Can Get Better at Getting Better represents accumulated learning from six years of programmatic activity at the Carnegie Foundation for the Advancement of Teaching. It also reflects some hard-learned lessons from decades of work by the authors at trying to improve teaching and learning in some of our nation's most challenging schools and districts. In the broadest of terms, *Learning to Improve* is a synthesis that integrates the work of many others throughout the field of education and beyond. We are deeply indebted to all from whom we have learned much.

We would especially like to thank all of the educators who have participated in the Community College Pathways (CCP) and the Building a Teaching Effectiveness Network (BTEN) for our opportunities to learn with them in making their respective networked improvement communities (NICs) come alive. Numerous community college educators helped develop the CCP network; several took up residence for a period of time at the foundation to lead it. We wish to acknowledge the special contributions of Bernadine Chuck Fong, Karon Klipple, Jane Muhich, Cinnamon Hillyard, Lawrence Morales, Nicole Gray, Rachel Mudge, Rikki Blair, and Myra Snell. Likewise, many academic colleagues shaped the ideas driving the Pathways initiative and also rolled up their sleeves to assist in moving these ideas into action. We thank Uri Treisman, Magdalene Lampert, James

Stigler, Guadalupe Valdes, Bill Saunders, Karen Givvin, David Yeager, Kim Gomez, and Rose Asera. We also thank Nisha Patel, Miguel Socias, and Cathy Casserly, who in varied and different ways supported the CCP as it began and grew. Throughout the work, we were inspired by an extraordinary group of faculty, deans, administrators, and institutional researchers in the fifty-plus institutions in the Pathways network. Their improvement efforts are now reclaiming the mathematical lives of thousands of students across the country every day.

For BTEN, we owe a debt to Sandra Park, Sola Takahashi, Kareen Yang, Holly Szafarek, Dave Williams, Jarrod Bolte, David Kauffman, Laura Baker, Rob Weil, Dyan Smiley, Justin Stone, Ross Wiener, Nancy Pelz-Paget, Sharon Greenberg, Joaquin Tomayo, Bob Hughes, and Susan Moore Johnson, who shaped and guided BTEN through its learning journey and from whom we in turn learned much. We also wish to acknowledge all of the school leaders and improvement facilitators in Austin, Baltimore, and New Visions for Public Schools Network who became our colleagues. Their efforts enlivened BTEN. The transformations that they have effected in their own work and in their respective schools and districts have convinced us that quality improvement can be a powerful force supporting educators' efforts to advance better outcomes for all students.

Our learning about improvement has been guided by numerous individuals and organizations, especially in the field of health care. We call out a special thanks to Lloyd Provost, Brandon Bennett, Uma Kotagal, Penny Carver, and Lindsay Martin. They have been coaches extraordinaire. We also acknowledge a deep learning-debt to the Institute for Healthcare Improvement, the Associates in Process Improvement, and Cincinnati Children's Hospital Medical Center.

Our interviews with a handful of people were crucial in the development of the case examples detailed throughout this book. For this, we'd like to thank Jeffrey Simmons, Mona Mansour, Ted Quinn, Steven Farr, Laura Baker, David Kauffman, Jenn Russell, Jon Dolle, Jane Muhich, Krissia Martinez, and Elyse Eidman-Aadahl.

Several others assisted us in the writing of this manuscript. Caroline Chauncey, our senior editor at Harvard Education Press, offered support and keen advice throughout the process. She was enthusiastic about the initial ideas. She gently but also firmly pressed us as deadlines slipped to move our ideas into words and finally into print. She was our beacon as the book was forming. Her critical reads and sage reactions to an early draft strongly reshaped the final product. Along related lines, a special thanks is owed to Sharon Greenberg, who read early drafts of selected chapters and offered feedback about both content and writing style. Her critical commentary pressed us to sharpen our focus about the audiences for the book and how we might make the ideas and practices of improvement more accessible to them. Susan Headden, along with Tom Toch, provided terrific editorial assistance. Tom advised during the beginning stages as the arc of this book was laid out, and read and reacted to early drafts of the various chapters. Susan, along with Tom, relentlessly edited our prose, uncovering tortured passages and helping to simplify the text so that key points might emerge more clearly. We owe a special debt to Corey Donahue. He "herded us elephants" throughout the process of developing the various chapters and provided extensive editorial and production assistance. He too read and offered critical commentary as we drafted and redrafted each chapter. We would also like to acknowledge and thank all of our colleagues at the foundation for their patience, understanding, and support as we struggled to complete this book. Frustration arising out of a conversation among the authors about some particularly nettlesome idea sometimes carried forward into a subsequent meeting that others had with one or more of us.

Finally, we wish to acknowledge the good colleagueship and support that we have received from the trustees of the Carnegie Foundation for the Advancement of Teaching and from our funding partners: the Bill & Melinda Gates Foundation, William and Flora Hewlett Foundation, Lumina Foundation, Kresge Foundation, Institute of Education Sciences, W. T. Grant Foundation, and our "big brother"—the Carnegie Corporation of New York. As we began this work, notions about improvement science and networked improvement community were totally foreign to education.

Each of these institutions trusted that we could transform a promising set of ideas into productive action. They supported and encouraged us, and sometimes asked tough questions, as we pursued an uncharted course. There is no way to fully express our gratitude for their confidence in us throughout this endeavor. Without their support, neither BTEN nor CCP would have come to life, and the learning from these efforts that are at the heart of *Learning to Improve* would never have emerged.

About the Authors

Anthony S. Bryk is the ninth president of the Carnegie Foundation for the Advancement of Teaching, where he is leading work on transforming educational research and development, more closely joining researchers and practitioners to improve teaching and learning. Formerly, he held the Spencer Chair in Organizational Studies in the School of Education and the Graduate School of Business at Stanford University from 2004 until assuming Carnegie's presidency in September 2008. He came to Stanford from the University of Chicago, where he was the Marshall Field IV Professor of Urban Education in the sociology department, and where he helped found the Center for Urban School Improvement, which supports reform efforts in the Chicago Public Schools. He also created the Consortium on Chicago School Research, a federation of research groups that have produced a range of studies to advance and assess urban school reform. He is a member of the National Academy of Education and was appointed by President Obama to the National Board for Education Sciences in 2010. In 2011, he was elected as a member of the American Academy of Arts and Sciences. He is one of America's most noted educational researchers. His 1993 book, *Catholic Schools and the Common Good*, is a classic in the sociology of education. His deep interest in bringing scholarship to bear on improving schooling is reflected in his later volume, *Trust in Schools*, and in the most recent book, *Organizing Schools for Improvement: Lessons* *from Chicago* (Chicago Press, 2009.) Bryk holds a BS from Boston College and an EdD from Harvard University.

Louis M. Gomez holds the MacArthur Chair in Digital Media and Learning in the Graduate School of Education and Information Studies at the University of California Los Angeles. Gomez has served since 2008 as a senior partner at the Carnegie Foundation for the Advancement of Teaching, where he leads the Network Development work. Beginning in 2009, he held the Helen S. Faison Chair in Urban Education at the University of Pittsburgh, where he was also director of the Center for Urban Education and a senior scientist at the Learning Research and Development Center. From 2001 to 2008, he held a number of faculty appointments at Northwestern University, including the Aon Chair in the Learning Sciences at the School of Education and Social Policy. Prior to joining academia, he spent fourteen years working in cognitive science and person–computer systems and interactions at Bell Laboratories, Bell Communications Research Inc., and Bellcore. His research interests have encompassed the application of computing and networking technology to teaching and learning, applied cognitive science, human–computer interactions, and other areas. Gomez received his bachelor's degree in psychology from the State University of New York at Stony Brook in 1974 and a doctorate in cognitive psychology from UC Berkeley in 1979.

Alicia Grunow is a senior partner and codirector of the Center for Networked Improvement at Carnegie. In that role, she oversees the core capacities that support all networked improvement communities: analytics, developmental evaluation, design and development, program technologies, and improvement research.

Grunow completed the Improvement Advisor program at the Institute for Healthcare Improvement in 2011 and currently leads the foundation's efforts to adapt these methodologies for the field of education. To this end, she teaches improvement workshops and coaches improvement teams both in and outside the organization.

Before coming to Carnegie, Grunow was an instructor in Stanford's Teacher Education Program (STEP), where she taught practices to support the academic achievement of English language learners. Her research at Stanford used a range of quantitative methodologies to examine policy issues regarding English language learners. Grunow received her BA in psychology from Reed College. She has a master's degree in economics and a doctorate in educational administration and policy analysis from Stanford University. Before graduate school, she taught for seven years in transitional bilingual and dual language elementary school programs in both Denver and New York City. She completed the Bilingual and ESL Teachers Leadership Academy at Bank Street College. At the core, she will always identify as a practitioner.

Paul G. LeMahieu is the senior vice president for programs at the Carnegie Foundation. Previously, he directed the work of the Carnegie Hub, which supports the networks the foundation convenes to engage problems of education practice in the field. He is also graduate faculty at the University of Hawai'i, Mānoa. LeMahieu came to Carnegie from his post as director of research and evaluation at the National Writing Project (NWP) at the University of California, Berkeley. He has also served as Superintendent of Education for the state of Hawai'i, the chief educational and executive officer of the only state system in the United States that is a unitary school district. He has held the top educational research position for the state of Delaware as Undersecretary for Education Research, Policy, and Development and professor at the University of Delaware. He also served for eleven years as Assistant Superintendent for Research, Evaluation, and Student Assessment in the Pittsburgh Public Schools. LeMahieu has published extensively on issues as diverse as testing policy and practice, educational accountability, issues in data analysis and use, staff development, school effectiveness, nontraditional work roles for women, minority achievement issues, science education, and vocational education. He has a BA from Yale College, an EdM from Harvard University, and a PhD from the University of Pittsburgh.

Index